'An uplifting and passionate response to a government whose slogan of 'taking back control' lies in tatters, framing a hopeful programme of socialist liberation for the present.'

– Jeremy Seabrook, author of *Cut Out: Living Without Welfare* and *Pauperland: Poverty and the Poor in Britain*

'*Taking Back Control* is a meticulously evidenced and indispensable survey of the catastrophe of late British capitalism. Its searing analysis of the way that work, the economy, the political system, and the media is organised will have you reaching for your pitchfork.'

– David Whyte, author of *Ecocide and How Corrupt is Britain?*

'This is an impassioned dissection of many of the important problems facing our society. It challenges most of the widespread and damaging preconceptions perpetuated by political, business, and media elites, and offers a hopeful vision of a different world. It deserves to be widely read.'

– Charles Umney, author of *Class Matters*

TAKING BACK CONTROL

CONTROL

PUTTING WORK, MONEY,
POLITICS, AND THE MEDIA IN THE
HANDS OF THE PEOPLE

REECE GARCIA

The Book Guild Ltd

First published in Great Britain in 2022 by
The Book Guild Ltd
Unit E2 Airfield Business Park,
Harrison Road, Market Harborough,
Leicestershire. LE16 7UL
Tel: 0116 2792299
www.bookguild.co.uk
Email: info@bookguild.co.uk
Twitter: @bookguild

Typeset in 11pt Minion Pro

Printed and bound in the UK by TJ Books LTD, Padstow, Cornwall

ISBN 978 1914471 889

British Library Cataloguing in Publication Data.
A catalogue record for this book is available from the British Library.

For Maya

Your smile, playfulness, innocence, and unconditional trust belies the version of human nature that is sold to us. I hope that your future is everything that you deserve

CONTENTS

CONTENTS

INTRODUCTION

You would be forgiven for having never heard the name Nick Hanauer. He is not a household name as some of his shrewd investments are, notably, a younger Jeff Bezos and Amazon, but he is a venture capitalist who can boast of being incredibly wealthy. He wrote a memo to 'my fellow zillionaires' that reads:

'If we don't do something to fix the glaring inequities in this economy, the pitchforks are going to come for us. No society can sustain this kind of rising inequality. In fact, there is no example in human history where wealth accumulated like this and the pitchforks didn't eventually come out. You show me a highly unequal society, and I will show you a police state. Or an uprising. There are no counterexamples. None. It's not if, it's when.'[1]

And yet, despite a further eight years of this upward trajectory in gross inequality the pitchforks have barely surfaced. For extended periods there has been very little sign of them. Curiously, not only do swathes of people generally seem quite accepting of this state of affairs, many actively defend those who are faring much better than themselves and continue to elect those who oversee it. Contemporary Britain is characterised by any number of things: a stutter in life expectancy (pre-Covid), increased numbers of children living in poverty, an almost tripling in the number of people who are homeless,

---

1   Nick Hanauer (2014) 'The Pitchforks Are Coming... For Us Plutocrats' *Politico* Magazine

insecure employment, long working hours yet a fall in 'real' terms income, undertaking roles wholly or partially made up of meaningless tasks, increased debt, exorbitant house prices, underfunded and worsening public services, tax avoidance for those financially positioned to contribute more, unprecedented wealth growth for the richest in our society, unrepresentative politicians, corporate greed, a loss in worker power, a media not fit for purpose, and an increase in the rates of suicides and those suffering from poor mental health. And yet, we continue to turn up to work exploited and exhausted, and to the ballot box misinformed or disillusioned.

The four chapters that follow establish just how worse off the majority of us have, and continue, to become. They aim to illustrate how this grossly unequal situation has arisen and how it is maintained. This is achieved by examining four key 'pillars' in our society: work, money, politics, and the media, recognising that these intersect in many different ways. In the process, it becomes clear that our governing elites will not be the vehicle for the progressive change we deserve and that a more proactive approach is required from people themselves. The book finishes by outlining alternative futures to the status quo in a bid to help break from any ideological impasse regarding what exactly it is that we can do. The structure of the book is as follows.

The first chapter provides answers to questions such as: how did the wealthy obtain their wealth? Is it possible for me to join their ranks? Do we rely on the Amazons of this world more than they rely on us? Who are today's working class? In doing so, we dispel the mythology of work by exploring its roots as we currently engage in it. In essence, despite the illusion of choice when applying for jobs wage labour is essentially forced, partly due to historical processes of land enclosure and trade financed by colonial activities. We examine how work has transitioned from a means to an end, where it would stop once people's needs were met and they could enjoy the fruits of their labour, into an end (in of itself). This is evidenced in the apparent ways that we have normalised taking little enjoyment from the first five days of each week, positing that the work ethic has effectively been ingrained into the masses 'from above'. As such, we become unwilling philanthropists[2] to the rentier classes who are spared such toil by our exploitation. That jobs can be unfulfilling is made worse by the fact that many offer little, if any, utility to society. The chapter contends that we could solve the simultaneous problems of unemployment for some

---

2   As termed by Bhaskar Sunkara (2018) in *The Socialist Manifesto*. Verso

and overwork for others by abolishing pointless jobs, accelerating widespread automation, and striving for full employment on reduced hours, in a smaller number of occupations – those that perform a clear utility for society. This would enable us to join the real 'idle classes' by not being so work-focused and having time for leisure, more direct democratic participation, environmental conservation, and other pursuits.

Chapter 2 explores issues ascertaining to money. Beyond evidence of the continued accrual of money to the wealthiest in our society via corporate welfare, tax breaks, and more, there are discussions regarding how money is created via private debt, which is a wholly political choice. Relatedly, how the 'government as household' logic pedalled by politicians is remarkably effective in fuelling the cynicism and distrust people direct towards welfare recipients, migrants, and acceptance of key services being underfunded for fear of tax hikes. Further, how debt has become normalised and thus an effective means of controlling ostensibly free persons, before an account of various methods of tax avoidance and evasion that ultimately enables billionaires to pay less tax than their secretaries. This discussion closes with a look at privatisation and how the taxpayer becomes something of an impotent cash cow for private interests under neoliberalism, with the revolving door between public and private office creating ample opportunity for corruption among politicians.

Following this, Chapter 3 illustrates that democracy in Britain equates to choosing – typically on a four-yearly basis and from an increasingly narrow sub-section of society – those who effectively make all the decisions. We know that trust and satisfaction in politicians is consistently low, but what are the causes and why is there such widespread, reluctant acquiescence to this? We will take a look at who they are, where they come from, and how their careers develop in order to better understand why our interests are under- and mis-represented. Key political issues such as austerity (a term beginning to reappear as part of a post-Covid 'recovery') and Brexit are used as departure points to discuss government action as a continuous classist project. This leads into a discussion of how to convincingly articulate true nationalistic pride via things like properly funded services, our being the birthplace of modern worker co-operatives, and how re-nationalisation truly equates to 'taking back control'. The chapter questions whether a transition away from a first-past-the-post electoral system and caps on campaign spending would result in a truly participatory democracy, or whether we need a new political system entirely.

In Chapter 4 we study the pervasive and largely unregulated influence of a small number of billionaire press barons on political and social matters. That just five outfits own and control the seventeen most circulated media outlets is well documented, as is their partisan nature. Discussed is the insidious nature through which Oxbridge-educated journalists write in what they perceive to be working-class prose, in order to divide such an audience and direct them into behaviours that stand in apposition to their own material interests. Meanwhile, the supposedly liberal media outlets harbour journalists who crave the 'soft centre' and ultimately refrain from upsetting the establishment. We outline just how important transparent and accountable media is to an informed democracy.

Once we examine the scale of the task we face, we are in a position to begin discussing solutions. This should be the goal for all of us; figuring out ways to improve the relatively short time we spend revolving around the sun. Chapter 5 begins with a wider discussion about how to articulate a message of progressive change that stimulates mass appeal. This involves recognising the challenges of appeasing a heterogeneous group with disparate values and interests, invoking such things as the universal provision of quality healthcare, education and housing, and a *real* living wage. Essentially, the utopian vision conjured is one where people are relinquished from both pointless jobs and mundane work as much as possible. The case is presented for worker co-operatives so that people are not alienated from their labour and receive rewards consummate with their efforts. Re-evaluating consumption patterns will aid a transition beyond capitalism to more localised forms of production and consumption as we aim for a life post-capitalism, or 'post-growth', and a reconnecting with non-material conceptions of the good life. There is also an account of the benefits and rationale for occupying unused, privately owned land for communal or environmental re-purposing.

These changes are not going to be achieved overnight, nor are they going to be easy. Some are certainly going to be met with hostility, including by those who actually stand to benefit from them. What I can say with great certainty is that the futures proposed here and the work required to get us there will not be as arduous as rituals such as hitting the snooze button multiple times, the daily commute, and the existential dread that often accompanies a 9–5 job that we perform weekly. Despite feelings of powerlessness, positive change has only come about when groups of people have joined together to say enough is enough. We owe it to ourselves and those who will follow to outline alternative futures for society and have concrete ideals to aim towards. After all, there is still a world to win!

ONE

WORK

'What the world wants is a good job. Humans used to desire love, money, food, shelter, safety, peace, and freedom more than anything else. The last thirty years has changed us. Now people want to have a good job, and they want their children to have a good job'[3]

This is a quote from Jim Clifton, Chairman and CEO of Gallup, the global analytics and advice firm renowned for its worldwide opinion polls. Naturally there are debates regarding what constitutes a 'good' job, but for Jim Clifton this merely translates to a regular salary. This feels somewhat underwhelming. If we are forgoing the rather loftier ambitions of engineering world peace, eradicating poverty, and avoiding environmental catastrophe to focus on securing a regular income then this represents a huge victory for our prevailing economic and social system. It is the goal of this chapter to de-mythologise work and create the foundations for alternative futures, not least because our fetish for work is inextricably linked to the aforementioned goals of eliminating poverty and avoiding ecological suicide.

It is widely acknowledged that Brits work some of the longest hours in Europe and beyond. That this is willingly facilitated by the state is well evidenced in our ability to opt out of the 48-hour working week as stipulated in the EU's Working Time Directive. Yet this extends beyond paid working hours with Britain claiming the undesirable title of 'unpaid capital of Europe'. Research by ADP finds that

---

3   Jim Clifton (2011) *The Coming Jobs War*. Gallup Press

people in Britain average an additional 6.3 hours of unpaid overtime per week (equating to around £5,000 of additional free work for our employers), which works out to £164.8 billion of unpaid overtime annually[4]. Workers polled by the credit report and score website TotallyMoney reported an average of 10 hours of discretionary overtime per week – which equates to someone's pay stopping on 16 October once those hours are totalled. After offering up so much of our time to employers one might expect to eventually enjoy the fruits of their long labour, yet the retirement age has not only gone up, it has disappeared entirely. Former Secretary of State for Work and Pensions (and architect of Universal Credit) Iain Duncan Smith fronts the right-wing think-tank, and seemingly ironically named, Centre for Social Justice. In 2019 they proposed that the state pension age be incrementally increased to 75: this at a time when the government's own figures had the average UK life expectancy at 79.4 years. So even if you are fortunate enough to not live in one of Britain's most deprived areas where you are quite literally forced to work until you die, the average Brit can expect just 4.4 years of relaxation after a life of toil if the elitist class has its way.

That we have succumbed to this state of affairs is partly a result of the 'fetish' for work being drilled into us for a very long time, with the Bible making reference to St Paul's admonition '*if any would not work neither should he eat*' (II Thessalonians 3:10). It is enshrined in key legislation; for example the 1948 Universal Declaration of Human Rights (Article 23 (1)) pays credence to the 'right to work' of all humans as fundamental. While the opportunity to work is positioned as a positive here (as something we need or want the right to do) it actually translates as a duty in most societies, for example ours where unemployment is punished and entitlement to welfare is increasingly dependent on the obligation to work[5]. The pantomime villain to capitalism – our system where everyone has a chance to 'make it' via working hard – similarly harbours a compulsion to work. In the *Principles of Communism*, Friedrich Engels draft version of *The Communist Manifesto*, it clearly states that there is an equal obligation on all members of society to work. The Soviet Union was driven by this same notion, with Alexey Stakhanov the benchmark for ordinary people[6].

---

4   ADP, 'Workforce View in Europe 2019' report
5   Points well-argued by Schutt (2010) in *Beyond the Profits System: Possibilities for a Post-Capitalist Era*, ZED Books
6   Stakhanov reportedly mined 14x his quota during one shift and Stalin's party officials pushed 'Stakhanovite' propaganda, encouraging workers to follow suit, i.e. to take pride in producing more than was necessary. See Siegelbaum (1990) *Stakhanovism and the Politics of Productivity in the USSR, 1935–1941*, Cambridge University Press

Practically every aspect of our upbringing and life thereafter revolves around work. Children who are naturally curious, unmoulded and above all else interested in play, are set about what is essentially a 40-hour week in school, with the tedium of assemblies, classes and so forth akin to a job, and the regimented hours and uniforms preparing them for a life of work. The question 'what do you want to be when you grow up?' reaffirms that we become our chosen occupation, recognising that this choice is often a constrained one depending upon the perceived and actual opportunities available to us. How are taxes worked out? In a way that will stimulate job creation. Legislation regarding workers' rights and protections? Deliberately non-interventionist so as not to compromise job creation. The two groups in our society that are most openly chastised are done so on the basis of work: both immigrants ('taking our jobs') and scroungers ('never worked a day in their lives'). In the US, Donald Trump's electoral success was built around notions of 'making America great again', which centred on bringing jobs back to the immiserated Rust Belt. Here in Britain the Conservative Party manifesto claimed that 'work is the best route out of poverty' following the mantra of the Tory-Lib Dem government to 'Get Britain Working'.

And yet, despite work being mythologised, the clue is in the very language itself. The word for 'work' in French is travail, which derives from the Latin word trapaliare, meaning 'to torture'. The German equivalent arbeit connotates effort, hardship, and suffering. In Slavonic languages rabota (from which English has taken 'robot') is tied up in definitions of serfdom[7]. Democracy, the great principle on which our society is purportedly founded, is thrown out of the window for many people when assuming work roles. And what exactly is a job? A requirement to perform a small number of productive tasks repeatedly on an or-else basis; ejected once your exploitation is no longer required. To have a 'superior' who tells you where to be, at what time, for how long; how much work to do and how fast; what to wear; and the freedom to control a person to humiliating extents, where voicing one's concerns can be deemed insubordination. Bob Black likens work to 'factory fascism' and 'office oligarchy'[8]. Peter Fleming describes the fate of workers as resembling that of criminal offenders in open prisons: 'free but also incarcerated, mobile but ultimately tracked, with tentative rights that are always on the verge of being

---

7   See Jeremy Seabrook (2013) Pauperland: Poverty and the Poor in Britain. C. Hurst & Co
8   Bob Black (1985) The Abolition of Work and Other Essays, Loompanics Unlimited

revoked'[9]. Where individuals are not confined to a workplace and a regimented routine (clocking in, clocking out, etc.) they may live under abstract work commitments that are never fulfilled and always hanging over us.

PAID WORK IS INHERENTLY EXPLOITATIVE

Because work is so ingrained into our psyche it is now perceived to be the natural order of things: in effect you go to school, college (or start work), university (or start work), get a job, get a house, get married, all of which costs lots of money and require you to continue working. But the employment relationship is as unnatural and unhealthy a relationship as one can be in. We are effectively commodities: putting a price on our time, energy, skills and knowledge, and renting ourselves to an organisation that meets what we think is a 'fair' valuation of ourselves. And once we do, we put to one side the things we would much rather spend our time doing, which, when it comes to commuting, sitting behind a desk and engaging in oft-soul-destroying tasks for much of the day, is quite an extensive list. As it was put to me by an undergraduate student looking to delay their foray into the world of work for as long as possible, 'your salary is the price you are paid to forget your dreams'. Perhaps this is cynical, but having to suppress our true selves and aspirations, five days out of seven, until we are nearly 70 or even beyond lends some support to this assessment.

This whole thing would perhaps make more sense as a way to organise society if attempts were made to make work more enjoyable, satisfying, or at the very least not exploitative. Naturally, there are people who do enjoy the work that they do, and even the act of going to work if for nothing but the sense of structure, functionality, and ultimately purpose it brings to their day. People meet friends and even partners at work. Yet, there are any number of reasons why paid work is exploitative by its very nature. Here we will focus on two: one refers to life before accepting employment; the second refers to life during employment.

THE ILLUSION OF CHOICE

The employment relationship is often positioned as one that we freely opt into. In effect, we have a choice to accept the terms and conditions on offer,

---

9   Peter Fleming (2015) *The Mythology of Work: How Capitalism Persists Despite Itself*, Pluto Press

therefore if we do accept a job offer then we lose some entitlement to complain about it. In other words, we can simply walk away if we find the conditions unpalatable. The first problem here is this illusion of choice – there is only so much walking away from jobs and job offers that do not meet all of our needs and desires before we are compelled to accept work we would otherwise abstain from. If you do not own the means of production, i.e. the capability to employ other people to work for you and derive your livelihood from their labour, you are eventually forced to use the only tools you do have, which is your own productive labour. And yet, how often is the valuation we have of ourselves met? Are we not forced into conceding lower terms and conditions than we would like? A quick glance at any recent data tells us that around three-quarters of the British workforce believe that they are not paid a fair wage[10].

The reason for this partly stems from the fact that the employment relationship is not an equal one. The balance of power sits with the employer as our livelihoods depend more on them (as finding new employment is not always quick or easy) than theirs does on us, unless we bring scarce, difficult-to-replace skills to the table. Eventually if one's pre-disposition is to avoid work this attitude will have to change as your situation becomes more desperate, unless you are to inherit a large sum of money. There are not many alternatives – crime? Become one of the stigmatised welfare recipients currently coerced into work for welfare benefits? All roads inevitably lead back to the starting point, being compelled to work. In effect, employment is therefore commonly forced labour, via economic and political means.

Secondly, other people are in exactly the same position. They too may be saddled with student debt, rent or mortgage payments, and dependents to provide for. Employers know this; indeed, the Office for National Statistics publishes monthly updates telling us approximately how many people are unemployed, the number of temporary workers who would like a permanent position, and those working part-time but desire longer hours. As a result of this there is little incentive for employers to improve wages and working conditions as there is always someone else who may be willing to accept a job for terms you are not wholly satisfied with. Naturally, this effectively forces people to work for less than what they believe and indeed they may deserve. This is particularly acute during times of economic uncertainty, which now

10   CIPD, 'Reward Management Survey' 2019

appears to be a permanent fixture after a decade of austerity, Brexit, and the Covid pandemic.

Simultaneously, this causes people to become individual, competitive, cynical, distrusting, and all the other characteristics you would not want in a cohesive, well-functioning society. In order to get ahead at work someone else does not get the job, promotion, or pay rise. This further creates a situation where some people will work harder to make themselves more attractive to employers, whether that equates to spending time outside of work becoming more 'employable', to unpaid overtime becoming normalised for those in work (as already noted) irrespective of the consequences, not least relationships outside of work suffering. If a colleague is replying to emails at 9pm by virtue of a work phone or laptop, employers might perceive that others are less committed to the organisation if they do not follow suit – despite the fact that this is beyond one's paid remit. Even firms with chequered histories have started to do something about this; for example, Volkswagen became the first company to ensure that emails sent after 6pm and during someone's annual leave do not make it to the recipient, to reduce the stress induced by an ever-brimming inbox[11]. But such a practice is not commonplace. Even your hobbies and interests outside of work may be scrutinised by employers, as they might demonstrate transferable skills or give more insights into your personality. So-called 'cybervetting' of private social media accounts by employers demonstrates that control is no longer confined to what people do at work but has expanded to life outside of the workplace too.

THE WAGE-EFFORT BARGAIN

The second issue to briefly focus on here concerns our value as workers, and how this relates to what we are paid. We go to work with the implicit understanding that we are exploited. If we were paid an amount of money that truly reflected the value we produce while at work then the company could only ever break even. In order to turn a profit and keep our employment going, we have to accept that we are underpaid, and that we are creating surplus value for our employer. In effect, *we* are basically paying *them* (the difference between the value we produce and the value of the wage that we receive) for the privilege of working for them. Yet, without the ability (usually necessary capital) to live off anything other than our labour power, it can seem that alternative options are few and far between.

But that is not all. As employers are not guaranteed a fixed amount of work

---

11   BBC News, 'Volkswagen turns off Blackberry email after work hours', 8 March 2012

from us – we are human beings, after all, who can tire towards the end of a long shift, resist unfair work targets, and so forth – there is a continuous drive to extract as much surplus value from us as an organisation can. How else can they compete with the Amazons of this world who have exploited workers in order to gain a competitive advantage? Particularly if you are not doing your 'dream' job, the chances are that an employer expects more work from you than you would like to give, or would without supervision, meaning that a degree of control is inevitable. There are reminders that time at work is not our own, that we have sold our time and ourselves to an employer for a fixed number of hours, with assertions such as 'you're on my time now' or 'I'm not paying you to lounge around'. This is the inherently antagonistic nature of the employment relationship: management is required to both control labour (i.e. ensure that they maintain maximum effort) and harness their motivation and commitment, which is a contradictory dynamic (i.e. your commitment to something is prone to wane if they are making you work harder than you feel you are rewarded for). Historically this has led to a range of managerial ideologies and tactics, from work intensification to increased automation, simultaneously fragmenting tasks into simple, thus unskilled and low-paid series of actions from which little intrinsic reward can be derived. Due to the nature of capitalism where firms compete with other firms on the global stage, in chasing competitive advantage workers will be subject to tight controls so that they work harder than is 'pleasant'.

Work can therefore be replete with daily humiliations: being told off by a superior, having to accept a rude disposition from customers, maintaining social ties with colleagues you have nothing in common with, the indignity of repeating the same monotonous task over and over, anything at all. Often people have to carve out ways to make the working week more bearable, from venting 'backstage' with other colleagues, to imagined or actual acts of civil disobedience against the organisation. That conflict remains at the heart of the employment relationship is evidenced via a range of different measures – be it dispute cases making their way to an employment tribunal, the workload of the Advisory, Conciliation and Arbitration Service (ACAS), working days lost due to strike action, frequency of disciplinaries and grievance proceedings, and much more. More than one-in-three employees in the UK report experiencing conflict at work[12], with managers spending nearly two days per week dealing with conflict at a cost of billions to the economy.

---

12   CIPD, 'Managing conflict in the modern workplace' report, January 2020

So we have established that paid work is inherently exploitative, that we do not perhaps have the degree of choice proponents of capitalism say that we have when it comes to making decisions about work (and consequently non-work commitments), that typically we do not share the balance of power with employers which allows them a degree of control over our behaviours and even emotions, and as we will see wages have been stagnating while we are effectively forced to work more (paid and unpaid overtime) for less. It does not make great reading. But if work is necessary then it is just an unfortunate fact of life that we must live with. So, is it necessary?

MOST JOBS ARE POINTLESS

In an enthralling yet terrifying assessment of jobs in contemporary society, David Graeber distinguishes between different types of work:

> 'Shit jobs tend to be blue collar and pay by the hour, whereas bullshit jobs tend to be white collar and salaried. Those who work shit jobs tend to be the object of indignities; they not only work hard but also are held in low esteem for that very reason. But at least they know they're doing something useful. Those who work in bullshit jobs are often surrounded by honor and prestige; they are respected as professionals, well paid, and treated as high achievers – as the sort of people who can be justly proud of what they do. Yet secretly they are aware that they have achieved nothing; they feel they have done nothing to earn the consumer toys with which they fill their lives; they feel it's all based on a lie – as, indeed, it is'[13]

There is a burgeoning literature reporting that while the need to be paid is the main motivation for working, people look for a deeper meaning in the work that they do, to the point where they would be willing to earn less money to do more meaningful work. In effect, pay satisfies us enough to turn up for work but to actually be motivated while there we need to find some value or purpose in what it is that we do each day. Naturally what constitutes 'meaningful' work will differ from person to person, but there are likely to be some common

---

13   David Graeber (2018) *Bullsh*t Jobs: The Rise of Pointless Work and What We Can Do About It*, Penguin Books

characteristics; for example, feeling like you contribute to society or the planet, garner unity with others, and such like.

To illustrate, presumably most people would take much greater satisfaction working in a turtle conservation role on the beaches of Costa Rica than they would a cold-caller in a Dewsbury call centre attempting to sell people something they do not need. I once worked a three-hour unpaid shift masquerading as a 'trial' in a call centre trying to shift overly expensive house alarm systems. As soon as a call ended the next victim was automatically dialled as I readied the script which began 'due to increased crime in your area...'. When not being understandably berated for disrupting people's mealtimes, some would ask questions like, 'Oh yeah, what area is that then?' I never knew. Occasionally a speculative guess such as 'South Yorkshire?' was correct, but not enough times to overcome the constant reaffirmation that I most certainly *was* contributing to society, just negatively.

A recent YouGov poll found that despite 87% of British workers describing a job that feels purposeful as important to them, only 26% find their work 'very meaningful'[14]. Our friend Jim Clifton drew attention to the fact that this is a worldwide phenomenon, when a Gallup survey of 142 countries found that globally just 15% of people are engaged in the work that they do[15]. This means that swathes of people suffer the indignity and intolerability of spending the vast majority of their lives doing something that they would prefer not to be doing. It is remarkable when you think about it. Whatever your view of work this is indicative of a flawed system: an independent review for Theresa May's Tory government found that there are more people working with mental health conditions than ever before and that poor mental health costs employers as much as £42 billion per year[16]. Beyond this, these are hardly the ingredients for a healthy and happy society. Taking some crude figures:

- There are (24 x 7=) 168 total hours in a week.
- If you are lucky enough to get 8 hours sleep per night, (8 x 7=) 56 hours per week sleeping[17].

---

14 YouGov, 'Quarter of British workers find jobs lack meaning', 20 February 2020
15 'The World's Broken Workplace', 13 June 2017
16 'Thriving at work: The Stevenson / Farmer review of mental health and employers', October 2017
17 See Jonathan Crary (2014) *24/7: Late Capitalism and the Ends of Sleep* for a fantastic account of how sleep, representing an affront to the theft of time from us by capitalism, has eroded to around 6½ hours per night

- If you work a standard week (9am–5pm, Monday to Friday) and are lucky enough not to have to bring any work home with you as either paid or unpaid overtime (8 x 5=) 40 hours per week working.
- If you are also lucky enough to have a relatively short commute, say 30 minutes there and 30 minutes back home, (1 x 5=) 5 hours per week commuting to/from work.
- You are left with just 67 hours per week spent not working or restoring your energy for more work. This is disconcerting enough, but if your job is essentially pointless or society would not be worse off without it, surely this is time that could be better spent doing something else.

This is the life that is sold to all young people. In your early teenage years you are already forced to pick subjects to study, and then again at college: which is likely to encourage young people to pick certain courses that are associated with a relatively well-paid income. This might explain why we have so many accountants – approximately 280k, much higher than anywhere else in Europe. To put this into perspective we have circa 50k family doctors. Even if you perceive accountants to be important to our society and doing work that has great purpose and meaning, we simply do not need that many. If you have an over-supply of people in any one occupation then you are of course going to have accountants who are out of work or under-employed on the one hand, and others overworked or setting up accountancy firms to create their own jobs (which simply are not needed) on the other. What a bizarre way to organise a society given that said society simply does not need so many people engaging in this type of activity, many of whom may not even be wholly fulfilled by this work they are doing. These people could be either a) doing more meaningful work, or b) they could all be accountants, if that is what they wish, but share the overall accounting workload and all work less, thus each getting to enjoy more leisure time. Either way, the reality is less favourable than the alternatives.

Even jobs that are likely to attract a degree of consensus as 'meaningful' to society seem to have experienced a drive towards ever-increasing amounts of pointless busywork. This is often bureaucratic, administrative 'time-intensive' activities whose necessity and value we might question. British workers estimate that they spend more than two hours each day on meaningless tasks when there is more important work to be done, which equates to fifteen weeks per year[18]. Such tasks will resonate with many, such as working out how to use old or failing technology, or reading emails that have no relevance to you whatsoever, but someone elsewhere in the organisation has decided 'we better send to this to everyone, just in case'. OVO Energy calculate that Brits send as many as 64 million unnecessary emails per day, which aside from wasting people's time amounts to the same yearly carbon footprint as over 81,000 flights to Madrid[19]. Most people sit in meetings either wondering what the point of them is, or that the key messages could have been conveyed much more quickly. In looking at figures for the US, ACAS report that managers typically attend as many as 60 meetings per month[20], which translates at 720 meetings per year and 21,600 meetings for anyone who spends 30 years in a managerial position. These figures are as alarming as they are wholly unnecessary. The fact is, between waiting for the day to end, chatting, having a quick look on Twitter, and everything else, we are paid to look like we are working some days as much as we spend actually productively working.

Those performing meaningful work tend to be exploited precisely because of it. Take care work, demographically we are an ageing population and already do not have a sufficient care sector to take care of those who need it. Instead of incentivising more people to enter into this occupation, care work is fraught with zero-hour contracts, low pay, and a lack of training or advancement opportunities. Are the reasons for this sexist given that care is a female-dominated sector? For example, do we see caring as an inherent skill for many women and therefore does not deserve the remuneration people get for developing other 'technical' skills? Do we expect carers to be intrinsically rewarded by the work they do, and therefore they do not need to be well-paid too? Each justification is as controversial as its predecessor. When you consider that other professions such as teaching are largely underpaid also, it becomes apparent that those who engage in meaningful work are somewhat punished for it by being undervalued and underpaid. In a way, we are therefore accepting that the only way to get people to put in long hours for the very many bullsh*t jobs that make up our society is to pay them more.

We would be well served to discuss, democratically, what it is that we

---

18 *Independent*, 'Employees feel they waste 15 weeks of year on 'pointless' tasks, poll claims', 11 June 2019

19 OVO Energy, 'Think Before You Thank', 26 November 2019

20 ACAS, 'What makes a business meeting worthwhile?', Workplace snippets 2015

collectively want from society. This should serve as the starting point from which we dispense with jobs that either are not required or create enough permanent existential dread to those who undertake it that they simply are not worth it. We are talking about jobs that exist solely to fulfil unproductive commercial means that line the pockets of very few, that use up valuable ecological resources, and add little fulfilment to people's lives – both those that consume such products and services and those that provide them. Yes, marketing executives, that includes you[21].

ROBOT WARS

'Labour Process' theory has demonstrated that capitalism breeds the expansion of wide-ranging tedious jobs, not least as technology has advanced. Traditionally skilled craftwork that offered autonomy and inherent value to those who undertook it has largely been replaced by automated, de-skilled, and thus lower-paid and increasingly precarious employment. And this feels entirely unnecessary: we find ourselves in a situation via technological advancement that machines can be doing much of the tedious, monotonous work for us. Instead of fearing technology taking our jobs, why not accelerate it to liberate us from as much work as possible? Unfortunately, this is another impossibility within the system we find ourselves. Capitalists would like to be rid of human labour in the sense that we are the most unruly part of the production process – we can resist, we can unionise and strike, we can make mistakes, and we can take too long during breaks. Equally, it is in their interests to implement technological change insofar as it trims the required human labour, ensuring that there are always people looking for work and thus wages and conditions can be contained. Likewise, technology acts as a digital panopticon[22] that enables ever more intrusive monitoring and surveillance of employees, including the need to police one's activity during non-employment hours. In sum, most capitalists would probably like nothing more than for technology to take on all of the work, yet capital needs labour as much as labour needs capital (in lieu of other ways to

---

21 William Morris was among those making similar arguments as far back as 1885 (see *Useful Work versus Useless Toil*)

22 The architectural form of prison pioneered by Jeremy Bentham in the 18th century, designed so that even when inmates were not actively being monitored, their behaviour could be controlled by the constant feeling that they were being watched

earn a crust). If we do not work, there is no-one to buy their products or use their services. This is not to say that such a situation is idealistic beyond all possibility.

Should we harness the ability of technology to produce much of what humans *actually* need outside of capitals control of said technology, say under the democratic control of society, the realms of possibility began to expand. Such an idea is not new. Bertrand Russell's 1935 essay *In Praise of Idleness* calls us to arms:

> 'Modern methods of production have given us the possibility of ease and security for all; we have chosen, instead, to have overwork for some and starvation for others. Hitherto we have continued to be as energetic as we were before there were machines; in this we have been foolish, but there is no reason to go on being foolish for ever'.

Products and services only have a value because people are willing to pay for them. If effort no longer went into making things as technology stepped in, and people therefore were working less and had less money to spend, said products and services would lose their value. Let us take this further: if workers or a democratically elected government decided to take over the production of goods and services and utilised technology to make or provide as much of it as possible, the system of producing products and services for private profit would fall apart at the seams. Although we currently feel very far removed from such a situation, it strikes me that if enough people begin to move away from this idea that technology will make us all jobless and this is a terrible thing, to consider what other possibilities this might bring, then such discussions can become more frequent and nuanced.

THE RIGHT TO BE LAZY[23]

One of the most important theorists on the development of modern Western society, Max Weber, observed workers that were paid piecemeal rate for their output simply stopped working halfway through the day[24]. The logic for this is pretty clear, as why would anyone continue to toil once they meet their basic

---

23   Title borrowed from a classic essay of the same name by Paul Lafargue, written while in exile during 1883
24   Max Weber (1905) *The Protestant Ethic and the 'Spirit' of Capitalism*, Unwin Hyman

needs in a satisfactory manner? His suggestion is that historically work was viewed as a means rather than an end, something done to provide subsistence instead of something to revolve our lives and identities around. There are countless examples throughout history calling on us to question our priorities and way of living. In 18th-century America, many colonisers decided to join Native American communities but there were no recorded instances of this exchange happening the opposite way. In a letter entitled 'The support of the poor' written by founding father of the US Benjamin Franklin in May 1753 he said:

> 'The proneness of human nature to a life of ease, of freedom from care and labour appears strongly in the little success that has hitherto attended every attempt to civilize our American Indians...When an Indian child has been brought up among us, taught our language and habituated to our Customs, yet if he goes to see his relations and make one Indian ramble with them, there is no perswading him ever to return, and that this is not natural to them merely as Indians, but as men, is plain from this, that when white persons of either sex have been taken prisoners young by the Indians, and lived a while among them, tho' ransomed by their Friends, and treated with all imaginable tenderness to prevail with them to stay among the English, yet in a Short time they become disgusted with our manner of life, and the care and pains that are necessary to support it, and take the first good Opportunity of escaping again into the Woods, from whence there is no reclaiming them[25]'.

Fast forward and work appears to be a calling from within rather than something merely imposed from outside, what Weber attributes to the Protestant work ethic; to not work hard is sacrilege, leading to feelings of anxiety and guilt, with others on hand to remind you of your duties. Work ethic has been central to (particularly male, breadwinning) working-class pride and identity. Is it cynical to suggest that this has been drubbed into us so that the masses work hard – almost inevitably for the benefit of those in control of the means of production who they actually work and thus generate profit for? Furthermore, to contribute to notions of meritocracy and the belief that those who work

---

25   As ever, the elitist class could not afford for people to down tools or seek otherworldly pleasures as their labour was necessary to sustain the elite's idleness. Many European defectors were shot, hung or burned at the stake by their lords as a way to dissuade more Europeans from joining the natives, yet the defections continued

hard will reap the rewards? And to not only individualise the working-classes so that they act in a more competitive and selfish manner, but to divide them among those who are seen to work hard and provide, and those who do not – to be castigated as layabouts and scroungers. Countless anthropologic studies in remote corners of the world document happy people living without much by way of material possession, in nature, working only insofar as it is necessary to provide for a sufficient standard of living. Those considered to be the greatest minds the world has ever known, including the father of logical thought Aristotle, had only contempt for work.

One may then question why we work such long hours. The answer may partly be because society has developed such that we have little choice given that living costs are expensive and generally rise (despite the whole point of neoliberalism, so we are told, is to increase competition and reduce costs/prices) and there is a constant influx of bills to pay. Added to this, we are continually marketed products we simply do not need, or feel peer pressured into purchasing trends as dictated by a society focused on deriving a large amount of life satisfaction from material possessions that go beyond what we do need[26]. This is of course aided by a drive from the capitalist class 'to discover consumers, to excite their appetites and create in them fictitious needs' (Lafargue *ibid*: p. 40). In a similar vein, to make a life far too taken up by work seem more bearable people may seek solitude in things like holidays, which tend to come with high price tags too. Naturally there are practical reasons from an employer's perspective, such as the greater costs incurred by hiring multiple people (training them, etc.) for a job one person can do. From their perspective, it is also a means of control, as someone working long hours at a company forces a level of dependency from employee to employer, as their livelihoods are thus tied up in that job role and the need to sustain it. It also helps to build a culture of presenteeism, where employees will vie with each other to look the most committed to the firm in order to be offered promotional opportunities and so forth.

There is another more cynical reason, alluded to notions of control at work above. Peter Fleming (*ibid*) suggests that our ruling class cannot allow working people to enjoy the independence that progress (such as in technology) could so easily bestow on us as we would become profligate idlers. In other words,

---

26   Websites exist with domain names like 'uselessthingstobuy.com'. Partly in horror, partly as a victim of capitalism forever curious in what is on offer, I scrolled through more of these products that I care to admit

because there are other things outside of work that we would prefer to do, and such self-preservation is not in the interests of our masters, we must be kept at/doing work as much as possible. And there is logic to this: capitalism is a continuous quest to enhance competitiveness, which means cutting costs and increasing efficiency. It therefore does not follow that millions of people would be doing meaningless jobs, or meaningful jobs that incorporate meaningless tasks. If endless hours of pointless work are not designed to keep us busy then what are they designed for? For as long as people are kept busy, the less opportunity they have to become politically engaged, to educate themselves on how the world works, to become accustomed to a different way of life that is not work-centred – most likely a better one. Allowing the proliferation of meaningless work would not even be the most ingenious or nefarious thing that the elitist class has concocted in a bid to maintain the status quo, so it is not beyond the realms of possibility or imagination.

It is certainly a time-honoured tradition, with deliberate impoverishment (via enclosing common land and forcing people into waged labour, as discussed below) a common occurrence in the historical records of landowners. As one example, Joseph Townsend noted in 1786 that 'Hunger will tame the fiercest animals, it will teach decency and civility, obedience and subjugation to the most brutish, the most obstinate, and the most perverse… In general, it is only hunger which can spur and goad them on to labour'[27]. In 1650 the Diggers (or so-called 'True Levellers') led by Gerrard Winstanley, were driven from enclosed land by the military, local officials and landowners when attempting to farm it as part of an early attempt at a society without private property, wage labour and thus class hierarchy[28]. For centuries priests have convinced peasants and the poor that their suffering was all part of God's plan and that eternal bliss awaited them in this intangible, unknowable location called heaven, and thus salvation is not something worth fighting for here on earth. In-between beheading his wives Henry VIII proclaimed that 'idleness is the mother and root of all vices' and oversaw the Punishment of Beggars and Vagabonds Statute in 1531, effectively forcing people into work (not before punishment via flogging). This was all largely due to the fact that – although few of us would be envious of how our medieval ancestors lived – they were

---

27   Joseph Townsend (1817) *Dissertation on the Poor Laws*, Ridgways
28   Writing in *Tribune*, Rebecca Tamás notes the irony that the former home of the Diggers is now a private gated community (home to none other than the likes of Tom Jones and Elton John)

keen to work only the required amount needed to survive. It is suggested that the medieval calendar was replete with holidays, accounting to as much as one-third of the year; explorers of the time suggest that their Spanish compatriots had as much as five months of celebrations and rest days[29].

Those with money often choose to do less work, or rather, prefer to have others doing the majority of it. As early as 1827 William Thompson referred to capitalists as the 'idle classes', for is it not those who do not have to labour (i.e. those who live off inheritance; money received through rent for their various properties; the toil of others) that truly have the right to be lazy[30]? This is something that was widely expected to await we, the majority, also as technology was supposed to liberate us from work. Indeed, the father of post-war economics himself John Maynard Keynes wrote in 1930:

> 'For the first time since his creation man will be faced with his real, his permanent problem – how to use his freedom from pressing economic cares, how to occupy the leisure… to live wisely and agreeably and well'[31]

Some problem! This has clearly not materialised in the way it was foreseen.

Still, there are many people who have attempted to give up the 'rat race' and work less, if at all. David Frayne offers an insightful account of the experiences and challenges faced by such people[32]. Perhaps most interesting is that income was not as significant an issue for many as one might expect. Unwittingly or otherwise, many of us structure our lives around work in ways that dramatically increase our costs of living, thus negating said earnings to varying degrees. For example, if you want to live in close proximity to where the 'good' jobs are, London being a typical example, house and rent prices and general costs of living are extremely high. If you want to live further afield where house prices, council tax, and so forth are more reasonably priced, you are likely to incur substantial commuting costs, particularly if you rely on Britain's rail network which has the highest fares in Europe. Not to mention the exorbitant pricing of childcare, high-caffeine drinks to perk

---

29   Juliet Schor (2008) *The Overworked American: The Unexpected Decline of Leisure*. Basic Books

30   *How to Secure to Labour the Whole Product of Its Exertion, by One of the Idle Classes*; see also *The Theory of the Leisure Class* by Thorstein Veblen in 1899 for a detailed critique

31   John Maynard Keynes [1930] (2010) 'Economic Possibilities for our Grandchildren' in *Essays in Persuasion*. London: Palgrave, pp. 321–332

32   David Frayne (2015) *The Refusal to Work*, Zed Books

us up for a day's graft, and the raft of high-convenience foods and products designed specifically to exploit the lack of free time our work creates. Some of the people in Frayne's study simply moved beyond materialistic notions of 'the good life', finding real, authentic happiness around others, hobbies and interests, community endeavours, and ultimately engaging in such activities in a less frantic fashion than we have to when the next impending work day hangs over us. While not everyone has the practical means, particularly financially, to slow their lives down and work less, it is equally implausible that they will find true happiness in consumption patterns that will ever-stretch their finances.

Another key point to make here is that 'not working', or 'working less', is only synonymous with idleness because this is the dominant narrative we have been fed for a sustained period of time. In the 1877 essay *An Apology for Idlers* Robert Louis Stevenson stated that, 'Idleness… does not consist in doing nothing, but in doing a great deal not recognised in the dogmatic formularies of the ruling class'. Think about the kinds of things people would do with reduced working hours: learn to play a musical instrument? Play sports? Read literature? Climb mountains? Have children? The things we enjoy the most often involve immense amounts of effort[33]. Consider for a moment where British culture would be without the degree of freedom a welfare safety net has provided past generations: for example, four out of five members of the original Oasis band were on the dole as the group formed and began the process of orchestrating *Definitely Maybe*, which hit #1 in the music charts less than one week into its release. The UB40 form issued to people claiming unemployment benefit forever immortalised by Brummies with a penchant for reggae offers another example. Particularly women already spend a great deal of time undertaking work outside of employment (the clue is in the title with 'housework'), so why would we want more? Less time spent in employment could encourage more egalitarian sharing of housework and childcare, while simultaneously reducing the pressures around breadwinning many men face[34], with both fathers and children potentially benefitting from more time together.

---

33   As argued by Srnicek and Williams (2015) in *Inventing The Future*, Verso

34   Mental health has received much more attention in recent times, but we cannot ignore the propensity to crime, drugs and even suicides in men who are unable to meet cultural norms around the provider role. Linda McDowell has long done excellent work on this very issue (see, for example, 'The Trouble with Men?' *International Journal of Urban and Regional Research*, Vol. 24, Issue 1, pp. 201–209)

Ultimately, the title of this section is a tad misleading. What we are talking about here is the decommodification of labour: moving beyond having to sell your labour (your time, effort, expertise, postponed dreams) to someone with the means to effectively rent you for a period of time, in order to survive. Simultaneously, this means moving beyond exploitation, whereby people are paid less than the value of work they produce. Creating a situation where being a work-horse for the betterment of an individual capitalist or group of shareholders is not held on a pedestal and thinking about the conditions where this could be made possible. As Bhaskar Sunkara describes it, we are 'unwilling philanthropists, subsidizing the lavish lifestyles of the rich'. A life of working hard, stagnating wages, precariousness, not enough time for oneself, and more, all to enrich the lives of an elite who do not need to work themselves, if they wish.

In the utopia we will begin to imagine as we work through these ideas, anyone who enjoys what they do for a living needn't panic. You would not lose the ability to undertake the activities that provide you with a sense of meaning or enjoyment, merely you would have the scope to complete these in your own free time, without the pressures that accompany it in the employment sphere. 'Work' will remain for any society to function, but 'jobs' are something we can fashion into something more palatable. They are neither necessary nor desirable once we begin to think about what is good for the body, mind, and soul. Any of the more unpleasant types of work that technology cannot do for us would be bestowed with meaning and purpose, as well as other intrinsic rewards such as the gratitude of those who thus do not have to do it, thus rendering them much more pleasant. There will always be people with a desire to work on something productive, if not for themselves but the betterment of society, and we can cater for such people in this currently imagined utopia.

FECKLESS, WORKSHY SCROUNGERS

Politicians and the press have created the perception that one of society's central problems is incredibly straight-forward: the hardworking majority are not seeing an improvement in their lot because they are having to pay too much tax in order to support a section of society that does not work, and seemingly never intends to[35]. When the Tory-Lib Dem coalition came to power in 2010 announcing significant benefit cuts the public appeared to be strongly in favour of this. As one example, a YouGov poll found that 73% of respondents supported the idea of the long-term unemployed having to undertake compulsory work placements or risk losing their benefits. 66% supported the withdrawal of Jobseeker's Allowance benefit from anyone who turns down a job offer or interview. 69% supported more stringent testing of people claiming disability benefits[36]. Encapsulated by John Hills in *Good Times, Bad Times: The Welfare Myth of Them and Us*, the situation is often portrayed as 'people with their curtains drawn mid-morning versus alarm clock Britain, "Benefits Street" against the rest of the country, undeserving versus deserving. It's them against us. We are always in work, pay our taxes and get nothing from the state. They… pay nothing to the taxman, and get everything from the state' (p. 1).

The evidence, however, clearly demonstrates that people have a grossly inaccurate picture of exactly how much of taxpayers' money goes to the unemployed, and also who the main recipients of welfare are. Returning to YouGov for a moment, in a joint poll conducted with the TUC during the austerity period, the public's belief that there is a 'scrounger' issue in Britain was evidenced by the fact that respondents believed that 41% of the entire welfare budget is spent on benefits to unemployed people. In reality, the figure was 3% and more recently was just 1%[37]. Another major finding was that, on average, people felt that 27% of the welfare budget was claimed fraudulently. The government's own figure on this? 0.7%. And more recently this has hovered around 1%. Other misconceptions included a gross over-estimation of how many people are on benefits for more than a year, and the amount of benefits received[38].

Again, a quick glance at these figures, freely available to anyone with a few spare minutes and an internet connection, tells us that the proportion of people long-term unemployed (i.e. for a year or more) at the start of the Covid

---

35 In *Scroungers: Moral Panics and Media Myths*, James Morrison (2019) highlights how the term 'scrounger' was used 2,103 times in UK press articles about claimants in 2013, more than five times its use in 2007. It was also a popular year for terms such as 'shirker', 'skiver', and 'benefit tourist', as Universal Credit was rolled out by the Tory-Lib Dem coalition

36 YouGov, 'Strong public support for benefit cuts', 16 May 2011

37 ONS, 'How is the welfare budget spent?', 16 March 2016

38 TUC, 'Support for benefit cuts dependent on ignorance, TUC-commissioned poll finds', 4 January 2013

pandemic was 306,000[39]. This is not a trivial number, but the maths does not stack up that this amount of people – given that Jobseeker's Allowance ranges between £59–75 per week – are responsible for Britain's macro-economic problems. That an unemployed life on the dole is not tantamount to 'the good life' nor the first choice of most people is reflected in the reality that over a quarter of JSA claims end before three months has elapsed, and nearly half before six months. That a huge sect of society is living the high life at our expense is accurate – but it is not the people we are led to believe it is.

The 1% of the welfare bill spent on those unable or unwilling to work is dwarfed by the amount spent topping up the income of those who are in work but do not earn enough to ensure a modest standard of living – second only to the money spent on pensions. Indeed, the figures clearly show that the number of working households claiming welfare is much higher than the number of workless households who do so. As such, much of the welfare bill is actually for the benefit of business rather than individuals, with tax credits and so forth effectively subsidising corporations who are not paying their staff a living wage. Considering the burgeoning trend in zero-hour contracts and bogus self-employment contracts offered by the likes of Deliveroo, research suggests that the treasury loses out on £4 billion per year due to both the tax shortfalls and greater reliance on in-work tax credits[40]. This is yet another example of the taxpayer picking up the slack for corporations who are given an easy ride by the government; with corporate *welfare* conservatively estimated at £93 billion per year – but potentially double that according to non-profit organisation Corporate Welfare Watch.

We have been duped enormously in this notion that too much taxpayer money goes towards the 'feckless' and the 'workshy'. The real winners when it comes to taxpayer money are the same corporations who many of the public defend when it transpires that they have not been paying their full tax obligations, due to some vague notion that they are job creators and thus above the law. It is quite a feat to convince hordes of people to vote against their own interests, but the idea of scrounger Britain is a very effective method by the ruling class to divide those below them, tapping into people's frustration that others even further behind on the social mobility ladder might enjoy a similar, low, standard of living as they do despite working less. We can see this most

39 Office for National Statistics, 'Employment in the UK: March 2020' statistical bulletin
40 TUC, 'Rise in insecure work is costing Exchequer £4bn a year, warns TUC', 14 February 2017

clearly in the lies peddled by both politicians[41] and the media who position Labour as a party who makes life too easy for those who do not wish to work.

It is certainly true that Conservative politicians tend to hold more abhorrent views about those not in work, as demonstrated by Tory MP for Mansfield Ben Bradley, whose 2012 blog post 'Give us the benefits "cap" – before we all drown!' targeted unemployed benefits claimants with the words 'vasectomies are free'[42]. Yet, once again the facts belie the argument that Labour have made life 'too easy' for benefit claimants. The clue is even in the title: the 'Labour' Party represents those who labour, i.e. it was founded to ensure acceptable working conditions for the labour movement. If we look at their last time in office, it was under the Gordon Brown 'New Labour' government that Work and Pensions Secretary James Purnell introduced many new conditionality criteria for claimants, not least the introduction of Work Capability Assessments, where people were tested to see just how disabled and sick they were. Literally forcing people to work in order to receive benefits for reasons that stop them working reinforces the point that work is no longer a means to an end (to survive); work has become an end in itself. If there is a party that represents idle layabouts, is it not the 'leisure society' of rentiers that do not need to work in order to survive and live comfortably? Likewise, rather than those living off £400 per month, are the real 'scroungers' not those hiding £400 million in tax havens to avoid paying their share into public services? The political affiliation of both these groups are unlikely to be the Labour Party.

The 2015 Tory election win had £12 billion worth of 'welfare savings' at its core – to follow the many billions in the five years running up to this point. John Hills (*ibid*) calculates that the share of total income received by the middle-income group in Britain stood at 18% of the total in 1979. This fell to 16% by 2011, demonstrating that there has indeed been a pinch on 'middle Britain'. However, this squeeze has not come from the bottom group, whose share of total income went down from 10% in 1979 to 8% in 2011. Between 1979 and 2011 the top income group increased their share from 35–42%, a trend that has accelerated over the course of austerity, as will be discussed in the next chapter.

---

41 David Cameron made the bold claim (see *The Telegraph* 19 February 2014) that the number of workless households doubled under Labour's governance. In reality, the number actually fell between 1997 (where it stood at 20% of households) and 2010, even in the immediate aftermath of the global financial crash

42 *The Mirror*, '"Vasectomies are free": Tory party's new vice chair urged jobless to stop having kids or UK would 'drown in wasters'", 16 January 2018

It is perhaps unsurprising that masses of the public would respond to rhetoric and images of worklessness. In terms of real pay and living standards, the last decade and more have been pretty rubbish for many of us. In an age of insecure employment, soaring housing and fuel costs, and so forth, it is perhaps easier to rile people up with assertions that others are living off their hard-earned taxes while their lives do not improve. One has to question whether the misgivings of middle Britain are somewhat misplaced, and whether blame is apportioned to welfare recipients so that 'decent' hardworking folk blame them for society's problems rather than those who are actually in charge and unwilling or unable to make hard work translate into a happy life.

The pervasiveness of this 'them' and 'us' ideology has been found to exist between benefit claimants themselves: illustrated by Sarah Teather, former Lib Dem MP for Brent Central, who noted how claimants would distance themselves from others in the same boat and reference labels such as scroungers themselves[43]. This all feeds into wider narratives around a so-called 'deserving poor' versus the undeserving (or involuntary, working, or 'people like us') poor. This whole narrative of 'them' and 'us' is flawed: the Office for Budget Responsibility reports that over half of UK families receive at least one benefit as a primary or supplementary source of income, with the vast majority receiving benefits for at least one-third of their lives. For example, this could be child benefit in earlier years, and pensions in later years (pensions making up over half of the welfare bill: £94 billion compared to £2 billion spent on Jobseeker's Allowance). In reality there is only an 'us' given that practically everyone accesses welfare across their life course (be it via pensions, the NHS, etc.) and heaven forbid we experience a spell of unemployment and could use the support on offer.

It is understandable that people resent work and therefore look unfavourably on those who choose not to subject themselves to its repetitive, mind-numbing nature, but the outcome is not much different if such people *did* want to work, as the jobs are simply not there. Employment in a capitalist society is a zero-sum game: if one person gets a job, another person does not. There simply are not enough jobs to go around, particularly during a recession or in areas affected by deindustrialisation. Where employment does proliferate – for example, pretty much anyone can become a courier for platforms such as Deliveroo and Uber Eats, employment is precarious, low-paid and characterised by other issues. We

---

43   *The Guardian*, 'Skivers v strivers: the argument that pollutes people's minds', 9 January 2013

already know that work does not pay for some – testified by the numbers of people who live below the poverty line yet do not belong to workless households. I cannot imagine that anyone actually believes that every single person who is unemployed is workshy. So, if there are people genuinely looking for work that are unemployed, surely it follows that there are not enough jobs available for them? And by extension, there are not enough jobs for those who would rather not work too? On that basis, if we successfully convinced those who did not want to work to do a U-turn, and they gained employment, then without full employment across Britain they would simply replace someone else who then becomes an unemployed welfare recipient themselves.

As such, there are always going to be people claiming unemployment welfare unless the system changes and we achieve full employment. Full employment seems most plausible if you abolish meaningless work and have everyone working a reduced number of hours in those capacities that society genuinely needs. We need more social and affordable housing, more green spaces, better education, and so forth. It is therefore clear that there is much work to be done in our society. However, work is simply not related to satisfying our needs; rather it is tied to someone else's profit. As such, we are left with both unemployment and unsatisfied needs. Simultaneously, if you believe people claiming welfare (unemployment or otherwise) is one of society's main problems then what you are actually advocating for is a change to the system. Indeed, the more unequal a society is then the more there is a need to redistribute some wealth; it follows that if people wish to reduce the amount spent on welfare the most effective way to do so would be to work towards a fairer society. As another example, if we want less money to be spent on housing benefit, why not advocate for more affordable housing to be built so that less people rely on support? Cutting such benefits or making their eligibility more stringent results in people put out onto the streets – is the former idea not better? Ultimately, if more quality jobs, housing, and so forth were available not only would people's lives improve but the welfare bill would be reduced as a consequence. This logic is subordinated by governments who prefer to use welfare as a political stick to continue beating the poorest in society, and act like it is a drain on taxpayers' money while simultaneously keeping top tax rates and loopholes favourable to both them and their associates – at a greater cost to the public purse.

In *Cut Out: Living Without Welfare* Jeremy Seabrook offers an illuminating insight into the lives of our society's downtrodden. He argues, as have others, that the poor in a given society serve a primary function: to be scourged and punished but must on no account vanish. Their presence is essential as a deterrent to the respectable, well-to-do members of the public who must see this destitution and thus a sense of insecurity is maintained among the better-off. As such they must not become complacent, i.e. they are to continue working and striving for economic growth or such misfortune may befall them too. This insecurity is compounded by the notion that there is a 'reserve army of labour' waiting in the wings to take our job, should we not put in the additional discretionary (typically unpaid) overtime demanded in many occupations, further helping to constrain wages and conditions. For this reason, countries whose economies produce trillions of pounds in GDP each year have to find very deliberate ways of ensuring that enough people remain poor.

There are many reasons why someone may find it difficult to find or retain work, which, in our society, can very easily lead to homelessness and other forms of destitution. These things may include psychological trauma (e.g. caused by domestic violence, childhood abuse, bereavement, war, crime, or natural catastrophe), a range of mental, social and intellectual conditions and disorders, and physical impairments (with 70% of those classed as disabled becoming so during the course of their working lives). Personally, I can understand why those whose choice is between low-paid menial work that does not lift one out of poverty, versus a life enriched in other ways, such as more time with children and focusing on a family role rather than being employment-centred, would make such a decision. Tackling the burgeoning number of crap jobs, ludicrously expensive private childcare and lack of publicly provided childcare might be a better alternative to getting people into work rather than simply ostracising folk and letting children go hungry. There are many who understand this: we Brits generally consider ourselves a relatively civilised, conscientious folk. Full of goodwill and vague notions of world peace and human brotherhood, who can be counted upon to respond moderately to appeals made in the name of charity, and who are genuinely distressed at the sight of unwonted forms of misery and suffering[44]. For some people, the thought of supporting 'the poor' is a nice one but it is an expense we cannot afford; partly because, despite our good qualities, there are few things we feel such conviction about that we would over-sacrifice or jeopardise our material comforts for. Meanwhile, for others it is travesty that some people

---

44   Borrowing from George Couts (1978) *Dare the School Build a New Social Order*, Southern Illinois University Press

avoid the seemingly naturally pre-determined requirement to work many of the hours that God sends: 'If I have to, you have to as well.'

There also seems to be those who argue that more stringent eligibility and reduced benefits is important to protect against 'pathological poverty', i.e. this idea that intergenerational unemployment and dependency spawns a cycle of repeat. This was the justification given by some of the 322 Tory MPs who voted against extending free school meals for children in 2020, the idea that a couple of weeks' extra respite from hunger might breed a new generation of dependents. Research does not find a clear and convincing link between these two things at all, with MacDonald et al. (2014) failing to find such families but finding many people who felt very confident they exist (without being able to actually point to any for the research to go ahead)[45]. The same authors noted that figures from the UK Labour Force Surveys suggest families with two generations that had never worked amounted to less than 0.5% of all workless households.

Poverty exists not because we cannot feed the poor but because we can never satisfy the rich. The richest 1,000 families in the UK were worth £547 million each on average in 2015 and their share of overall wealth has continued to skyrocket while everyone has been subject to wage stagnation and a fall in 'real' terms income during a decade of economic uncertainty. Within the confines of the planet's natural resources, we are capable of ensuring that everyone's basic needs: adequate food supply, clean water, decent sanitation, housing, education, healthcare, etc., are met. The fact that they are not reflects the system we are led to believe is some kind of natural order yet is a politically chosen one. It is the insatiable desire for more by those who already have enough that are diminishing our natural resources. Not providing everyone with their basic needs might be understandable if our resources could not take it – for example, the planet became too over-populated – but not doing this because it impinges on those who already have 'a lot' is very difficult to justify[46].

Capitalism creates an endless series of products and services, most of which we do not need, marketed to ensure that we have a steady supply of wants – which often present themselves as needs. Both of these things within

---

45 MacDonald, Shildrick and Furlong (2014) 'In search of "intergenerational cultures of worklessness": hunting the yeti and shooting zombies'. *Critical Social Policy*. 34 (2) p. 199–220

46 To rebuff this myth of over-population, if everyone lived as densely as the population do in Hong Kong, every single human being could live in just Egypt alone (see *Financial Times*, 'Jamil Anderlini's guide to Hong Kong', 18 January 2021)

the realms of affordability for most people and many beyond. This creates a situation where we all feel like we are without things we want – that we are all deprived in some way, exacerbated by the aforementioned stagnating and falling wages in real terms. This 'poverty', unlike the absence of the necessities of life which can be cured via government intervention, the charitable actions of others, etc., cannot – it is an inherent feature of capitalism's perpetual expansion and has become the perceptibly natural condition of humankind. This ever-constant feeling of inadequacy, of being un-rewarded irrespective of whether disposable incomes increase or not, helps to sustain a situation where the majority are less likely to sympathise with the poor because most feel like they cannot satisfy their own desire either. Likewise, it is more likely to deter people from sympathising with the unemployed because they cannot fulfil their own desires despite working, 'so why should those who don't work get more of what *they* want?'. We increasingly measure ourselves against what we would like to have rather than what we do have. Again, David Graeber makes a stinging assessment of the situation:

'*Working long hours, in jobs that are either meaningless, exploitative or (likely) both, and resenting those who do not live this way, suggests that we have become collectively acquiesced to our own enslavement*' (Graeber: Bullsh*t Jobs; p. xxiv)

NOT ALL RICH PEOPLE HAVE WORKED HARD FOR THEIR WEALTH

'*They hang the man and flog the woman, that steal the goose from off the common, But let the greater villain loose, that steals the common from the goose, The law demands that we atone, when we take things we do not own, But leaves the lords and ladies fine, who take things that are yours and mine*' (Poem by anonymous, circa 1760)

We are led to believe that we live in a meritocratic society, and that you get *out* what you put *in*. In other words, if you are not where you need to be in life it is because you've not worked hard enough. The chief proponents of meritocracy in this country have largely, if not entirely, been privileged and born into rich families: your Blairs, Camerons, and Johnsons. Thatcher liked to remind people that she was the daughter of a grocer, but we heard much less of her marrying a millionaire ex-public schoolboy who was able to pay for her barrister training and multiple homes in places like Chelsea. Upward social mobility is unrealistic for many people in today's climate: so unrealistic that the entire board of the government's own Social Mobility Commission all resigned in 2017 claiming that there is 'little hope' for a fairer Britain due to government inaction to tackle related issues[47]. This is reflected in the OECD's 'Going for Growth' report that ranked the UK bottom among developed countries in terms of social mobility. For the first time we have a generation of young people who are forecast to be less well-off than their parents at every stage of their lives; unable to afford homes, unlikely to have a 'job for life', and much more. In an unequal society, where so much depends upon your formative years, the local education system and many other mediating factors intersect such that people often do not get what they deserve[48]. The recent pandemic should tell us nothing if not that our hardest-working, who keep society ticking over, are grossly undervalued and under-appreciated. Meritocracy favours those with the advantages – from better schooling to the contacts who make up their 'social capital'.

Take (now Baron) Zac Goldsmith who in 2016 failed in his bid to become the London Mayor and lost his by-election seat. Upon regaining his seat by a slim 45-vote majority the next year, he then lost it again just two years later. Repeated failings have been of no detriment to his career, after being rewarded with a peerage to the House of Lords shortly after his 2019 election defeat. In thinking about why this is the case, it probably did not hurt that he is an Eton alumnus (see Chapter 3 for more of this) or that Boris Johnson's partner Carrie Symonds is a close friend, particularly after helping his electoral campaign in 2010. Undoubtedly someone whose father is a billionaire, and who inherits great wealth via a web of trusts (a useful mechanism for avoiding tax, as is discussed in Chapter 2) finds opportunity where others do not, and does not have their career spurned by a series of failures in the same way others might. Indeed, also inheriting his father's non-domicile status – further alleviating his tax obligations – was no inhibitor to his political aspirations at all. He eventually changed this status due to opposition party and public pressure given his candidacy as a Tory MP, and the impending New Labour policy disqualifying parliamentarians from claiming non-dom status. The fallacy of meritocracy is well illustrated by a man who failed to become democratically

---

47   BBC News, 'Social mobility board quits over lack of progress', 3 December 2017
48   Accepting that this is a rather vague notion of receiving the type of reward that befits the effort expended and the quality of work done

elected to a ruling position numerous times, before simply being fast-tracked into an (undemocratically selected) ruling position in our society by his friend the prime minister, on the say-so of the prime minister's fiancée. That this is born largely because of the financial and political capital he is able to accrue, that are beyond the realms of possibility for others, is unquestionable.

History shows that the rich have done everything in their power to improve their lot, which typically involves subordinating and stifling the attempts of everybody else to improve theirs. The minimum rights and protections that we 'enjoy' today in the world of work – breaks, a minimum wage, sick pay, annual leave, and so on – were not handed out voluntarily by generous employers or sympathetic governments; they were fought for by workers themselves. 'May Day' bank holiday, formally International Workers' Day, speaks for itself[49]. Consider weekends: there was no such thing before 1850, with Sunday the only day of rest as instructed by the Bible. As more and more workers in Britain decided to take Monday off too (in what informally became known as 'Saint Monday' as an ode to the imaginary religious figure spawning this self-appointed holiday) employers were forced to concede a cut-off of 2pm on Saturdays, at full pay, in order to get their Mondays back. Incidentally, this is how the Saturday 3pm kick-off in British football matches came about[50].

Consider freedom of association: the much-famed Tolpuddle Martyrs were six farm labourers in Dorset who were shipped off to Australia in 1843 for seven years of hard labour, simply for *collectively* protesting three years of wage cuts, after collective bargaining and trade unions had been outlawed by the Combination Acts of 1799 and 1800. If we go back even further, feudalism only ended partly due to unrest, but largely because the Black Plague decimated nearly one-third of the workforce and suddenly labourers were in short supply, thus able to demand more favourable working conditions; and even that was ground to a halt by the Statute of Labourers in 1351, disqualifying them from an increase in remuneration. English history is replete with workers collectively organising and, more often as not, being met by the full force of the elitist class

---

49   The idea spread from Australia, with hundreds of thousands of British workers first holding a mass demonstration in Hyde Park, London, on Sunday 4 May 1890. They were vying for an eight-hour working day to be enshrined into legislation, and this celebration of the working classes occurred each year thereafter

50   Ben Tippett (2020) *Split: Class Divides Uncovered*, Pluto Press

and the law (not always two distinct entities)[51]. At one point, the crown and parliament sent more soldiers to crush the Luddites than they did to fight one of the greatest military minds to ever exist in Napoleon Bonaparte[52]. As a final example, in post-feudalist England when workers made lives for themselves on common land, the elites again fought back with a spate of land enclosures declaring it their own personal property. In one of numerous uprisings, Robert Kett led a rebellion in 1549 which led to his being drawn publicly through the streets and publicly hung from Norwich castle[53].

In an excellent book entitled *Who Owns England?* Guy Shrubsole presents, via countless freedom of information requests, meticulous mapping, and physical trespassing, an alarming picture of who owns much of the land, and therefore wealth, in this country. He broadly distinguishes numerous waves of wealth accumulation, beginning with 'old money'. While many people spend much of their lives working to pay a debt incurred on patches of land just big enough for a home, and garden if you are lucky, approximately 25,000 landowners (out of a population of approx. 67.5 million) own more than 44% of England, much of it inherited on the back of conquest and enclosure. After the Norman invasion of 1066 William the Conqueror dispossessed the English thegns and common land used by the peasantry, distributing the country between himself and approximately 190 Norman barons and clergy. This lineage has remained remarkably intact one thousand years later, via these aristocrats gifting themselves titles and creating laws – during times when common folk did not have a vote to sway Parliament – ensuring that others could not come along and fight them for the land as they had done themselves.

An illustration of this is the seventh Duke of Westminster, Hugh Richard Louis Grosvenor, a direct descendent of Hugh Le Grand Venour (roughly translating as the 'great huntsman' of King William's court, Anglo-fied to

---

51 There are many examples of this, not least the army firing on (both killing and injuring) workers during the Liverpool general transport strike in 1911, and army tanks deployed during 'Bloody Friday' in Glasgow 1919

52 Claire Wolfe (2005) *Dark Satanic Cubicles: It's Time to Smash the Jobs Culture!*, Dojo Press. The 'Luddites' were self-called after a mythical, Robin Hood-esque figure Ned Ludd, a young apprentice who was rumoured to have wrecked textile apparatus in 1779. From 1811 in Nottingham (and spreading further afield) they began breaking into factories and smashing textile machines hoping to deter further installation. On the contrary the government made machine-breaking punishable by death. With the army deployed, many Luddites were shot and killed, some hanged, and others transported to Australia

53 For a full account of such rebellions see Martin Epsom (2018) *Kill All the Gentlemen*, Bookmarks Publishing

Grosvenor). He inherited a £9 billion fortune made from owning a vast, 130k acre estate in land and property largely managed under the family business Grosvenor Group. A statue of the first Marquess of Westminster can be found today situated in Belgrave Square, London, proclaiming:

> 'The Grosvenor family came to England with William the Conqueror and have held land in Cheshire since that time'.

It is estimated that between 1604–1914 around one fifth of common land in England (approx. 6.8 million acres) was enclosed by Acts of Parliament. This stands in great contrast to the stipulations of Magna Carta two centuries before, which recognised the importance of common land to any free person's right to subsistence and to roam freely. Those part of the aristocratic class were able to use their wealth to wield great political influence. Their ranks were also swelled by those whose fortunes were made via unsavoury means, not least colonialism and slavery. Consider Edwin Lascelles (First baron Harewood), who built Harewood House in Yorkshire from inherited wealth his father accrued both from owning thousands of slaves in the Caribbean, and a hefty pay-out of £23,000 in 1835 for his loss of 'property' once slavery was abolished – worth approximately £3 million in today's money[54].

The history of Britain that we are not taught much about centres on the fact that money earned off the back of slavery in the West and using India as a cash cow in the East, bankrolled much of the land enclosures. Upon returning from their exploits abroad these obscenely wealthy individuals built huge homes and erected walls around their land[55]. As such, there is a direct link between this money and the partitioning of the commons upon which ordinary people

---

54 The Slave Compensation Commission's records detail names of British slave owners, where they lived and how much compensation they received (available on the UCL website, 'Legacies of British Slave-Ownership'). Over 80 MPs at the time made compensation claims to the Commission, including Richard Godson, who vocally supported the Slavery Abolition Act of 1833 through the House of Commons and then claimed £5,018 for the freedom of his own slaves (over £350k in today's money). Today over 40 peers in the House of Lords enjoy privilege bestowed on their families by such generous settlements, with the former slaves and their descendants left empty-handed

55 In another hugely valuable resource *The Book of Trespass*, Nick Hayes cites the estimated figures of India's GDP being drained from 27% to 3% by the time the British left (at what others such as economist Utsa Patnaik estimates to be a stolen $45 trillion), and up to 29 million Indians dead via famine, murder, and organised genocide. Over 3 million African slaves were transported to British colonies with 400k not making it there

had cultivated, in order to provide for their own subsistence and modest lifestyles. As private ownership spread, more and more people had no other option but to survive the only way they could – sell their labour power to those who had taken the land for themselves and work it for them. As a further consequence, the formation of two distinct classes was entrenched between those who were able to live off the labour of others and those who eventually left the countryside to motor the industrial revolution across the major British cities. In other words, enclosures (often bankrolled by the ills of colonialism, so too the provision of raw materials such as cotton for the mills in Lancashire) were the pre-cursor to capitalism as we know it today.

Nowadays, the ancestors of those land-enclosing aristocrats earn their crust a number of ways. If you have found yourself wandering through the plush gardens or inside a stately home the chances are it is because the law states that they became exempt from inheritance tax and capital gains tax if they are made available for Joe Public to view on a given number of days per year. These wealthy individuals also benefit from the old adage 'socialism for the rich, capitalism for the poor' via substantial handouts and subsidiaries. In 2016 alone, billionaire James Dyson received £160 million for his swathes of land. The irony is that many of those taking taxpayer money do their best to not contribute. As one example, in North Yorkshire the grouse moor Gunnerside estate, encompassing 27,258 acres, is registered via an offshore company in the British Virgin Islands and thus exempt from tax obligations, yet has received around £400k in taxpayer subsidies. All told, annual subsidies gifted to land used for grouse shooting – an activity enjoyed by fewer than 0.01% of the population – has been over £17 million, alongside protection for the environmentally destructive practices it involves.

Some descendants are fortunate enough to be able to live very comfortably off the rent their inherited assets accumulate, particularly if lucky enough to have ancestors that bought land in areas such as central London. Others were graced land with great natural resources and have made a lot of money by exploiting minerals or allowing private companies to do so, of which the resources and proceeds should really have been public. Or, to uphold the values of feudalism, as a voting constituent you can simply elect the wealthy landowner near where you live into government so they can maintain their wealth directly through lobbying and policy. There are innumerable examples of this, but just to pick one: former Tory MP for Newbury, Richard Henry Ronald Benyon. Richard has the crown of single biggest landowner in West Berkshire after inheriting the 12,000-acre Englefield Estate, with an estimated fortune of £110 million ensuring that he was also the richest MP in parliament. In what is a non-trivial occurrence among the ilk of Richard Benyon, his father was an MP (first for Buckingham, then for Milton Keynes) and his great-great-grandfather was Tory prime minister Lord Salisbury.

Maintaining positions in parliament has aided the family interests very well. While serving as junior environment minister in David Cameron's government, Richard pressed ahead with plans on his vast estate that had been subject to protests by the local wildlife trust, such as felling trees, destroying ancient woodland, and the permanent loss of heathland. His other interests include running pheasant shoots at Englefield, and the family is also in possession of an 8,000-acre grouse moor in Scotland. Naturally, you would want someone with a passion for shooting wildlife to be in charge of conservation. As an illustration of this obvious conflict of interest, with the power bestowed by his ministerial position Richard refused to make the possession of poison carbofuran a criminal offence, as this is used by gamekeepers to kill birds of prey suspected of targeting game birds. His commercial activity is as you would expect: notably buying up land and property on the New Era Estate in Hackney, dramatically increasing the rent and kicking out working-class families in the process, so too his voting behaviour. He has always voted against welfare benefits, backed the bedroom tax, and one assumes views the unfortunate as scroungers; a label that could arguably extend to someone effectively handed a vast fortune and not being above EU handouts worth millions of pounds for the upkeep of his inherited land. Alas, he is but one of many[56].

Not known for his socialism, even Winston Churchill was scathing of the land rentier in a speech delivered to the House of Commons, 4 May 1909:

'*Roads are made, streets are made, services are improved, electric light turns night into day, water is brought from reservoirs a hundred miles off in the mountains – and all the while the landlord sits still. Every one of those improvements is effected by the labour and cost of other people and the taxpayers. To not one of those improvements does the land monopolist, as the land monopolist, contribute, and yet by every one of them the value of his land is enhanced*'

---

56   Shrubsole references the likes of Sir Geoffrey Clifton-Brown, Tory MP for the Cotswolds; Sir Henry Campbell Bellingham, Tory MP for North West Norfolk; and the aforementioned Richard Grosvenor Plunkett-Ernle-Erle-Drax, Tory MP for South Dorset, who all similarly own huge, inherited estates and regularly vote in ways aligned to such interests and not those of the majority in their constituencies

Such aristocrats own about one-third of England, although likely more as the Land Registry is incomplete. We cannot understate the role that land and property ownership has played in exacerbating distinct social classes, enabling those who possess it to raise capital during the early years of industrialisation. Even as private, small-scale land ownership proliferated (this comes with many caveats: not only the likes of leaseholders who are entangled in multiple forms of ownership, but consider the need for planning permission to undertake work on your own property as another example), this has had the effect of making ownership aspirational to the point where people became much more individualised, competitive, and ultimately instrumental.

In another highly recommended text, *Rethinking the Economics of Land and Housing* by Josh Ryan-Collins, Toby Lloyd and Laurie MacFarlane, the inextricable link between land ownership and political power is noted. Most obviously, such ownership is tied to wealth and naturally those with such wealth are inclined to protect it the best way they can. Linked to this, is the capacity for governments to expropriate landowners given that land is fixed and immobile, and thus landowners can be targeted for higher taxation and other means that would reduce their fortunes. The landowning classes therefore have plenty of motivation for controlling 'the state' and have done so via many different means, not least inherited peerages in the House of Lords. Chapter 3 discusses the proportion of MPs who own multiple properties and it becomes very clear that they make up a disproportionate part of the House of Commons too.

Again, this is not a new phenomenon. The very reason we have National Parks relates to our landowning elites viewing the public as an annoyance to be kept off hectares they consider their own. Clement Attlee's post-war Labour government proposed to complement the NHS with a change in access laws to Britain's countryside, enabling free roam of the land for those who had quite literally fought for it. Landowners were a dime a dozen in both the Commons and the Lords, and would hear nothing of it – the compromise being the National Parks Act designating, initially, ten areas the public could freely roam for recreation (the Lake District et al.). All told 92% of the country is off-limits to us, i.e. we are prohibited and thus considered trespassers if stepping foot on it. Little surprise then that tax obligations on property is not too burdensome, common land has been allowed to stay enclosed and affordable housing is kept scarce. There are many reasons to support the principle of private land ownership while recognising that if holdings become overly vast (as many are) and uninhabited land is not plentiful (which indeed it is not) then clear problems abound. It is also worth reiterating that in most cases those who previously habited land are generally forced out and into positions as wage labourers on the land, which poses many moral questions.

Shrubsole argues that there have been waves of 'new money' in England since the initial period outlined above. The first involved Middle Eastern oil wealth following the 1973 oil embargo imposed by the Organization of Arab Petroleum Exporting Countries (OAPEC) as the UK were seen to support Israel during the Yom Kippur War. As oil prices almost doubled over the course of a year many individuals in the Middle East became very wealthy. Consider Sheikh Mohammed bin Rashad Al Maktoum, prime minister of the UAE since 2006, who just happens to be one of the largest individual landowners in England (owning approx. 92,000 acres) via a number of offshore companies incorporated in Jersey and Guernsey. Again, wealth accumulated via questionable means is evident in this 'wave' of wealth: not least Saudi Prince Badar, son of the defence minister who brokered the controversial 1985 al-Yamamah arms deal with BAE and Thatcher's government. BAE were later forced to pay £285 million in corruption-related penalties due to this deal, Prince Badar was able to invest his money in the 2,500-acre Glympton Park in Oxfordshire.

The third wave of wealth in England came via oligarchs following the collapse of the Soviet Union, when the assets of the huge state-owned industries were sold off and a class of Russians (and to a lesser extent those in neighbouring countries) were able to profit very large sums very quickly. London property was a much safer and fruitful investment than the depleted Russian banks of the time, and Russians quickly became the largest foreign buyers in the city. The swathes of vacant, multi-million-pound mansions belonging to a series of offshore companies dotted around London raise further questions about the extent to which it is a place to launder (often dirty) money, superficially inflating house prices for everyone else in the process[57].

The super-rich of today effectively live off unearned income. Via their owning and controlling of assets such as land and property they can ensure that land is both scarce and privatised, thus being able to charge those who need it through various forms of rent. Land rentiers are often simultaneously

---

57 Notable examples include Britain's second richest street 'Billionaires alley', The Bishops Avenue in London

natural resource rentiers, i.e. in ownership of land with resources that other companies will pay for the right to access, mine, and such like. By rentiers we mean those who receive rent (money) purely by virtue of controlling something valuable[58], rather than actually doing much that is productive or value-creating themselves. As a further example, the banks have been effective financial rentiers. By creating money out of thin air with minimal production costs: the pressing of buttons on a keyboard in an age where only around 3% of money is represented by actual coinage, the charging of high interest rates is effectively a rent on money.

It could be said that the most recent transfer of wealth has been from public coffers to private via the neoliberalist drive to privatise national infrastructure and state-owned enterprises, with recent UK governments very rentier-friendly. Corporations own around one-fifth of England, much of it formerly of public (and thus taxpayer) ownership, which is down to just 8% now. Privatisation has often been on very favourable terms for rentiers, who typically have a near-monopoly on certain assets or industries and have been free to exploit resources that could have been of great benefit to the taxpayer. This has particularly been the case with land – for example, the controversial selling-off of 55,000 service family homes by the (taxpayer-funded) Ministry of Defence to Annington Property Limited for £1.66 billion in 1996 has cost taxpayers billions according to the National Audit Office[59]. Indeed, this estate is now worth over £7 billion – and is leased back to the MOD with a discount that expired in 2021, representing more bad business as rents will increase substantially. In some instances, land has been bought back by governments, albeit on very unfavourable terms. For example, Ealing Council in London bought back 516 abodes originally sold under the 'Right to Buy' scheme for over £100 million, more than five times what they had been sold for; and Network Rail has spent hundreds of millions of pounds buying back freight sidings and yards that were *gifted* to private-sector freight companies in the 1990s.

Ultimately, much of the wealth in this country is derived from bloody conquest and land enclosure[60]; more recently foreign investments, some of

---

58   As described by Brett Christophers (2020) in *Rentier Capitalism*, Verso
59   National Audit Office, 'The Ministry of Defence's arrangement with Annington Property Limited', 30 January 2018
60   In what Karl Polanyi called a revolution of the rich against the poor, enclosures were imposed through violence and backed by law; with 3,280 enclosure bills passed through parliament between 1770 and 1830, transitioning English society away from one that had been based on relatively self-sufficient communities operating autonomously from 'the market'. See Giovanna Ricoveri's *Nature for Sale* for more on the commons

which are from questionable sources or means; the corrupt use of public office for private gain; and only a very small minority of people who might constitute the tag 'self-made'. Jim Ratcliffe, founder of chemical company INEOS, was the UK's richest person according to the 2018 *Sunday Times* rich list, which described him as 'self-made' and from a 'humble' background. This champion of the working class regularly battled with trade unions (most publicly at Grangemouth oil refinery), changed his domicile from Hampshire to Monaco and moved his company to Switzerland between 2010–16, avoiding millions of pounds in tax in the process. He also personally met with then-Chancellor George Osborne to lobby a reduction in income tax and is an ardent proponent of fracking. His business is a significant contributor to greenhouse gases, the effects of which are not lost on Jim, who is attempting to build a mansion on stilts for the impending rising sea levels he is helping to create[61].

The truth of the matter is that unless you are an exceptional athlete, singer, actor, or inventor, you are not going to join the elite classes no matter how hard you work. By and large, meritocracy is just a pipe dream that we are sold to ensure that we continue to buy into an unequal system and work hard. And what our self-made heroes Jim Ratcliffe, James Dyson et al. demonstrate is that in the current system, if you do manage to beat the odds and make it from an 'ordinary' background, you are likely to align with the behaviours of the elites. This is the problem with our current set-up: human interaction in capitalist societies is often reduced to economic transactions. It is all about capital accumulation and when others are using offshore companies to avoid tax obligations, employing people on precarious contracts and cosying up to politicians in return for insider information or favours, the incentive is for others to do the same. How else can you compete with the giant corporations like Amazon that do these things? To compete on price and to gain a competitive advantage, someone in your supply chain is inevitably going to be exploited for you to be successful. Organisations are focused on shareholder value which naturally subordinates other stakeholders, from keeping labour costs low to not worrying about environmental impacts beyond legal compliance.

---

61   *The Telegraph*, 'Britain's third richest man Sir Jim Ratcliffe wants to build luxury summer house on stilts at his £6m mansion', 20 November 2019

THE GREATEST MYTH OF OUR TIME: WE RELY ON THE RICH[62]

'The patience and forbearance of the poor are among the strongest bulwarks of the rich' (C.L.R. James, *The Black Jacobins*)

So ingrained into our psyche is this notion that the rich are the source of employment and thus they are the wealth creators, integral to everything that we need and value. As such, people regularly defend the Amazons of this world for tax avoidance, deplorable working conditions, and such because they fear the 'flight of capital' – we need them more than they need us. In other words, we have to accept our subservient treatment because otherwise they will locate elsewhere in places where the indigenous populations will be more accepting of this ill fate. Firstly, this is simply not true: analysis of the *Forbes* list of billionaires shows that 95% remain in the country they were born or made their fortune in, with similar evidence found in the US specifically[63]. Having presence in and being located close to big markets is essential and Europe is no different. The UK has one of the lowest corporation tax rates in Europe, which we do not even make Amazon pay[64]. According to Corporate Welfare Watch Amazon have had around £20 million in direct welfare handouts and significant discounts on business rates, typically for establishing their 'fulfilment centres' in areas of high unemployment. In fact, some years (notably 2013) Amazon received more in corporate welfare than it has paid in tax[65].

Given these extremely generous conditions and the huge profits Amazon generates, they are clearly in a position to offer decent employment to the worker ants that keep it functioning at maximum capacity – many of whom are forced into claiming tax credits to top up this income. The decision in 2018 to increase employees' pay was a welcome response to enduring criticisms, which linger regarding wider employment practices at the company. Naturally,

---

62 Another excellent book, debunking many of the myths covered in this section, is Andrew Sayer's *Why We Can't Afford the Rich* (2015), Policy Press

63 Cristobal Young (2017) *The Myth of Millionaire Tax Flight: How Place Still Matters for the Rich*, Stanford University Press

64 In 2010 the corporation tax rate was 28%; this was cut to 21% in 2012, and has been 19% since 2017. As a comparator, the corporation tax rates in France, Belgium, and Spain are 33.3%, 29%, and 25% respectively

65 *Independent*, 'Revealed: Amazon earns more through government grants than it pays in tax', 16 May 2013

there are other costs which are rarely considered in sweeping statements about our need to keep such corporate giants in the UK. As one example, the number of people employed by the major corporations is of course high compared to the numbers employed by other organisations, but this still only equates to a very minor percentage of the total number employed. SMEs alone account for approx. three-fifths of private-sector employment, with the public sector home to some of the largest employers in the UK. It is entirely plausible that many local bookstores and the like have failed to compete with Amazon, companies more likely to pay their full tax obligations and employ staff on fairer terms and conditions, who are then out of a job. As such, it is not entirely clear if Amazon is responsible for more job losses than it creates. The underlying ideology that we depend upon the rich for our survival seriously lacks nuance – and on facts alone Amazon get a much better deal from us than we do from them[66].

The argument is typically premised on the idea that keeping taxation for corporations low and regulation light enables them to profit and create jobs. But we can note three things: 1) we are not exactly inundated with jobs, let alone 'good' jobs, as this line of argument would suggest; 2) during the 1960s and 1970s when there was greater taxation of the rich and other so-called 'anti-rich' reforms, the economy grew at double the rate seen since the (pro-rich) neoliberal turn in the 1980s up to the global financial crash; and 3) we have seen that the wealth of the 1% continues to skyrocket. So, the evidence tells us that rather than low taxation and the scrapping of employment rights and protections creating more jobs (a questionable trade-off in principle anyway), the rich are instead hoarding the extra money gained for themselves. The issues with this argument should have become clear when more money began being invested in finance and the knowledge economy (which is not always labour-intensive and therefore job-creating), but there is also a long history of profitable businesses acquiring other organisations and shedding employees during any merger, or simply investing any profit in more technology rather than workers.

66 Another argument I cannot pick up here (see, for example, *The Entrepreneurial State* by Mariana Mazzucato) is how often we downplay the role other parties, including the public sector, have when crediting corporations with innovations worth millions of pounds. Mazzucato illustrates this via the Apple iPhone, with state-funded research key not just to the more obvious examples, e.g. to the internet itself; the Department of Energy, who contributed to the development of lithium-ion batteries, the micro hard-drive, and multi-touch screens; military entities to signal compression and cellular technology, and so forth. The taxpayer (and early innovators) are crucial to such corporations' success, yet we still tend to place them above tax obligations despite their dependence on pre-existing, publicly funded banks of knowledge

Perhaps more counterintuitively, the economy only grows and jobs created when people are spending more money. Therefore, allowing the rich to accumulate even more of the wealth (the wealthiest 1%'s share of total national income has more than doubled since 1979 – discussed in Chapter 2) does not follow. This means that more money is being invested in stocks and shares, the purchase of assets, and stashed in offshore tax havens – the juxtaposition to greater spending that can fuel the type of economic growth required to generate mass job creation and so forth. For a while this was offset by people turning to 'credit' (bank and building society loans, credit cards, etc.) which enabled many to keep spending despite more wealth being syphoned off to the elites. However, the global financial crash exposed how unsustainable this model is. A much more effective way to create jobs would be to tax the rich more or to stop them extracting so much additional wealth in the first place, meaning that more people have disposable income, with a much greater propensity to spend, ultimately ensuring more money flows through the economy. A larger public sector, re-nationalising key industries, and worker co-operatives are all illustrations of exactly why we do not need to rely on the rich.

The argument that we should allow businesses to operate as freely as possible is also flawed when we look at how labour markets have operated over time. The closer we are to 'full employment', i.e. everyone who wants to work is employed for the number of hours they desire, the more power shifts towards workers. In such a situation employers have to offer better terms and conditions in order to tempt people away from their existing employment. This is therefore not a labour market that said employers will support; they rely on a 'reserve army of labour' waiting in the wings to replace anyone contemplating demands for a wage rise or improvements to their reward packages. A pool of unemployed people stagnates wages and conditions, which is precisely what employers want. As such, allowing businesses free reign will not lead to this job-creation utopia politicians glowingly refer to, as it simply does not serve their purposes.

It is also not the case that firms who become successful expand their workforces indefinitely. Even when labour market figures look rosy – as they have in recent times in the UK relative to the economic uncertainty we have experienced – this usually masks the nature and quality of the employment on offer. For example, the figures for March 2020[67] (the onset of the pandemic, after which figures are of course skewed) proclaim 'record-high' employment

---

67   Office for National Statistics, 'Labour Market Statistical Bulletin, May 2020'

figures and many fewer vacancies as more people entered into work. Leaving aside the growth in precarious forms of employment (particularly with the rise of platform work via the likes of Uber Eats and Deliveroo), over a quarter of people working in temporary roles cited that this was the case due to the fact that they could not obtain permanent jobs. More than one in ten people working part-time do so because they cannot secure full-time employment. Likewise, 1.87 million people declared economically inactive state that they do want a job, with the number describing themselves as 'discouraged' up on previous years. So clearly there is demand for work among those who are either currently 'under-employed', temporarily or long-term unemployed to work more.

Ultimately we find ourselves in a situation where the bulk of the population upholds a system that makes them grossly unhappy, they are exploited in (and implicitly subject their children to the same fate), and destroys the planet, all so that a small group of elites can sustain their lives of luxury. This seems absurd, and we should at the very least be having a debate about how much wealth is too much per household. It is not to say that people cannot strive for upward social mobility and to improve their 'lot', nor is this a bitter rant from someone who will never belong to the elitist classes. It is merely posing questions about how much wealth is excessive and unjustifiable, both given how it is often accumulated in ways that are exploitative or essentially unearned, and way beyond that required for their own well-being. The wealth of the richest 1,000 people in the UK has increased from £450 billion in 2013 to £771 billion in 2019[68]. To put this into perspective, this effectively equates to the same wealth possessed by the poorest 50% of households in the UK and is enough to sustain both the National Health Service and the welfare bill comfortably. Given the means through which this wealth is acquired, and its meteoric increase, it might be time to think about effective ways to redistribute some of this wealth – via the (actual) tax obligations already in place would be a starting point.

WORKERS OF THE WORLD, RELAX!

The widespread scorn that met the Labour Party's pledge to advance the debate around a four-day working week in the run-up to the 2019 general election was

---

68   The Equality Trust, 'A Nation of Ferraris and Foodbanks – UK Rich Increase Wealth by £253 Billion Over Five Years', 12 May 2019

somewhat bemusing. Seemingly, huge swathes of people who spend much of their lives working do not want to reduce this time spent 'on the clock', despite the fact that research continues to show that most people would choose more time off over an increase in pay[69]. Typically, feigned hysteria centres on how businesses could not possibly survive as they would lose a day's labour, and thus people's jobs (and livelihoods) would be at risk. And this assertion does seem to make sense – less time working implies that less work is done. Actually there is evidence to the contrary, and proponents of the four-day week are not a bunch of workshy idealists but management scholars and practitioners[70]. The rationale is thus: the UK has experienced weak labour productivity growth since 2008, to the extent that the Office for National Statistics describe it as 'the defining economic question of our age' despite the fact working hours have remained constant at around 39.1 hours per week for full-time workers[71].

This very same workforce reports high levels of stress, fatigue, dissatisfaction, and a range of other negative indicators of workplace well-being, all of which contribute to increased absenteeism, lower levels of motivation, commitment, and productivity[72]. The idea is that a four-day week offers an innovative solution to these issues: with a better work-life balance, reduced tiredness and stress employees are more likely to be engaged, which presents a business case as well as the ethical case that people can actually spend additional time outside of work leading more holistically fulfilling lives. This is not to say that there will not be challenges in introducing a four-day week to boost both well-being and competitiveness, but the current situation is not really benefitting either party in the employment relationship. A shorter working week does not mean that we transition to everybody simply not working on a Friday anymore. As a society we have developed complex flexible working arrangements and have the technology to facilitate a situation where businesses can be fully operational from Monday–Friday but each individual employee works, say,

---

69 Although of course there is nuance here, with a four-day working motion passed at the Trades Union Congress annual conference in September 2021, meaning that a three-day weekend with no reduction in pay potentially has the backing of more than 6 million workers

70 Even the self-proclaimed 'centrist' cross-party think-tank Social Market Foundation have argued that technology could facilitate a 32-hour (or four-day) working week: '4IR in the Workplace: Ensuring employers and employees benefit', October 2018

71 ONS, 'Labour productivity, UK: October to December 2019', released April 2020

72 The World Health Organization and International Labour Organization attributed 745,194 deaths worldwide to long working hours in 2016 alone (see WHO, 'Long working hours increasing deaths from heart disease and stroke: WHO, ILO', 17 May 2021)

a four-day week. This could be managed most plausibly by alternating shift patterns, flexitime, compressed hours – all things that are commonly used by organisations already.

Previous periods of rapid paid working hour reductions (notably the 1920s and 1960s–'70s) were periods of exponential productivity growth and these trends can be seen in the contemporary global labour market. For example, Mexico has significantly lower productivity than the UK despite working a six-day work week, while German workers are considerably more productive than UK workers despite working nearly 300 fewer annual hours[73]. A wealth of academic and think-tank research points to productivity lowering significantly after a certain amount of weekly work hours (e.g. for the Institute for Labour Economics it is 35 weekly work hours). These arguments are far from new, with Henry Ford an early proponent of the shorter working week, and the cereal entrepreneur W. K. Kellogg enjoying unmitigated success by doing the same thing during the 1930s Great Depression. The world's largest ever trial of a four-day working week, involving over 1% of Iceland's working population between 2015–2019, witnessed a cut in hours and no reduction in pay boosting both productivity and well-being[74].

As highlighted above, we spend an awful lot of time engaging in pointless work, so even shedding tasks that simply are not necessary would bring us down to a four-day week at the very least. So obsessed with time are we that it does not even make sense to work more efficiently, because you will then either have to look busy for the remainder of your working day, or will be given pointless busywork until it is time to go home. It is as hard to believe that businesses want to pay people for engaging in pointless tasks as it is people wanting to undertake them. Workers are themselves reporting that they could complete a week's work in four days without any drop in the quality of that work, and businesses report that they would be in favour of a four-day week (64% in favour compared to 36% who are opposed)[75]. Andrew Barnes, chief proponent of the four-day working week after trialling it in his own New Zealand company Perpetual Guardian with much success, also points out the environmental benefits of people travelling less (to work), reduced energy usage in workplaces, and so forth[76]. As an illustration, moving the economy

73   IPA and Friedrich Ebert-Stiftung, 'Is Thursday the new Friday?', July 2019
74   Alda and Autonomy, 'Going Public: Iceland's journey to a shorter working week', June 2021
75   YouGov, 'Business backs a four day working week', 23 September 2019
76   See Andrew's website '4dayweek.com' or his 2020 book *The 4 Day Week* (published by Piatkus)

to a four-day, 32-hour working week (with no reduction in pay) would reduce the UK's carbon footprint by 127 million tonnes per year[77], which equates to taking over 85% of cars off the road.

WE ARE (NEARLY) ALL WORKING CLASS

Since their inception the Tories represented the aristocracy and latterly a loose alliance of the affluent, and were opposed by the Whigs, then the Liberals, then Labour. Thatcher did an excellent job of destabilising the class basis of the different parties by asserting that there was no such thing as class, or even society for that matter. In her famous 23 September 1987 interview for *Woman's Own* Margaret Thatcher said:

'...there's no such thing as society. There are individual men and women and there are families. And no government can do anything except through people, and people must look after themselves first. It is our duty to look after ourselves and then, also, to look after our neighbours'

There is such a thing as society – you and I live in one. Indeed, there are innumerable sub-societies in our shared, collective society based on a variety of things, from religious communities to grassroots movements. The fallacy of this notion was laid bare when the Conservatives asked us to come together as a society during austerity, again after the prolonged embittered aftermath of the EU referendum, and again as part of the Covid pandemic response with Boris declaring 'there really *is* such a thing as society'[78]. There are countless contradictions to this idea across history via the many acts of solidarity seen by communities across the country[79]. Our altruism is also well documented in the sciences and psychology fields: if anything, we are the biological outlier from other species such is our ability to care for the welfare of others beyond egotistical reasons[80]. Think for a moment about how you feel when things are

---

77 Platform, 'Stop the Clock: The environmental benefits of a shorter working week', May 2021
78 *New Statesman*, '"There is such a thing as society". Has Boris Johnson repudiated Thatcherism?', 31 March 2020
79 A great read that casts our cynicism of human nature into doubt is offered by Rutger Bregman (2020) in *HumanKind: A Hopeful History*, Bloomsbury
80 As examples, see *Altruism in Humans* by Daniel Batson (2011), Oxford University Press; and *A Paradise Built in Hell* by Rebecca Solnit (2010), Penguin

going well for you, but how this would be impacted if those around you – family and friends – were in dire straits. People donate to the victims of famine in far-flung corners of the world or adopt snow leopards that have no tangible impact upon our lives. We are mindful of others in many different ways in day-to-day life, often at our own expense, as that is our nature.

Such acts of solidarity frighten those who rely on our division to maintain their place at the top of the pecking order. It is clear that the majority in such a society would be better positioned to share humour, dissent, common experiences, and ultimately articulate a shared set of goals[81]. This building of intra-competition among the masses was crucial to expanding cynicism against others, who may take your job; whose welfare receipt must be assessed for worthiness; undermining solidarity and ultimately the class basis underpinning Britain. Key to this process was gaining widespread support for meritocracy and making people believe that they are in complete control of their own destiny (and have the freedom and wherewithal to get rich). Any reading of class theory immediately brings to light that this freedom is of course a constrained choice in reality – if you do not own the means of production then for Karl Marx you are constrained into a life of wage labour as a member of the working-class. For Pierre Bourdieu class encompasses economic capital (wealth and income), cultural capital (education through to things like understanding what constitutes 'good taste' among the elites), and social capital (contacts, membership of clubs and societies, one's name/familial reputation). Whichever conception of class one uses alludes to there are various ways in which people's life experiences and opportunities differ.

Opposition parties going along with the idea that class was no longer a key feature of British society played right into the hands of Thatcher and her allies. This is best illustrated by Thatcher's response when asked what her greatest achievement was, 'Tony Blair and New Labour. We forced our opponents to change their minds'[82]. The architect of New Labour himself, Peter Mandelson,

---

81   One of Britain's most influential thinkers John Stuart Mill indicated as far back as 1848: 'I am not charmed with the ideal of life held out by those who think that the normal state of human beings is that of struggling to get on; that the trampling, crushing, elbowing and treading on each other's heels, which form the existing type of social life, are the more desirable lot of humankind… The best state for human nature is that in which, while no-one is poor, no-one desires to be richer, nor has any reason to fear being thrust back by the efforts of others to push themselves forward' (see *Of the Stationary State of Wealth and Population*)

82   Conor Burns, 'Margaret Thatcher's greatest achievement: New Labour', Conservative Home, 11 April 2008

had famously claimed 'we are all Thatcherite now' when writing in *The Times* in 2002 about the economy. So much so, that Blair became the first Prime Minster to be jeered during his last speech, to the Trades Union Congress (TUC), those who perceived (quite rightly) that he had turned his back on them.

Class still matters. Conservative politicians[83] have attempted to create this idea that it does not for a number of reasons: our elites do not wish to make it visible that there is an oppressive class in our society, one that opposes the majority – who could quite easily change society for the better if they forged a collective identity. The contradictory messages of 'there is no such thing as class' and 'we are all middle class now' aside, Hadas Weiss argues that such a widely used yet ill-defined concept like 'middle class' has to be a manufactured, and thus socially constructed, ideology[84]. Indeed, categories like middle class only exist because certain people at some point in history decided to make it so. It is worth thinking about why this would happen.

For one, this idea of 'middle' suggests that there are 'others' below to whom we need to maintain distance (the workshy, uneducated, and other marginalised groups), which requires ever-renewed effort, as does aspiration to join the ranks of those above[85]. This is the cornerstone of meritocracy: the false idea that if we have not become rich, it is a mixture of poor choices or use of resources such as time and energy, or as not having as much guile, luck, or foresight as others such that they manage it while most of us do not. Meritocracy necessitates more instrumental, individualistic behaviours, which is more in tune with what our lords and masters desire: solidarity, a lack of hierarchies, and egalitarianism are what they seek to avoid. Such aspirators will also work hard (which ultimately benefits their employer more than anyone); assimilate via measures such as taking on mortgages (with debt, as will be discussed, a potent tool of control); compete with their neighbours over scarce resources such as 'good' schools, jobs and housing; and begin adopting the same views as the elites, not least a dim view of anyone who does not see the world as they do – the unemployed being one such grouping. Wider implications include an inherent subscription to capitalism, continuous over-consumption, environmental suicide, and more.

---

83 John Major vowed to make Britain a 'genuinely classless society' as one example; with the opposition offering up similar sentiments, e.g. Labour's Deputy PM John Prescott declaring that 'we are all middle class now'

84 See *We Have Never Been Middle Class* (2019), Verso

85 Such a philosophy is useful for governments not wishing to invest in things like social housing, as the impression of desiring one (or needing help in general) becomes somewhat more demeaning

But most importantly, unlike historic notions of the 'working class', the middle class does not really have a shared identity and certainly does not stand in opposition to any other group: 'it replaces cohesive and demarcated groups with an image of multitudes of disconnected individuals' (Weiss, *ibid*: p. 22). Weiss argues that 'middle class' has come to represent individuals who stand on their own two feet and that this is seen as indicative of the investments and sound choices they have made – albeit this needs to be sustained or they may slip from their achieved social standing. This stands in sharp contrast to any conceptual engagement with 'class', as seen above, all of which recognise that our positions in society are determined by many more factors than simply desire or perceived effort.

A further issue with meritocracy is that it compels us to constantly adapt, upskill, and so forth without even a guarantee of future reward. Consider the vast number of students who saddle themselves with debt and often wind up in employment that historically a degree was not needed for. Yes, the university experience can be a positive one and thus worth the investment beyond eventual employment outcomes, but with the 'leisure society' that is going to be posited in this text, people are afforded time for the joys – reading, socialising, debating, all of which could happen without debt. Most people have bid to improve their 'human capital' at some point, only to find that due to economic factors outside of their control, wages have stagnated, and opportunities for permanent, meaningful employment are few and far between. What is it all for? A slightly bigger house with slightly bigger bills to worry about, that compels us to be slightly more worried about work to cover the costs of? I suppose that we could ask the same politicians who tell us meritocracy is alive and well in Britain to relinquish their inheritances, or stop sending their children to £40k+-per-year fee-paying schools, to refrain from joining exclusive members' clubs, or owning property in 'nice, affluent' areas, since apparently none of those things really matter.

Weiss notes that tying oneself to a thirty-year mortgage, raising children in such a way to improve their life chances (investment in a good school, etc.) takes at the very least 'two committed, working investors': the chief irony being that people are making less visible their position as exploited workers to identify as 'self-determining investors of work, time and resources' (p. 118). Naturally, as we will never be fully remunerated for our work, investing in things like property whose value may go up seems a shrewd and understandable endeavour. We spend almost our entire lives toiling for a slightly better social standing (which, in accordance with the rules of the game as they stand, for the current generation seems likely to be a fallacy as their parents achieved more upward social mobility than they can hope to) and safeguarding against any decline in this standing. One has to question whether this truly is the sum of what we want out of life, and whether changing the end goal could make things significantly better for much of the population.

It would be impossible to collect data on this but I do wonder what proportion of people who vote for the Conservative Party, despite the fact this party rarely advances the interests of people in their income group, occupation, and the other usual criteria for being middle class, because it makes them feel like part of such a class. An attitude of the Labour Party is for those who a lifetime of blue-collar, manual work beckons, which a) is not me, and b) will therefore not serve my aspirational interests. It is truly admirable in its effectiveness that by asserting there is no such thing as class, and preaching meritocracy, the Tories have been positioned as the aspirational class given that it is almost exclusively the actions of post-war Labour governments that provided the upwardly mobile working class with the means to do so. We are of course referring to things like the expansive welfare state, including free healthcare and education, full employment and trade unions/collective bargaining ensuring better wages and conditions.

The attack on trade unions and other attempts to divide those outside of the elitist group shows how considered and deliberate this strategy is. We regularly hear about how trade unions were a scourge on society in the '70s[86] but we hear much less about the wider context. For example, 1971 saw the end of the Bretton Woods system that pegged all international currencies to the US dollar as part of a fixed exchange rate. For years the pound had been over-valued in this system and its inevitable depreciation was compounded by an increase in the costs of imports and consequently prices too, which led to both a demand for higher wages and also unemployment. This was followed closely by the OAPEC oil embargo in 1973, with energy prices as much as quadrupling, further heightening the pressure for higher wages.

---

86 Derek Jameson, then editor of the *Daily Express*, later wrote in his book, *Last of the Hot Metal Men: From Fleet Street to Showbiz*, that this now-mythologised notion that greedy unions were the cause of rubbish piling up in the street and the dead lying unburied was a deliberate ploy: 'We pulled every dirty trick in the book. We made it look like it was general, universal and eternal, whereas it was in reality scattered, here and there, and no great problem.'

We also hear much less about Ed Heath's Tory government who were in power for the first half of the decade, overseeing a significant rise in unemployment; creating palpable tension with the Industrial Relations Act; his Housing Act a contributing factor to council tenant rents increasing by 23% in just three years (culminating in rent strikes[87]); politicising the dispute with miners – spending more money and creating more disruption by confining commercial and industrial users of electricity to a three-day operating week than if he had settled with them; and much more. Unemployment between 1976–79 peaked at 5.8%, which is half of what it stood at by the end of Thatcher's first term as PM, and the Gini coefficient measure of income inequality fell to its lowest point in '77. As one would expect seeing these figures – which should be viewed positively – union members' wages did indeed increase, but this was in line with the cost of living: inflation during the final year of Ed Heath's Tory government ('73–74) increased dramatically from 10.2%, reaching 24.6% in 1975. During the initial stage, trade unions had abided by the 'social contract' introduced by Labour whereby pay demands were curbed in return for rent freezes, pension increases, and so forth. On the back of the post-1973 oil crisis, Harold Wilson and his successor Jim Callaghan sided with the capitalists and financiers demonstrating some unity of thought with the Tories that working-class power was a threat to democracy, with the 'social contract' putting a block on wages, and the rest, as they say, is history. Actually sticking to principles of nationalisation and worker co-operatives, as propagated by the likes of Tony Benn at the time, may have led to a very different outcome.

There are many entities, the International Monetary Fund included, who suggest that financial crises tend to happen – and deepen – when workers are not paid enough and their bargaining power ineffective[88] as happened in the '80s. In terms of the economy and its competitiveness, labour productivity and output fell after 1979[89]. Much of the large-scale industrial action of the time was in response to real wage decreases, job cuts, or political attacks (as with the 1972 Industrial Relations Act) too. One only needs to look at the devastation caused to de-industrialised communities and wider inequality since that time to understand the bitterness with which changes were resisted. British uncompetitiveness was

87   See *The People: The Rise and Fall of the Working Class, 1910–2010* by Selina Todd (2014), John Murray

88   IMF working paper, 'Inequality, Leverage and Crises', 1 November 2010

89   Ken Coutts and Graham Gudgin, University of Cambridge (April 2015) 'The Macroeconomic Impact of Liberal Economic Policies in the UK', p. 21

partly due to the progression of other countries, often via deliberate state-planned and supported investment. Instead 'the City' and its financial institutions (which carried much favour with our governments) opted more towards overseas investment, short-term profits, and thus speedy shareholder dividends.

Notions of 'the working class' as white men stood on picket lines in grainy footage are clearly a thing of the past. But the working classes have not simply disappeared – indeed, analysis of the British social attitudes survey by University of Oxford researchers tells us that 60% of British people still consider themselves to be working class, a figure that has not changed since 1983[90]. Even those who attended university and work in managerial and professional, i.e. 'middle-class' occupations, were still just as likely to describe themselves as working class as those who do not. Much of this stems from the belief that familial background determines your class, and as we enter a period where generations are worse off than their parents it will be interesting to see if people associate themselves as being working-class or associate with their parents' materially better off standing. The fact is that the 'working class' look different to before: they are multi-ethnic[91]; much less likely to have as proud an occupational identity (where work truly defines who one is) as the miners, steelworkers, and so forth; they are the (bogus) self-employed couriers delivering our food via mobile phone apps; those working in retail and supermarkets; nurses and carers; basically a who's who of people who got us through the Covid pandemic. True working-class spirit – solidarity, looking out for one another, community. The evidence tell us that these people are working long hours, often for low pay, precariously, unable to get on the property ladder, and a range of other 'metrics' befitting those outside of what might constitute the 'middle class'.

Given the diverse complexity of the present-day working classes a political agenda that appeals to this proportion of the population based on class will be difficult. Appealing to more universal rights and protections around work, at least initially, would be most fruitful here for any kind of resurgent Labour Party. Despite the nonsense we hear about the younger generation being indoctrinated with 'leftist' ideas at university, their views are instead formed by the awful

---

90 University of Oxford, 'Most people in Britain today regard themselves working class', 30 June 2016

91 Office for National Statistics data via Trade Union Bulletins show that trade-union membership is more likely among those female, black, older, and/or disabled than they are white, able-bodied men

deal our current system is offering them – low rates of home ownership, huge debt for their education, little social mobility, and a planet heading for climate Armageddon. They have many overlapping concerns with the wider population given the raw deal most people are contending with. It is worth noting that the so-called 'centre' New Labour and others have been obsessed with capturing is itself an opaque, non-homogenous group; and while we may theorise about the types of policies that would appeal to such a group, it does not follow that we cannot for the changing complexion of the working class. Likewise, it takes real work for the elites to create divisions along such lines as ethnicity, sex, immigrant[92], welfare recipient, leave or 'remainer', some opaque notion of 'leftie' or 'the left', supposed Marxists, and so on. Fostering solidarity among the masses, many of whom face the same issues (be it extortionate housing or university tuition fees) and indeed care about the same things (be it the NHS or a real living wage) will of course be difficult, but it cannot be dramatically harder than convincing swathes of the population to vote against their own interests.

CAPITALIST REALISM

'[Capitalism] is not a success. It is not intelligent, it is not beautiful, it is not just, it is not virtuous – and it doesn't deliver the goods. In short, we dislike it, and we are beginning to despise it. But when we wonder what to put in its place, we are extremely perplexed' (John Maynard Keynes)

Margaret Thatcher's slogan denoting that *there is no alternative* still reigns supreme. Indeed, Mark Fisher suggested that it is easier to imagine the end of the world than the end of capitalism[93] – something that may actually come to fruition over the course of this century. It has been positioned to us that the only viable alternative to free-market capitalism, communism, died a death with the collapse of the Soviet Union in 1991. There is also good reason for unfettered confidence by proponents of capitalism as it has survived and indeed 'thrived' (depending

---

92 The assertion that immigrants 'take' jobs has been used to disguise the fact that capitalists lay people off in order to take advantage of immigrants to increase their profits – undoubtedly they are pleased to hear immigrants being blamed and not they themselves. As noted by Neal Ascherson, even those apathetic to the plight of others ought to be weary of how our governments and employers treat refugees (and migrants), as it shows how they would treat the rest of us if they thought that they could get away with it

93 Mark Fisher (2009) *Capitalist Realism*, Zer0 Books

upon where you fit into said system) through a great deal of economic, political and social upheaval – the industrial revolution, the great depression, world wars, and recently the global financial crisis. The economic system that caused this collapse barely received scrutiny, despite revealing what the 'free' market actually is: socialism for the rich, and market capitalism for the rest of us. Previous zealots for minimal state interference were left with no alternative but to bail out their domestic banks (or receive the government's help) to the non-trivial tune of approx. £550 billion. In the main, Labour governments have shared the belief in 'the market' of both the Tories and Liberal Democrats helping to create this notion that we do not possess the means nor appetite for something different.

The reality, however, is that capitalism has not been functioning effectively across many of the usual performance indicators for quite some time. In post-war Britain, rising labour productivity was matched by rising average wages, as did rising employment. Average economic growth between 1949 and 1979 was 2.6%. As Thatcher's ascension brought in neoliberalism, economic growth dropped to 1.7% as wages have stagnated and productivity has been sluggish also[94]. In the decade from the 2008 financial crash this fell to 0.2% due to many reasons, not least austerity measures. On top of this the proliferation of low-paid, precarious work, which – combined with increased thresholds for paying tax – mean that many people do not meet the threshold and tax revenues have not increased either, as typically they would when more people are in employment. Shareholders are paid whopping dividends that mean less money is reinvested into businesses (which would potentially allow them to create new jobs and all of the usual trickle-down economy tropes) nor money into people's back pockets to then spend and boost the economy that way. Instead, more and more is hidden offshore. We are in a situation where copious amounts of unneeded goods are produced and thus wasted (190 million meals worth of food each year by just the top 10 supermarket chains in the UK, for example[95]), millions of people work yet are in poverty, many more cannot find work, and the planet simply cannot handle it.

---

94 Centre for Business Research, Cambridge University, 'The Macroeconomic Impact of Liberal Economic Policies in the UK', April 2015

95 Globally, an area the size of China is required to produce the billions of tonnes of food wasted. This is even less likely to go to those without food in the UK as a government subsidy scheme incentivises food producers and supermarkets to dump edible food, which is then used to create biogas for the renewable energy sector. Our neighbours France introduced legislation whereby supermarkets who do not donate food (and are seen to allow it to spoil) face fines, with tax breaks rewarding donations. Carrefour alone donates thousands of tonnes more than the entire UK supermarket sector

The economic 'recovery' post-2010 was largely attributed (and accumulated to) rentiers of property, finance, and insurance; with land rent on residential and non-residential property by far and away the primary source of UK economic 'growth'[96]. The UK finance sector has been funnelling money into speculative and rent-extracting endeavours rather than productive (and/or labour-intensive activities) and lending to emerging and recently established global competitors such as China: essentially meaning that the UK finance sector has served itself rather than the UK economy[97]. As rentiers effectively have whole or partial monopolies in their sectors, it is difficult to see how the situation is going to change more favourably – if you do not own assets the future is not so bright for you. Despite the proclamations of politicians who manipulate figures or rely on dogmatic insistence that something is a 'fact' with no supporting evidence, there is little to suggest that the situation is going to change without a change in the system itself – plutocrats will continue to thrive; the rest not so much. Brett Christophers argues that at the very least there needs to be some competition introduced into monopolistic sectors to drive innovation, potentially curb price hikes, and so forth; a change in the tax system which stops millions of pounds being paid to shareholders by companies operating with massive debts to avoid tax obligations; and incentives to nudge corporations into non-rentier, preferably more labour-intensive, green industries. The rise of green industries will itself present great opportunities for rentiers of all kinds – finance, patents, and land – we must learn from the lessons of the past to ensure that the public sector goes back to building, owning, and operating: something rather unlikely under any Conservative or New Labour-type government.

If recent trends in work are anything to go by the situation will only worsen. More and more the burgeoning platform economy enables tasks that were traditionally performed by one person for a secure wage to be fragmented into even smaller, low-skilled tasks that are competed for on a global scale. For example, peruse apps such as Amazon Turk and a person in Newcastle can advertise for someone to undertake short, mundane admin tasks and people from as far away as French Guiana or Botswana can offer to complete the

---

96 See *Rentier Capitalism* by Brett Christophers (notably p. 334) for specifics. He also demonstrates how 'UK PLC', i.e. the corporations with the largest market value, are rentiers, e.g. Royal Dutch Shell top the list as rentiers of natural resources; HSBC are second as rentiers of finance

97 See Guy Standing *The Corruption of Capitalism* (2021), Biteback Publishing

service for much lower than the UK national minimum – rebadged 'living' – wage. Previously people gave up a great deal of control over their bodily and mental powers to their employers for much of their waking lives, in the hope that one day they would receive a decent pension. A pretty underwhelming bargain in the first place, but now most people do not even get that.

Our collective imagination has taken a hammering after decades of neoliberalism; with too few politicians offering an alternative and a media that fails to even deliberate on fundamental issues with the system narrowing what the public view as possible. We can be shown images of anything from queues of cars at petrol pumps and empty supermarket shelves, to learn of totalitarian murmurings among employers or politicians[98] with accompanying messages of 'a glimpse at life under communism'. The irony being that these are real-world instances of life under the untouchable capitalism. We are confined to dystopian views of 'there's not enough money' (for public services, etc.), 'everyone must work', 'government is inefficient'. As David Harvey suggests in *The Anti-Capitalist Chronicles* neoliberalism is very much a class project – to accumulate more wealth and power within a small elite class[99]. It is no coincidence that neoliberalism came to the fore at a time when the labour movement was at its most powerful, wealth more evenly distributed, the public having a stake in most of the key services, legislation passed that served the interests of the majority rather than the wealthiest (from consumer protections to employee health and safety, environmental protections, and so forth). Of course, economic principles were needed to rationalise the injustices and inequality that were to follow: the need for 'free markets', low taxation, privatisation, limiting labour power; everything that served the interests of the few and not the many.

There are innumerable flaws in the whole idea itself. There is no such thing as a free market given that there are always rules governing behaviour within it – and we have seen how much the free marketeers rely on government intervention whenever there is a crash or crisis (2008 being prime real estate here). There are rules that we take for granted, such as the banning of

---

98 Well illustrated by Deputy Prime Minister Dominic Raab seeking to introduce ad hoc legislation to 'correct' judgements made in the courts that ministers felt were 'incorrect', i.e. did not like or benefit from. See *Independent*, 'Raab threat to "correct" court judgments is "deeply troubling"', 18 October 2021

99 Neoliberalism being economic practices that see individual well-being as best advanced by deregulation and a 'free' market, thus congruent with reduced labour power (nominally trade union influence) and public sector(s)

child labour, the requiring of licences to practice certain medical and legal professions, a minimum wage, and so forth. Each progressive intervention was fought for by our working-class ancestors, always against people who opposed the modifying of the 'free' market. Where is the free market when governments hand over industries that have a monopoly to private corporations? Would the free market not collapse within weeks if the taxpayer was not on hand to subsidise them with in-work tax credits? In *23 Things They Don't Tell You About Capitalism* Ha-Joon Chang perfectly illustrates how subscription to a new regulation as supposedly restricting the free market is always a political objection masked as an objective economic truth. The vast number of think-tanks, lobby groups, and donating to political parties in order to lend the ear of government ministers offers a good illustration of how much governments intervene in the markets, with any decision not to do so itself a deliberate political approach. Neoliberalism is not then a shrinking of the state (albeit it certainly is in terms of its workforce) but the maintenance of its might in order to recalibrate whose needs and interests it serves. The state more than flexed its muscles during the Covid pandemic, with the population literally sat waiting for permission to leave the house.

The government's response to the recent pandemic included the Covid Corporate Financing Facility, an initiative to support large companies making a 'material contribution to the economy' effectively through loans with interest of between 0.2 and 0.6%. Meanwhile, small businesses have been paying anything up to 6% interest on taxpayer-backed Covid support loans during the same period. Justifications for such a move were tied up in the usual tropes of job creators needing to survive months of uncertainty, but the evidence paints a rather different picture. While nearly one-third of the companies accessing these (emergency) taxpayer funds cancelled their dividend pay-outs this year, another third paid out an estimated £11.5 billion in dividends – some shortly before accessing CCFF money and others just after[100]. At the same time, companies using the CCFF had, or were announcing, job cuts that could reach over 42,500. This is yet another example of corporate welfare and government refusal to monitor businesses who are meant to be supporting workers: although with the likes of Ryanair (receiving £600 million) among those using the scheme this may have been wishful thinking from the start. As Dan Hind notes, the premise of neoliberalism that self-seeking individuals

---

100 *Vice*, 'Corporations receiving bailout billions have laid off staff and paid investors', 4 August 2020

compete under the watchful eye of an enabling state is largely at odds with the reality, where large corporations dominate and governments subsidise favoured sectors and organisations[101].

Capitalism has indeed improved the fortunes of many and lifted many out of abject poverty. There are good reasons why proponents are so confident in what capitalism has achieved. That should come with a note of caution, however, given that capitalism as we know it would have looked very different without the interjection of the working-class. When we praise capitalism, despite its ills, we must remember how worse those ills (not least working conditions) would be if capitalists had been able to completely have their way[102]. And much of what was achieved by the working class happened under Labour ministers who are as socialist as we have been given (Nye Bevan and the NHS being the obvious example). This is precisely why the impact of class struggle on our history has been effectively airbrushed out of our dominant national myths – the ruling class do not want to give us any reminders of this.

The moral case against capitalism is clear: it is a system that effectively forces the ill and disabled into meaningless, low-paid work; where changes are made to the benefit system that forces people to compete for jobs that simply are not available, in a process fraught with stigmatisation and de-humanises those who may have perfectly valid reasons for not being 'employable', as narrowly defined by our capitalist demigods; where employers welcome cheap migrant labour who are then scapegoated, subject to overt ridicule and even violence. The number of billionaires in Britain hit a record high in 2021 (thanks to the biggest jump in their number for 33 years – despite the Covid pandemic), as did the number of food parcels handed out by food banks. Capitalism is failing us so badly that pre-Covid UNICEF reported that nearly one in five children lacked sufficient safe and nutritious food, with over two-thirds of those in families where at least one parent was gainfully employed. Indeed, for the first time in the charity's 70-year history they began supplying food to hungry children in 2020 in what was termed a domestic emergency for thousands of

---

101 *The Return of the Public* (2012), Verso
102 Outside of trade unionists and labour scholars the power of workers is downplayed enormously. Sure, we are not in the 'heydays' of millions taking to the streets, often in solidarity with other workers, à la the 1926 general strike or 1968–74, where over 90% of all strikes were unofficial acts of grass-roots resistance. But not only is the labour movement responsible for the things we take for granted nowadays (sick pay, annual leave, etc.), recent cases of 'winning' Uber drivers basic rights and protections, abolishing employment tribunal fees, etc., all point to the enduring influence of workers collectivising

children suffering from food poverty. This at the same time the Tory *Children's Minister* Vicky Ford voted against extending free school meals for families facing financial hardship. Now it is clear that capitalism is not working even from an economic perspective like before – if we can even say that any form of pure capitalism deserves the plaudits, it is clearly time to change the system to one that works for the majority of people rather than just a select few.

TWO

MONEY

'It is true that if care is taken to use only a language that is understood by graduates in law and economics, you can easily prove that the masses have to be managed from above' (Frantz Fanon, *The Wretched of the Earth*)

Oxfam caused a stir in 2015 with their 'Even It Up' bus tour, visiting such cities as Glasgow, London and Cardiff, proclaiming that the world's 80 richest people own the same wealth as the poorest half of the world and could thus fit on said bus. Just two years later, Oxfam's calculations had just eight of the richest men on the planet possessing the same amount of wealth as the poorest 50% of the global population (which equated to over 3.9 billion people)[103]. This is representative of the wider trend whereby wealth has been accumulating more rapidly among those at the top of the 'wealth charts' recently. Consider the following figures compiled by the High Pay Centre:

Year	FTSE100 CEO pay (£)	FTSE100 employee pay	Pay ratio CEO:EE	Avg. UK worker pay	Pay ratio FTSE100 CEO:Avg. UK worker
1980	115,000	n/a	n/a	6,000	18:1
2019	3,610,000	32,818	110:1	30,353	119:1

---

103 Oxfam, 'An economy for the 99%', published on 16 January 2017, one month before they themselves became embroiled in a sexual misconduct scandal in Haiti, demonstrating that even those we see as advocates for positive change require scrutiny

The High Pay Centre found that by 9am on the 7th January 2022, these CEOs have already received the median annual British wage. As one would expect from the above, the share of total national income accruing to the wealthiest 1% of the population has more than doubled since 1979 (Thatcher's ascension) from 6% to 13%. Between 1920–1970 this had dropped from more than 20% to the figure of 6%. Meanwhile, the average UK worker is actually down in real-terms pay (pay when factoring in inflation and higher costs of living) by 2.9% since 2008[104]. It is quite interesting that FTSE100 CEO pay has itself dropped over the last few years, as there is now an increasing divide both internally between the top 1% of earners, and this group versus the rest of the top 5 or 10% of earners (i.e. the top, top earners are pulling away from the rest of the pack even more).

Far beyond any reasonable doubt, senior management pay is a sham. Naturally, people warrant greater remuneration if they take on additional responsibilities and risks, and have skills that are not easily replaceable. But if you take Tim Steiner (CEO of Ocado), whose pay was £58.73 million for the year, this is 1,935 times the median salary of the average full-time UK worker. Is it possible to work 1,935 times harder than those who also contribute to a company's success? This at a time when their couriers were allegedly earning as little as £3.80 per hour[105]. We assume that such individuals have steered their organisations to great success via heroic strategic decision-making, being a visionary and great leader. But the evidence just does not stack up: for example, the Chartered Financial Analyst Institute UK reports that CEO pay for the FTSE350 between 2003 and 2014/15 increased by 82% in real terms, yet the median firm generated less than 1% economic return on invested capital[106]. Clearly pay is not proportionate to performance in any objective sense.

Jeremy Corbyn incited much debate in the run-up to the 2019 general election when he tweeted, 'There are 150 billionaires in the UK while 14 million people live in poverty. In a fair society there would be no billionaires and no-one would live in poverty'. A YouGov poll indicated that 51% of the general public agreed, citing that nobody deserves to be a billionaire, illustrating that this is a hugely divisive topic. Although the number of billionaires is disputed – e.g. *Forbes* have the figure at 54, New World Health report 95[107] – the key issue is that wealth continues to accumulate rapidly among this small group,

104 ONS, 'Employee earnings in the UK: 2019', statistical bulletin
105 *The Observer*, 'Ocado drivers 'paid less than £5 an hour', 21 August 2021
106 CFA, 'CFA UK Executive remuneration report 2016', 27 December 2016
107 New World Wealth, 'UK Wealth Report 2019', 6 November 2019

to the detriment of the wider population. As one illustration of this, a study by the Money Advice Service in late 2016 reported that around 17 million Brits of working age (amounting to around 40%) have less than £100 in personal savings at any one time[108]. Money is obviously central in any capitalist society. We are pretty obsessed with it, rarely leave the house without it, yet very few people properly understand it. While it does not guarantee you happiness, it helps to alleviate many of the pressures that can be a source of unhappiness and anxiety. It is worth considering where it comes from, i.e. how it is created, and whether our current monetary systems are the most effective that we have at our disposal.

DO GOVERNMENTS HAVE A MAGIC MONEY TREE?[109]

One of the many things that has happened during the Covid pandemic is that our government have, as if by magic, found money for an array of programmes and supports that were deemed fantasy just months before. One of the most pervasive myths in our society is that governments are constrained by their income – that spending must not exceed income from taxes – otherwise they will run up a high deficit. In other words, that governments must 'live within their means'. There are a number of problems with this, which we shall address, but the consequences are to normalise under-funding our key services (like the NHS), deep cynicism of anyone receiving welfare, and notions that running a deficit is tantamount to financial profligacy (a key justification for austerity in the aftermath of the global financial crash). The problems with these ideas are numerous.

Firstly, running a deficit is not actually a bad thing. If a government had a budget surplus, i.e. received more money than it spends (perhaps to pay down some of its debt), this reduces the quantity of money circulating through the economy. As a result, the public will be spending less, companies are less likely to be able to expand operations, and ultimately economic growth (and everything that comes with it, such as reduced unemployment levels) will be

---

108 The Money Advice Service, 'Low savings levels put millions at financial risk', 29 September 2016

109 For those who, like myself, are not economists, Stephanie Kelton (2020) *The Deficit Myth*, Mary Mellor (2015) *Debt or Democracy: Public Money for Sustainability and Social Justice*, Ann Pettifor (2018) *The Production of Money: How to Break the Power of Bankers*, and Mitchell and Fazi (2017) *Reclaiming the State: A Progressive Vision of Sovereignty for a Post-Neoliberal World* have largely informed the thinking here and are must-reads for those unconvinced

adversely affected. To be clear, when government spending – particularly on key public services such as healthcare, education and housing – is greater than its income, this is not automatically a cause for alarm. This stands in contrast to the typical portrayal that deficits are to be avoided simply because they lead to unsustainable debts. In June 2011 David Cameron echoed similar sentiments by George Osborne at the 2010 Conservative Party conference[110] when he likened what he called reckless Labour spending to that of a household, stating that 'if you maxed out your credit card, if you put off dealing with the problem, the problem gets worse[111]'. It was a view popularised by Margaret Thatcher who in 1983 said 'the state has no source of money, other than the money people earn themselves. If the state wishes to spend more it can only do so by borrowing your savings or taxing you more'[112]. The government as household is a flawed analogy for the reasons cited below.

Unlike households, governments can increase their revenues by raising taxes. Unlike households, governments can borrow large amounts of money at low levels of interest by issuing bonds. Unlike households, many sovereign governments (including our own) have the power to create money if it wishes. Despite suggestions that they should not as they tend to be inefficient and such a system would impede competitiveness, this is effectively what happens anyway, as is well illustrated with the bank bail-outs after the global financial crisis. The government holds an account with the Central Bank, where tax receipts are recorded and payments are made from. If the government wants money, typically an instruction is sent from the treasury to the Central Bank who then transfer funds out of this account and into that of the recipient (of the public spending). Actual material currency makes up just 3% of that in public circulation, these transactions simply take place via computer operators who record sums in and out of said account. If there are insufficient funds in this account to cover spending, government bonds are sold (essentially at a debt auction with select, private banks) who then credit the treasury's Central Bank account with reserves of equal value[113].

110 *The Telegraph*, 'George Osborne: Britain risks lost decade due to "credit card", economy' 4 October 2010

111 *New Statesman*, 'An economics lesson for David Cameron', 16 June 2011

112 Margaret Thatcher Foundation, 'Speech to Conservative Party Conference', October 14, 1983

113 Private banks generate money in much the same way: they borrow money from the central bank (which creates it out of thin air) at a lower interest than they charge on the loans they themselves issue – to households, businesses, etc.

The significance of this is that our government can technically create money out of thin air, via 'overt monetary financing' in co-operation with the central bank, thus they do not have to fund their spending via taxes or create money through (private) debt. Mitchell and Fazi (ibid) note the mainstream view that this would create severe inflation is flawed, because overt monetary financing does not carry any intrinsic inflationary risk: it is government spending that does, irrespective of how it is financed. Any spending is inflationary if it drives nominal aggregate spending faster than the real capacity of the economy to absorb it. Therefore, it is perfectly logical and possible for a government to issue its own currency and pursue goals that increase the productive capacity of the economy (e.g. by facilitating high levels of employment) without increasing spending growth beyond this productive limit. In effect, just because a government can create as much money as it wants, it would not make sense to actually do it. Between the onset of the 2008 financial crisis and December 2021 (effectively after two years of responding to the Covid pandemic) the UK government created approximately one trillion pounds' worth of money, and no unforeseen inflation of everyday prices occurred. Overt monetary financing is not a new idea having been propagated by the likes of John Maynard Keynes and Milton Friedman in response to the 1930s Great Depression. In the same period it was successful in Japan, Canada, New Zealand, and used by the German government between 1933–37 to transform itself from bankruptcy into the strongest European economy.

There is no 'natural' way to create money, therefore the decision to do so via tax and debt is a voluntary, political one[114], not to mention complex and unnecessary. The motivations for doing so are therefore unclear, but a cynical view would be that this is deliberate obfuscating. If the government simply created money of its own accord with no third-party involvement, then it would be under immense pressure to not underfund services and would have greater difficulty rationalising a range of neoliberal fiscal policies. Neoliberalism dictates that markets are the sole creators of wealth (and thus provide income for households and public services). Resultantly, this acts as the catalyst for privatisation, de-regulation including of workers' rights, cuts to corporation taxes, and incentives for private-sector expansion. Public debt can

---

114 It is worth stressing that bond sales and taxation *do* have their uses within monetary policy (e.g. taxes transfer money back to the government 'sector' enabling a redistribution of wealth) but, simply, they are *not* required as a source of funds to finance government spending

easily be manipulated such that citizens accept – and even demand – policies that are not in their own best interests for fear that any improvement would need higher taxes and so forth. A widespread view is that public services are dependent upon the private wealth creators (to create tax-paying jobs, corporation tax, etc.) who we must then bow to, and not question tax reliefs and the like for fear of 'losing them' to fairer overseas lands. In effect, we are made out to be the parasites, not them. They are required as money appears in the economy as a result of commercial demand/economic activity and thus those who have it must have done something to deserve it. The fact is that this way of doing things could be legislated out of existence if the public had a better understanding of how the money system works and wanted to change it.

It is therefore problematic that the power to create and circulate money has come to rest with the central banks, rather than the state, and by consequence the people themselves. As such, macroeconomic policy is not wholly accountable to voters but is managed by unaccountable central bankers and dominated by private vested interests. Creating new public money via private debt makes the public sector just another borrower and this is detrimental to the taxpaying public, who are themselves reduced to mere borrowers, consumers and indeed taxpayers. In the wake of the global financial crisis the government effectively borrowed money to bail out the banks – taking on debt from the central banks to do so, despite the fact that this could be debt-free, newly created money – and thus a debt the public had to repay. In effect there is no public right to money. We as ordinary citizens can only access it through wage labour or debt in this system, and those who are unable to do so are left to vanquish. Those who do not work are scroungers, workers who unionise in an attempt to improve their lot are seen as trouble-makers or greedy, and government departments positioned as wasteful and part of profligate government bureaucracy that we simply cannot afford. We have seen the consequences of this: citizens become consumers, employee rights become zero-hour contracts, housing becomes an investment opportunity, and debt a way of life. As Mary Mellor suggests in *Debt or Democracy*, private wealth and private money do not drive prosperity – rather it accumulates among the elitist class – only public money and public wealth can do so, but not in its current form.

The result of this is that people expect little else than a vicious, competitive struggle for scarce resources and services in which most people lose or must wait long periods before accessing. The knock-on consequence is the generation of tremendous social resentment: every little bit that anyone else gets is suspect, it has to be interrogated, and the beneficiary's worthiness needs to be tested. Mitchell and Fazi call for a change in what we consider to be desirable fiscal outcomes. For example, instead of aiming for, say, a 'deficit of 3% of GDP' we should focus on the usefulness of government spending instead, in achieving its national socio-economic goals, such as full employment or whatever else.

DEBT AS A MEANS OF CONTROL

'Debt is the slavery of the free' (Publilius Syrus, Roman aphorist 42 BC)

There are many who feel that creating a monetary system that is primarily driven through debt is a clever tactic to exert control over masses who became increasingly emboldened through universal suffrage, social movements, a growing politically engaged student body, de-colonisation, and the like[115]. This so-called 'Crisis of Democracy', to borrow from the 1975 Trilateral Commission report warning Western elites that people were no longer satisfied by being passively governed, was a problem to those in government looking to maintain the status quo[116]. Under the auspices (perhaps real at one time, today disingenuous) of enabling people to realise the manufactured aspirations of home ownership, a nice car, and all other components of 'the dream' they are drawn into obligations and burdens that ultimately constrain people across most, if not their entire lives. As described by Andrew Ross in *Creditocracy: And the Case for Debt Refusal*, 'Short of armed repression, the loading of debt on to all and sundry has proven to be the most reliable restraint on a free citizenry in modern times' (p. 31).

Creditors operate with minimal regulation (the City of London a prime example) and are extremely powerful, as again demonstrated by the bail-outs after the global financial crisis. In fact, despite this cultural practice of debt getting us into a financial mess in the first place, there were barely any alternatives offered by mainstream economists or policy-makers other than to cut public expenditure and re-boot the debt-driven expansion of production

---

115 Debt serviced as punishment and control is perhaps best illustrated through colonialism, e.g. the annual compensation payment imposed by the French on Haiti between 1825–1947 for slave-owners' 'lost property'. The French receive money they do not deserve, and Haitians' progression is effectively restrained

116 Republished by New York University Press as a book, *The Crisis of Democracy: On the Governability of Democracies*. The Trilateral Commission is a global elitist body founded by the late David Rockefeller

and consumption all over again; with apparently little amendment to prior banking practices. It makes sense that the Conservative Party would create a favourable environment for the financial elites to profiteer through an economy based on debt, but New Labour did exactly the same – notably when Tony Blair controversially removed Clause IV from the Labour Party constitution, which had been added in 1917 outlining the party's commitment to nationalising key industries, including the Bank of England[117] and greatly expanding the use of private finance initiatives. Debtors do not enjoy the same conditions as creditors, with the latter essentially securing rights to debtors' future wages and supported legally to do so, even if this involves smaller payments across an individual's entire life course. As Scurlock demonstrates in *Maxed Out: Hard Times in the Age of Easy Credit*, banks make a lot more money by putting people into debt than they do encouraging people to save, 'banking is about selling a single product: debt' (p. 46). If we take the average credit-card arrangement – banks derive their profits from a continuous flow of merchant fees and late payment penalties so it is in their interests that the debt service is extended indefinitely and that we are not able to pay back our balances at the end of the month (within reason)[118]. In a competitive marketplace this has encouraged lenders to target the most 'profitable' groups, i.e. those on lower income who pay higher interest rates on their debts for longer periods, also being sold the same dreams necessary for over-consumption. One only needs to look at the 'advice trends' on the Citizens Advice Bureau website to see that issues around debt and welfare dominate, with those seeking advice tending to have interrelated concerns. This whole system is further aided by really poor interest rates paid by the banks on savings, thus encouraging greater spending too.

Debt has become such a routine way of life it is almost viewed as operating like a legitimate tax collection: education being a classic example, with undergraduates from poorer backgrounds accruing debts of around £60k for a three-year course somewhat normalised given the relatively stable

---

117 The clause read: 'To secure for the workers by hand or by brain the full fruits of their industry and the most equitable distribution thereof that may be possible upon the basis of the common ownership of the means of production, distribution and exchange, and the best obtainable system of popular administration and control of each industry or service'

118 Deloitte estimate that as much as 80% of banks revenue from consumer credit comes from the interest paid by consumers (on credit cards and loans). See 'The Future of Credit: A European perspective' (Spring 2019)

intake universities experienced pre-Covid[119]. According to Deloitte the UK is the 'credit-card capital' of Europe, with credit-card debt climbing to over £72 billion in February 2020, and another £150 billion in personal loan debt. Naturally, the situation for those who rely on debt to survive month to month worsened enormously during the Covid pandemic, with household borrowing and arrears increasing 66% between May 2020 and March 2021[120]. Even if you are unsure of whether access to affordable shelter, healthcare, and education is a fundamental right, it is problematic that these are being forfeited for a small proportion of society to derive vast profits from. In the context of stagnating wages and rising costs, the situation is not conducive for many debtors to live a life free of debt and begin to build beyond that. Rather than viewing a house as a 'home', they are increasingly seen as a financial asset, and thus instead of representing a place of security, stability, and comfort, it is transformed into one of anxiety and discomfort (over possibly eviction and/or repossession) when we are unable to actually own it and call it our own, as for much of our lives it belongs to the crediting bank or renter[121].

The suggestion in several quarters (see Wolfgang Streeck *How Will Capitalism End?* as one example) is that crises are inevitable in the current system. In effect, people borrow money to invest in assets when the prices of those assets are increasing, with the belief that such loans can be easily repaid when selling the asset, as it reaches a higher price. Prices continually rise as more people use this logic to borrow money with the intention to invest in such assets. Of course, this is a ticking time bomb as such speculative growth is unsustainable, triggering (periodic) economic crises that result in widespread repossessions, bankruptcy, and dangerous projects like austerity. The responses to crises also tend to be short-term 'fixes' that stabilise the economy for only a period of time, and usually only because neoliberal governments act as a guarantor – on behalf of the taxpayer. Therefore, while we may continually buy time through responses to debt crises, inevitably the day will come where the present unsustainable capitalist system propped up by debt will collapse.

---

119 Adjusting figures from the Institute for Fiscal Studies, 'Higher Education funding in England: past, present and options for the future', Briefing Note 2017

120 Tribune, 'Rebecca Long-Bailey: 'The Tories are ignoring the pandemic debt trap', 01 March 2021

121 For a good literature review of the sociological and psychological outcomes of debt see Mark Featherstone (eds) *The sociology of debt* (2019). Bristol University Press

TAX

Much of the argument to not raise taxation levels is the 'flight of capital' mentioned previously, but this assumes that those with wealth are indeed paying their fair share of taxes by way of higher rates. As such, is the idea that we cannot afford to lose their tax payments or the tax-paying jobs that they are said to create. Indeed, many do pay their share, but this is only half the story. Given that most people see the state as constrained by its tax income for spending on public services, it is somewhat surprising that there is not greater pressure applied on wealthy individuals who by rights should boost the treasury's coffers by billions of pounds each year (that could be used on schools, the health service, and so forth) yet choose not to. And the word 'choose' is not used lightly here, since it requires a very deliberate set of actions and often specialist help to funnel money and assets where the taxman cannot find it. Indeed, the House of Commons' own watchdog has explicitly noted how the 'big four' accountancy firms have a long history of advising the government on how to design taxation laws, before returning to their clients with the know-how regarding how to avoid their full obligations[122]. And why wouldn't they? It is their job as profit-focused organisations to be the best at offering financial services; insider info only benefits those aims. Before we consider the different ways in which this is accomplished, let us begin by assessing what those obligations are in the first instance.

TAX RATES
The total tax revenues for the year 2018–19 were £627.9 billion with the following overleaf an overview of the amount(s), and proportion of overall taxation received by HMRC, the different taxes make up for this tax year[123]. The most significant contributors being:

---

122 House of Commons Public Accounts Committee, 'Tax avoidance: the role of large accountancy firms', 15 April 2013
123 HM Revenue and Customs, 'Annual Report and Accounts 2018–19'

Tax	Total £ (billions)	% of total tax
Income tax	194	30.9%
Value added tax	135.6	21.6%
National insurance contributions	135	21.5%
Corporation tax	53.5	8.5%
Council tax	29.8	4.7%
Fuel duties	28	4.5%
Business rates	25	4%

The rest of total tax revenue is made up by things like stamp duty, tobacco and alcohol duties, inheritance tax, and so forth. While it would be foolish to argue that we do not benefit greatly from the tax contributions of the rich, with the Institute for Fiscal Studies reporting that the top 1% of earners contribute around one-third of *income tax* paid to the government[124], one has to question whether their contributions have been somewhat mythologised. For example, VAT as the second biggest contributor to tax revenue is a flat rate to be paid irrespective of earning capacity, and there is no evidence to suggest that the wealthy spend more on alcohol (which contributed £12.1 billion in tax revenue) and tobacco (£9.2 billion) that together contribute just under 4% of the total revenues. Naturally many of our wealthiest do contribute more income tax as a consequence of their higher earnings, but income tax itself represents less than one-third of all tax revenues and is often far removed from the actual wealth of this 1% (see below). Corporation tax contributes 8.5% and businesses benefit from a comparatively low corporation tax rate, itself down from 52% in 1973, e.g. Spain is 25% and France 31%[125].

Furthermore, research by the Sheffield Political Economy Research Institute in 2015 estimated that large private businesses extract more from the state in financial terms (via subsidies, grants, and tax relief) than they contribute via corporation tax[126]. Such 'corporate welfare' amounts to between £93 billion and £180 billion each year[127]: to put this into perspective, the

---

124 IFS, 'How high are our taxes, and where does the money come from?', briefing note, 13 November 2019

125 Combined statutory corporate income tax rates, via the Tax Foundation

126 SPERI, 'The British Corporate Welfare State: Public Provision for Private Businesses', July 2015

127 See the Corporate Welfare Watch database here: https://www.corporate-welfare-watch.org.uk/cww_database/

Department of Health and Social Care's budget (i.e. the NHS and wider sectors) is around £140 billion[128]. Taking the most conservative figure of £93 billion: the government's own statistics estimate that there are 27.8 million households in the UK[129], which means that each household effectively donates £3,345 to big corporations each year via their tax. That is after being ripped off by them as a consumer, or exploited by them as a worker; and in most cases both. This apparent dependence on wealthy job creators is not the full story, and this is before accounting for tax avoidance measures.

The desire of our wealthy peers to reduce tax contributions has been aided by government policy: based on Tolley's Income Tax archives, in 1974 the top rate of tax was 83%, with the basic tax rate 33%. These figures now are 45% and 20% respectively: which equates to a drop of 38% in tax paid by the most wealthy, nearly three times the reduction that has occurred for those on lower income. Meanwhile Value Added Tax, which everybody pays as a flat rate irrespective of income, has increased from 8% to 20% to help make up some of this shortfall. It is therefore unsurprising that the regular taxpayer would be amenable to cuts in the welfare budget and such like as their perception that they already pay a considerable amount of tax is correct, and the desire to not see taxes increased justified. However, not only do we know that our government could simply create the money to properly fund these services if it wished, it does not because any increase in tax for the regular citizen is primarily to subsidise tax breaks for the wealthiest in the country instead. Were we not doing this, and those with the most paid their fair share, there would be plenty of money to properly fund health, education, and housing – again, without having to increase tax for the regular payer by a penny.

Despite the pandemic, the wealth of UK billionaires grew by £106.5 billion between May 2020–2021. Instead of taxing this colossal wealth, the government cut £20 of universal credit from the poorest in society, threatened the unemployed with benefit sanctions if they refused jobs irrespective of skill-level or preferred occupation, and broke their election pledge by increasing National Insurance Contributions (NICs). Such contributions are set at a rate of 12% for earnings up to £50,270 and 2% for earnings over this sum, which means that those earning vast amounts of money will pay a lower proportion of their income in NICs compared to the less well-paid. It also does not apply

128 The King's Fund, 'The NHS budget and how it has changed', 13 March 2020
129 Office for National Statistics, 'Families and households in the UK: 2019', statistical bulletin

to unearned income – capital gains, rents, and so forth. Once again the plan is to disproportionately target everyone from the low- to middle-income worker during a supposed phase of 'levelling up' while the wealthy rentiers are spared by their friends in office. One cabinet minister acknowledged this by stating, 'They can't seriously be thinking about a tax raid on supermarket workers and nurses so children of Surrey homeowners can receive bigger inheritances'[130]. This proposed change will raise £36 billion over a period of three years, whereas a 10% wealth tax on assets exceeding £100 million would raise over £69 billion – at a time when British billionaires wealth grew by an astonishing £290 million per day.

At first glance, the suggestion that local public transport could be free at the point of use appears to be very radical, yet such a service that is also green and reliable is entirely possible if taxes are used to fund it rather than it being wasted and/or doled out to friends of the government. The Institute for Public Policy Research's Becca Massey-Chase asserts that the cost of doing so would be under £3.5 billion per year, a small dent in the government's £27 billion roads investment strategy fund, and we can take lessons from cities across the US, Europe, and Australia who already provide a free service to their citizens[131].

It is pretty clear who the winners have been over time, but altogether unsurprising given that it is wealthy people making these decisions. The clearest indication that the wealthy did not want to pay their fair share of tax came in 1989 when Thatcher attempted to introduce the 'poll tax', a single flat-rate tax for every adult in a local authority area to replace the existing system that was based on the value of the property one owned (and thus was linked to someone's wealth and capacity to pay). In fairness, elements of this issue exist with its replacement council tax amidst calls to review this. Much diluted from public outcry in 1989, of course, many of those sentiments remain today. For example, YouGov found that there is an overwhelming desire for the rich to pay more progressive rates of tax (92% of Labour voters, 86% of Lib Dem voters, and 70% of Conservative voters) yet only 5% believe that they would actually fulfil their tax obligations[132]. This latter view is perhaps well-founded, with a number of mechanisms used by the rich to avoid paying *current* levels of taxation, or any at all (e.g. of the *Forbes* list of 54 billionaires in the UK, only

130 *The Telegraph*, 'Tories at war over 'idiotic' National Insurance tax increase', 4 September 2021
131 *Tribune*, 'Local Public Transport Should Be Free', 26 July 2021
132 YouGov, 'Half of Brits say nobody should be a billionaire', 16 November 2019

33 actually claim residency here as it is). Billionaire John Caudwell, founder of Phones4U, eloquently indicated that there would be a flight of capital if Labour won the 2019 general election with, 'we'd just go and live in the south of France or Monaco. Why stay here and be raped?'[133].

The poor choice of wording aside, there is a problem here: if other wealthy individuals are utilising the various measures open to them that avoid 40+% taxation, does it not follow that others will too? To be fair to John Caudwell he does recognise that the British system (reliant on taxes) created an environment that enabled him to be a successful entrepreneur and thus was not opposing the act of paying tax itself, more an increase when loopholes enable others to pay nothing at all. But this logic of 'why would I stay here when I go elsewhere and be taxed less' necessitates a race to the bottom. Where would this stop? The worrying signs are evidenced by the World Bank's 'Doing Business' annual reports (all available online) that measure and compare the regulations of 190 economies, effectively inviting countries who require financial investment to compete on lax secrecy laws and the like.

TAX AVOIDANCE AND EVASION

> '...in this world nothing can be said to be certain, except death and taxes'
> (Benjamin Franklin[134])

This well-known statement might apply to the majority, but tax is not an inevitable part of life for some. This is not even a new phenomenon: in the first ever report from the Board of Inland Revenue in 1853 the number of those avoiding their duty of paying tax was described as 'considerable', with the first estimate appearing twenty years later at £1.5 million, which amounted to approximately 40% of all income tax due. Given the popular support for not shirking one's tax responsibilities it is astonishing that this problem has been sustained for so long. As with most things, without a political will change is unlikely, and here Tony Blair and Gordon Brown are as culpable as their counterparts in blue. In fact, there is a whole industry dedicated to aiding those who wish to avoid paying their full allocated tax rate, which incorporates many of the same big accounting and law firms that 'help' our governments to devise

---

133 *The Times*, 'Phones4U tycoon: I'll quit Britain if Corbyn wins power', 25 April 2019
134 Excerpt from a letter to Jean-Baptiste Leroy, 13 November 1789 (*The Writings of Benjamin Franklin*, Vol. 10)

and review regulations. Even the banks continued to operate tax avoidance schemes in the immediate aftermath of being bailed out by the taxpayer in 2008–9. Consider Lloyds TSB, a recipient of £17 billion of taxpayer money and 43% owned by the taxpayer at the time, while *simultaneously* fighting to save a tax avoidance scheme through the courts[135].

Not content with seeing the tax rates for higher income bands collapse and their money proliferate at ever-faster speeds, the super wealthy decide that they do not want to contribute to the countries that have helped them (via publicly serviced healthy, educated workers using publicly funded transportation and infrastructure) to become so. We are now in a situation where some billionaires pay less tax than their secretaries[136]. Research by the University of Warwick and the London School of Economics found that less than one-quarter of individuals with a total remuneration – income and capital gains – of over £100k paid the statutory average rate for their income[137]. One in ten people with a total remuneration of over £1 million paid a lower average tax rate than someone earning £15k per year. The study also found that the average person with total remuneration of £10 million or more had an effective tax rate of 21%, therefore even lower than the rate paid by someone earning £30k per year. This amounts to billions of pounds worth of tax revenues that HMRC do not therefore receive, but how do these individuals manage it?

There are various completely legal means through which wealthy individuals avoid paying the prerequisite tax amount. One method is to restructure their financial affairs such that their income is classified as capital gains (usually taxed at 20% or 28%) and corporate dividends (up to 38.1%): forms of remuneration that attract significantly lower tax rates than income tax (45% on earnings over £150k per year). Undoubtedly, more opportunities beckon offshore. It is not an accident that the City of London, British overseas territories (half of which are tax havens: Anguilla, Bermuda, British Virgin Islands, Cayman Islands, Gibraltar, Montserrat, Turks, and Caicos), and Crown dependencies (Guernsey, the Isle of Man, and Jersey) equate to around one-

---

135 See Richard Brooks (2013) *The Great Tax Robbery* for a comprehensive rundown of tax avoidance

136 See *The Triumph of Injustice: How the Rich Dodge Taxes and How to Make Them Pay* by Emmanuel Saez and Gabriel Zucman

137 University of Warwick and LSE, 'How much tax do the rich really pay? New evidence from tax microdata in the UK', June 2020 briefing paper

quarter of the global market share for offshore financial services[138]. In fact, it is a very deliberate, state-created legal space to protect wealth. The Tax Justice Network's 'Corporate Tax Haven Index' demonstrates that the UK has single-handedly done the most to break down the global tax system, with tax avoided each year the equivalent to three times the NHS budget, or the entire GDP of Belgium[139]: with figures for the UK ranging anywhere between £36 billion (according to HMRC) and £100+ billion in lost tax revenues due to avoidance, evasion and other illicit means such as fraud, embezzlement, insider dealing, and political funding. The government reports that the gap between the tax that should be paid and the tax actually paid is 5.5% and had a self-set target in 2017–18 for an additional £28 billion in tax revenue by tackling avoidance, evasion and non-compliance, which became £30 billion in 2018–19[140]. This represents an underwhelming target at best.

Since June 2012 the Serious Fraud Office have successfully prosecuted just 34 individuals for offences associated with offshore tax evasion. To put this into perspective, in 2018 the Common Reporting Standard passed on information relating to approx. 3 million UK taxpayers with offshore financial interests. To put it into further context, in 2018 alone there were 9,000 prosecutions of benefit fraud (unemployment, disability, etc.) by the Crown Prosecution Service with this type of fraud amounting to 'just' £1–2 billion[141], a figure over a hundred times less than that of the wealthier fraudsters. As ever, the poor feel the full force of the law as vast policing resources are mobilised not to deal with elite corruption but to control groups further down the social hierarchy.

It is important to reiterate that having ownership of an offshore company is not illegal, but one has to wonder if, given the size of 'the prize' for recuperating due tax and as a deterrent to others who might engage in similar behaviour, whether there is enough ambition and drive here. At the risk of being cynical yet again, perhaps it is because those in office are engaging in such activities themselves alongside associates. Tax evasion and those in government are often members of the same networks, and even family trees. For example, former PM David Cameron's father Ian chaired an offshore investment firm in Jersey known

138 The Tax Justice Network found that 8 of the 10 jurisdictions whose tax systems are most enabling of corporate tax avoidance are part of this network

139 *Independent*, 'UK by far the biggest enabler of global corporate tax dodging, groundbreaking research finds', 28 May 2019

140 HM Revenue and Customs, 'Annual Report and Accounts 2018–19', p. 22

141 Department for Work and Pensions, 'Fraud and Error in the Benefit System', 9 May 2019

as Close International Equity Growth Fund and was director of the investment firm Blairmore Holdings Inc, incorporated in Panama, which avoided paying any UK tax, and David profited £31,500 from when selling his shares just before becoming PM. It was later revealed that the PM sent a letter to then-EU president Herman Van Rompuy urging a drive towards more stringent transparency laws to not extend to trusts[142]. Conservative Home Secretary Amber Rudd naturally jumped to his defence, herself being director of two companies in the offshore tax haven of the Bahamas[143]. One might be forgiven for thinking that electing MPs who have (past or present) links to businesses that engage in tax avoidance would ensure our regulators have the knowledge required to plug holes in the system, but this requires the appetite to do so also.

Jersey's status as a Crown dependency gives the island constitutional rights of self-government and judicial independence, which it has used to establish an offshore industry that helps Brits (and others) to hide their money. Its speciality is trusts: essentially, a 'settlor' puts assets that could include money, buildings, land, or investments into a trust, which is a legally binding arrangement with a 'trustee'. The trustee manages the trust on the settlor's behalf, and a 'beneficiary' (typically family) reaps the rewards of the assets and/or income generated from them as per the agreement. The attraction of trusts is the legal separation from ownership it confers on the settlor, who is then not taxed on the assets, only the revenue it generates. For example, if you would prefer not to pay capital gains tax or inheritance tax, a sound investment might be a luxurious, spacious villa in the South of France. Simply put this under the ownership of a trust company in Jersey, thus absolving yourself of ownership duties, and the trust – as per your deed – will have a legal obligation to pass it on to your children at the appropriate time.

Ian Cameron's other location of choice for business, Panama, hit the headlines when 11.5 million documents were leaked out of law firm Mossack Fonseca to two journalists at Munich-based newspaper *Süddeutsche Zeitung* in April 2016 – the famed 'Panama Papers'[144]. Mossack Fonseca specialised in setting up anonymous offshore shell companies: organisations that exist legally but have no active business operations or significant assets (such as

---

142 *Financial Times*, 'David Cameron's EU intervention on trusts set up tax loophole', 6 April 2016

143 BBC News, 'Leak reveals Amber Rudd's links to offshore investment funds', 22 September 2016

144 For a full account the two journalists in question, Frederik Obermaier and Bastian Obermayer, wrote the book *The Panama Papers: Breaking the Story of How the Rich and Powerful Hide Their Money*, Oneworld Publications

an office or employees). In the documentary *Panama Papers: The Biggest Leak in History* undercover cameras are utilised to demonstrate just how easy setting up an offshore shell company is. For a nominal fee, photo ID, proof of address, a CV, and some brief semblance of a business plan, a Swiss bank sets up a shell company in the state of Delaware, the US tax haven. A British pensioner living in South Africa whom the French documentary-makers will never meet is named director, who presumably receives a very small fee for his trouble[145]. They receive a New Zealand bank account in the company's name and are directed to pay a contact of the original Swiss bank 6% commission to transfer money to said account, which is received via an organisation in Hong Kong. They are then free to spend this money without the French authorities knowing anything about it.

There are a few things going on here: countries like Panama offer total anonymity to foreign investors and a 0% corporation tax on all income earned outside of the country and are thus an attractive proposition for those wishing to hide their money from authorities with greater inclination to ask questions and/or expect tax payments. If money is obtained via illicit means or an individual wants to avoid tax obligations then creating offshore shell companies and manoeuvring money into them as above enables them access to spend this money with little chance of being caught doing so. Consider another offshore favourite – the small island of Nevis, which does not recognise foreign court rulings; there is no requirement for registered entities to keep financial documents on the island; and no reporting, accounting, or auditing necessities either. In sum, full privacy and lots of protection for anyone wanting to keep wealth or assets out of plain sight.

There are several offerings of influential tax evaders in this text, including our press barons in Chapter 4. It is important to put this into context to appreciate the damage that this does to our society. According to *The Economist*[146], owner of *The Times* and *The Sun* Rupert Murdoch saved at least £350m in tax between 1988–1999 by cleverly moving money around various international and offshore sites, resulting in a tax bill of 6% as opposed to the 30%< he should rightly have paid on profits of over £2 billion. This equated,

---

145 Indeed, the documentary-makers visit Panamanian Mossack Fonseca employees Yvette Rogers (who boasts directorship of over 7k offshore companies) and her colleague, 63-year-old Leticia Montoya (director of more than 11k offshore companies), albeit their cut of proceedings is very low indeed
146 *The Economist*, 'Rupert laid bare', 18 March 1999

based on BBC estimations at the time, to the equivalent of seven new hospitals or 300 primary schools[147]. Given that he is not alone in such endeavours, we begin to see the mammoth level of public services that we are deprived of by the refusal of wealthy individuals to *pay their way*, as most of the rest of us do.

David Cameron was not the only high-profile individual to be implicated in the Panama Papers; six members of the House of Lords, three former Conservative MPs, and dozens of donors to our main political parties were all listed as having offshore assets[148]. A year later there was a further leak to the same journalists in what became known as the 'Paradise Papers'. This time such household names were implicated as Lord Michael Ashcroft, former deputy chairman of the Conservative Party and donor of millions of pounds to said party, who – despite living in the UK – claimed domicile in Belize for tax purposes although he repeatedly said that this was no longer the case.

There are also other services offered by banks to the discerning tax avoider. They provide individuals the opportunity to own assets like private jets and yachts, but via complex and opaque structures that make it difficult to trace such assets back to the original owner. Typically the asset will be owned by a company rather than an individual, which itself will be owned by another company – registered to, say, Luxembourg, itself owned by a company registered to Panama, with this repeated multiple times until you reach a company with a phony director as the front wo/man à la Yvette Rogers and Leticia Montoya in Panama. Nothing is off the table – with 'global citizenship', i.e. passports available for purchase should you have plenty of money and require such an insurance policy. If your money is offshored, why not offshore yourself? In return for a donation, investment in capital or government bonds there are various tropical shores that will offer you citizenship, and a pathway to non-domicile tax status in the UK among other benefits.

Much of this happens closer to home than we might think. In *Moneyland* Oliver Bullough takes us initially on a tour of Eaton Square in London, on which 86 properties are owned via anonymous structures, obfuscating who the true owner is from the taxman and others. Thirty were held in the British Virgin Islands, 16 in Jersey, 13 in Guernsey, the Cayman Islands, Mauritius, and other known havens. He suggests that over 100k properties across England and Wales are owned offshore, and often stand empty. Essentially, if you own a property under

---

147 BBC News, 'Business: The Company File Murdoch "pays no UK tax"', 19 March 1999
148 *The Guardian*, 'The Panama Papers: how the world's rich and famous hide their money offshore', 3 April 2016

British law you have to declare it, but if it is owned in, say, Mauritius, you do not, thus ensuring privacy. Later on we visit 29 Harley Street also in London, home to a company called Formations House that had created 2,159 shell companies – as of April 2016 – starting at a very low price (<£100) enabling companies to list this prestigious location as its registered address. Bullough traced back one of the companies registered to Harley Street, Blythe (Europe) Ltd., which was itself owned by P & A Corporate Services Trust Reg. of Liechtenstein (a country that does not reveal who owns its companies), itself owned by various other companies that eventually led to the network of corrupt, ousted Ukrainian president Viktor Yanukovych. The lack of scrutiny when firms are being set up is well illustrated by Bullough's discovering names registered with Companies House like "Xxx Stalin" and that 4,000 company owners were detailed as being under the age of two.

What we find is that not only does such money laundering cost the UK over £100 billion per year (according to the National Crime Agency – the government's international law enforcement agency) but what George Monbiot describes as the perpetuation of colonial looting. Via means such as the 'golden visas' wealthy individuals from overseas can obtain by investing £2 million+ in the UK, irrespective of how this money comes about, money is siphoned out of poorer countries to be shrouded in secrecy here. Can we do anything about it? A more co-ordinated effort on the international stage (much easier said than done) and a better-resourced HMRC would be good starting points. We are also in an interesting position whereby consumers are now the key determinant of good organisational practice – in a climate where governments advocate de-regulation and trade unions are weakened. For example, known tax avoiders Starbucks suffered a drop in turnover in 2013 following the negative publicity when such stories hit the headlines, with organisations like Ethical Consumer leading the charge for customer boycotts in the contemporary marketplace. This requires public angst to be directed towards the elites, whose evasion deprives public coffers of hundreds of billions of pounds.

PRIVATISATION AND THE ROYAL BANK OF TAXPAYER

In *The Nanny State Made Me: A Story of Britain and How to Save It*, Stuart Maconie asks, what was so bad about properly funded hospitals, decent working conditions, and affordable houses? And what was so wrong about student grants, free eye tests, and council houses? And where did it all go so wrong?

When Thatcher came to power in 1979 much of Britain's economy and infrastructure were in state hands: a third of all homes were rented from the state. The National Health Service, most schools, the armed forces, prisons, roads, bridges and streets, water, sewers, the National Grid, power stations, the phone and postal system, gas supply, coal mines, the railways, refuse collection, the airports, many of the ports, buses, freight lorries, nuclear fuel reprocessing, air traffic control, much of the car-, ship- and aircraft-building industry, most of the steel factories, British Airways, oil companies, Cable & Wireless, Rolls-Royce, the arms makers Royal Ordnance, the ferry company Sealink, the Trustee Savings Bank, Girobank, technology companies Ferranti and Inmos, medical technology firm Amersham International, and many others[149]. In effect, we are talking about a time when the Brexit slogan 'taking back control' would have actually meant something as the taxpayer had a stake in this commonly owned economy and infrastructure. Thatcher's government was not the first to privatise – earlier that decade a Tory government had privatised travel agents Thomas Cook and the Labour government had sold some of its stake in British Petroleum. However, such moves were driven out of necessity; privatisation only became the desired *modus operandi* under neoliberalism.

Now, much of the electricity made and sold in England is owned by companies in Western Europe (e.g. of the 'big six' providers of energy in the UK, the French *government-owned* EDF provides approximately one-sixth of the country's electricity; with E.ON of Essen in Germany not far behind). East Asian conglomerates own much of the biggest English water firms (for instance Li Ka-shing, Hong Kong's richest businessman, serves the North East of England and Malaysia's YTL Power parts of the South). There are even civil servants in places like Canada, Australia, and the Netherlands unwittingly owning shares in the likes of Severn Trent, Southern Water[150], and Anglian Water through their pension funds. Compare Scottish Water, which has remained a public

---

149 This list compliments of James Meek (2015) *Private Island: Why Britain Now Belongs to Someone Else*, Verso

150 Despite being privatised in the 1990s with no debt, the likes of Thames Water, Southern Water, and Yorkshire Water have loaded themselves with billions of pounds' worth of debt in order to pay zero tax – despite £72 billion being paid out via dividends and other means to their owners. The harm caused by (private) corporate greed is not only financial. Taking Southern Water as one illustration, they flouted 168 previous pollution cautions by dumping c20 billion litres of sewage into protected sea near Kent and Hampshire, purely in a bid to avoid charges and penalties

utility, charging consumers much less and investing much more money than the water companies in England that have loaded themselves with debt – partly to reduce tax bills[151] and partly to receive government subsidies or aid with improving infrastructure – yet dish out generous dividends to shareholders and bonuses to executives[152]. At the same time, water bills have increased by over 40% since privatisation at the end of the 1980s. With '08 fresh in the mind, it is not lost on us that should any of the private monopolies over our utilities fold (after substantial dividend payouts) presumably it would be left to the taxpayer for a bailout.

Neo-liberalism as instigated by Thatcher, continued by Major and solidified as Britain's economic and market ideology by New Labour, has paved the way for an insurmountable level of corruption. Its chief goal is to reduce the size of 'the state' by transferring public services into private-sector ownership, effectively giving away control of our nationalised services and introducing private-sector-style management into the public sector. The promises of privatisation, namely lower costs and prices, improved services, and better working conditions have not been realised some forty years into the 'experiment'. In reality the opposite is true, with spiralling costs, under-investment, poor performance, a lack of transparency[153], and detrimental changes to working conditions have been the norm. This should not surprise us: private companies are driven by one thing, profit. Our basic needs and services have not been treated as the essential infrastructure of daily life but resources for corporations to plunder at will. They have also been able to take advantage of fables typically reserved for the public sector, i.e. with wholly or part-monopoly status, there has been little incentive to innovate and invest to actually improve customer experience[154].

---

151 As a glimpse into the magnitude of this problem: Charlie Elphicke (see 'Water companies' tax dodging is beyond the pail' for *The Spectator*) estimates that in the water sector alone public coffers lost £1 billion due to the deliberate debt tax relief measures of companies such as Yorkshire Water and Thames Water – in just a three-year period

152 Articulated with greater nuance by Guy Standing in *The Corruption of Capitalism* (ibid)

153 The government refuses to extend freedom of information requests to private-sector companies, even those who are providers of public services. That said, Ian Cobain's *The History Thieves: Secrets, Lies and the Shaping of a Modern Nation* illustrates the British state is more than adept at keeping the public in the dark

154 E.g. OECD data from 2018 shows that Britain's % of broadband subscriptions with a fibre connection was 1.52% (compared to, for example, S. Korea at over 78%, Sweden over 64%, Spain 52%) largely due to our comparatively poor fibre coverage (c4% compared to, say, Portugal at c89% coverage), denying customers – notably SMEs and businesses in rural areas speedy internet access. BT's Openreach division has been consistently criticised for a lack of investment in the transmission network they control

The issues of privatisation, wherein the public interest in the provision of essential services is relegated to those of private interest, can be seen time and time again, with the taxpayer becoming an impotent cash-cow for private profit. Thatcher claimed that shareholder capitalism would result in ordinary people having an ownership stake in their country: individual shares in British companies were nearly 40% when she came to power and are now around 10%. Let us take railways as an example:

TRAIN WRECK

The British public pay the most expensive fares in Europe, which is a sorry state of affairs in and of itself. But consider that in taxes, the very same public provide more than double the subsidy to rail as we did when British Rail was under public control. To illustrate, the taxpayer subsidy to British Rail was 15% in 1994, the year before John Major privatised the industry. It has risen over 200% in the time that has elapsed and now stands in excess of £6 billion per year[155] in what can only be described as corporate welfare. In that same time, the real increase in rail fare stands at over 20%[156]. A significant reason for these exorbitant costs to both taxpayer and rail user is that the costs of running rail are ludicrously high. Before privatisation, British Rail owned the entire operation, whereas now over 100 separate companies complete this (now-fragmented) operation, each collecting a profit mark-up at each stage. This is incredibly poor business for the public, yet, private companies are also free to walk away if their heavily subsidised rail operation proves to be unprofitable, meaning that they are effectively given lots of free cash to have a punt at making more money at further expense to rail users. In fact, our rail system makes so much financial sense to governments that they do own our rail operators: namely the French (Govia[157] being part-owned by the French National Railways Corporation), Dutch (Abellio owned by Dutch national rail company Nederlandse Spoorwegen), and German (Arriva UK is part of Deutsche Bahn, with the German state its biggest shareholder) governments.

To truly understand how bad rail privatisation has been in Britain, consider East Coast Main Line (serving Edinburgh–London). In 2009 it

---

155 Full Fact, 'How much does the government subsidise the railways by?', 7 November 2018
156 House of Commons Library, 'Railways: fares statistics', 30 November 2018 (and has increased in years since)
157 Govia were stripped of Southeastern train services in October 2021 after failing to declare over £25 million of taxpayer funding

was returned to public ownership when then-operator Stagecoach declared that profit margins were too low. During the following stint as the only rail provider in public ownership it received less taxpayer funding than any of the private ones, becoming a beacon of excellence, winning twelve industry awards along the way. In other words, it was a win-win for the taxpayer and rail users. As is typical of a Tory-led government, it was then privatised once again in 2013 – only to be temporarily returned to public ownership in 2018 after failing to make a profit – despite enormous taxpayer-funded subsidies for the private owners. In May 2021 the government heralded their own supposed renationalisation project as 'the biggest shake-up since the 1990s'; however, their plans saw Network Rail effectively rebranded as Great British Railways and the entire basis of privatisation not only remaining intact but consolidated. Private operators are now paid a flat fee, ensuring guaranteed profits for dividends while the risk therefore remains nationalised, i.e. with the taxpayer.

ROYAL FAIL

Privatisation also deprives taxpayers of revenues that could be used to provide more and better public services. Let us take Royal Mail as our second example, compliments of the Tory-Lib Dem coalition government.

Relying on banks and financiers (the likes of Goldman Sachs) that had been involved in unsavoury dealings in the past themselves for a recommended valuation, then-Business Secretary Vince Cable set an asking price of 330p per share. This was £1 billion under even conservative valuations of its worth. Naturally, the share price soared 38% to 445p per share within hours, effectively transferring over £750 million (as estimated by the National Audit Office) of money that taxpayers were due from the sale of this taxpayer-owned entity, straight into the pockets of private 'speculators'. How quickly this 'state-milking army of overpaid, underworked, Luddite ne'er-do-wells jamming the cogs of the British economy' became a priceless national asset[158]. Privatisation hardly coincided with this unforeseen upturn in Royal Mail fortunes: one of the speculators, Lazard Asset Management, had been advising government ministers on an appropriate price via their financial advisory arm (now called) Lazard Ltd., for which they were paid £1.5 million, and then made a tidy £8.74

---

158 James Meek, *ibid*

million profit selling their shares just 48 hours later[159]. An equally generous act from the government came in the form of Royal Mail being privatised, but its pension liabilities, which stood at around £8 billion, were kept on the taxpayers' books. A further piece of good fortune for the speculators was the decision of postal regulator Ofcom allowing the price of first-class stamps to increase 30% just before privatisation.

As ever, where there are losers (in this instance both the taxpayer and Royal Mail staff; as is typically the case following privatisation, whopping dividends were paid out to shareholders while staff were subject to redundancies, pension cuts, moves towards more precarious employment arrangements, and work intensification) there are winners. The winners here were the priority investors: 16 entities allocated greater shares than were made available to everyone else, on preferential terms, with the proviso that they would hold the stocks long-term. Among them were Singapore and Kuwait sovereign wealth funds, and UK hedge fund Landsdowne, whose co-founder Sir Paul Ruddock had donated over £700k to the Conservative Party and Senior Partner Peter Davies was the best man at George Osborne's wedding. The National Audit Office revealed that half of these priority investors sold their shares within weeks: making an absolutely killing at taxpayers' expense in the process and not upholding their end of the supposed bargain[160].

JAILHOUSE FLOP

Equally bad, is that abject failure and fraudulent practices present no barrier to new contracts to these private-sector companies. Prisons offer yet another example of privatisation being an abject failure.

G4S suffered a very public humiliation when failing to provide enough staff as per their London 2012 Olympic games contract, resulting in thousands of armed forces being deployed to cover the shortfall[161], which they were subsequently fined millions of pounds for. Less than two years later and there was more trouble when G4S were given the contract to manage the tagging of offenders, and it transpired that they were fabricating the numbers of people they had tagged, including giving the names of people who had died some years earlier (in order

---

159 *Daily Mail*, 'Firm that advised ministers on Royal Mail sell-off also made £8 million from shares', 30 April 2014
160 National Audit Office, 'The Privatisation of Royal Mail', 1 April 2014
161 BBC News, 'London 2012: G4S Olympics statement in full', 13 July 2012

to increase their KPIs), resulting in more fines[162]. Fast forward two years later and G4S were embroiled in another scandal, with undercover filming by BBC *Panorama* showing the mistreatment and abuse of children at the Medway Secure Training Centre in Kent[163]. Two years on from this and there was another feather in their illustrious cap, when uncontrolled riots at HMP Birmingham forced the public sector to reclaim ownership of the prison. This followed repeated warnings from the Independent Monitoring Board of insufficient resources, an alarming regularity when private-sector profits are put before quality of public service[164]. They are not the only company to repeatedly be given public contracts in spite of these failings, with the likes of Serco and Atos also culpable.

The fact is, we have been getting ripped off at the expense of our elites for quite some time. Trade and Industry Secretary Norman Tebbit privatised BT in November 1984, before joining the company as director a few years later. In *Westminster Babylon: Sex, Money and Scandal in British Politics*, Alan Doig reports on an investigation into the privatisation of British Telecom (BT) in 1987 where 101 MPs and 34 MPs' wives purchased shares in the company just as the House of Commons voted on it – with Tory MP Keith Best submitting multiple applications (illegally) under different names, resulting in a prison sentence and fine. Similarly, PricewaterhouseCoopers economist John Hawksworth *conservatively* estimated that had Britain not privatised its North Sea oil reserves (using much of the immediate gains to fund tax cuts for the rich) and instead retained ownership, renting out its fields to private companies and retaining profits in a national sovereign fund, like Norway did, we would now have a fund with £450 billion of assets[165]. Whatever way you look, privatisation has been nothing short of a disaster. Take the 2017 selling-off of £3.5 billion of student loans for less than half their value: an amount the government's own analysis forecast they would have recouped in just eight years had they not short-sightedly sold these off[166]. When public assets are gone, they're gone, as Meg Hillier, Chair of the House of Commons Committee of Public Accounts, noted. You are greeted by the failings of privatisation as soon as you arrive in Britain at one of the Mitie-ran

---

162 BBC News, 'G4S repays UK government £108.9m after tagging scandal', 12 March 2014

163 Vimeo: 'Panorama: Teenage Prison Abuse Exposed'

164 BBC News, 'HMP Birmingham: G4S loses permanent contract', 1 April 2019

165 *The Guardian*, 'UK "missed chance to build up £450bn sovereign wealth fund"', 27 February 2008

166 House of Commons Committee of Public Accounts, 'Sale of student loans: Sixty-Ninth Report of Session 2017–19'

immigration centres where its practices and conditions treat those seeking asylum as sub-human.

There will be divergence of opinion regarding what exactly is in the public interest, and certainly over which services should be renationalised or through which privatisation (better managed and regulated) could be successful. But what these examples do illustrate are things that surely cannot be in the public interest, i.e. a poor return on tax investment in services that then become private; less money to sufficiently fund schools and healthcare; worsening employment conditions for the (still substantially large) public sector; private monopolies that rip consumers off; and much more. Governments can borrow money at a rate that would make any other entity jealous: banks clamour to get involved in these secured, reliable loan deals. It makes much more sense to raise finance this way and properly fund public services than it does, say, via the Private Finance Initiative (PFI) schemes already mentioned. Private companies stumping up the cash (often largely via loans on much more unfavourable terms) instead of government borrowing is nearly, if not actually, always bad news for the taxpayer and end user. Take the council housing PFI scheme in Miles Platting, a stone's throw from where my grandparents grew up in Manchester. Private capital invested into this scheme totalled around £84 million, yet the total estimated repayments over the 30-year arrangement has cost the taxpayer (approximately) an eye-watering £566 million[167]. There are 19 other schemes just like this, each with extortionate consultancy fees attached alongside a range of other services such as maintenance with additional costs incurred.

PUBLIC OFFICE, PRIVATE INTERESTS

The blurring of boundaries between public and private affairs creates ample opportunity for questionable practice. For one, the revolving door of personnel between public and private office creates conflicts of interest in which the public interest may be subordinated to those of the private. Periodically we see key business leaders brought in to advise on government policy, which is tantamount to big business helping to determine the regulation of… big business. There are countless examples as this is routine practice, but instances include Winfried Bischoff (of *Lloyds*) and New Labour Chancellor Alistair Darling determining that de-regulation was the best policy for the future of financial services in 2008–

---

167 Gov.uk website, 'Private Finance Initiative and Private Finance 2 projects: 2017 summary data', current projects as at 31 March 2017 spreadsheet

09: a key contributing factor to the crisis that created untold woe for millions. Before him, then-New Labour leader Gordon Brown appointed chairman of J Sainsbury Philip Hampton to review business regulation, who (naturally) wanted a drastic reduction of government inspection in consumer watchdogs, food inspectorates, and trading standards. Brown obliged, cutting 26 of the 35 government agencies involved in inspecting and regulating businesses[168]. As the proportion of senior civil service appointments from the private sector increases (actually doubling to 40% during the 2000s), it is increasingly likely that lobbying interest is exerted, insider knowledge is gained, and so forth[169]. One high-profile example was CEO of GlaxoSmithKline Sir Andrew Whitty, paid £7 million in 2013, serving as lead non-executive director of the Department for Business Innovation and Skills – that responsible for legislation on executive pay.

Personnel moves the other way too. Between 2015–18 the Advisory Committee on Business Appointments (ACOBA) received over 700 applications from crown servants and former ministers for external appointments[170]. As the name suggests, this is simply an advisory body without the legal powers to actually enforce anything that may prevent questionable behaviour. Just the latest (at time of writing) in a long list of serving MPs accepting lucrative additional jobs is Sajid Javid, recruited as a senior advisor to banking giant JP Morgan six months after stepping down from his position as Chancellor of the Exchequer[171]. ACOBA acknowledged numerous risks in his taking this position, not least his 'privileged access to information' on government fiscal policy (including around Brexit) and inside knowledge of the Royal Bank of Scotland (RBS) which could give an unfair advantage to the company. Essentially, their concerns were entirely the reason for him being offered the job.

The revolving door between the major financial and political institutions is well-oiled; Javid became an MP after 18 years in banking (including at JP Morgan) and his replacement Rishi Sunak went straight into parliament from investment bank Goldman Sachs. It is hardly any wonder that the financial services sector has, and remains, under-regulated. It also makes it less surprising that the banks would be bailed out after the global financial crisis with disproportionately little scrutiny or furore – no bankers were arrested,

---

168 Public Finance, 'Four super regulators to replace inspectorates', 17 March 2005
169 David Whyte (2015) *How Corrupt is Britain?*, Pluto Press
170 All ACOBA annual reports available on gov.uk
171 Following in the footsteps of the likes of Tony Blair, who was paid handsomely by JP Morgan in 2008

whereas Iceland jailed 26 for their part in proceedings. In fact, this practice is so common Facebook alone systematically recruited ten former policy officials between January 2019 and August 2020[172], with big tech companies the latest in a long line of corporations (banking, pharma, oil, and the like) seeking inside knowledge and networks.

As a final point here, private corporations are very keen to see the size of the state limited to reap many of the aforementioned benefits: fewer regulations to have to adhere to (including employee rights and protections), less stringent tax rates and laws, multi-million-pound public-sector contracts, and so on. Yet, they are very quick to look to the government in times of need. Lest we forget the words of Mark Ridley, Northern Rock CEO two years before the bank's £3 billion bailout of taxpayers' money, who wrote in online magazine *The Edge*, 'Government is the problem not the solution', going on to say, 'In all times and in all places there has been too much government… the more we limit the growth of government, the better off we will all be'[173]. Or how about Richard Branson, who vehemently opposed the bailout of Virgin's competitor British Airways in 2009, claiming that unsustainable businesses need to perish, but was keen to secure over a billion pounds in bailout money for his own airline during the Covid pandemic. The same Richard Branson who is a tax exile, having paid no income tax in the UK for fifteen years; whose train operations are heavily subsidised by the taxpayer (including £58 million in 2018 alone); whose healthcare company pays zero corporation tax on the multi-million-pound NHS contracts it is handed; and sued the NHS, which was forced to settle out of court in 2017 to the tune of £2 million of taxpayers' money, after their contracts for community children's services were not renewed in Surrey. Having socialised all of his business risks to the taxpayer while taking the profits for himself, Richard is using that money to travel into space – handy with the impending ecocide.

CRONYISM IS REAL - AND WE PAY FOR IT

On 14 May 2002 there was a legislative amendment made to the Code of Conduct for those presiding in the House of Commons, which allowed MPs with private business interests to initiate parliamentary proceedings on

---

172 *The Times*, 'Facebook accused of poaching UK officials to influence policy', 25 August 2020
173 '"What's your dangerous idea?" responder, Matt Ridley, "Government is the problem not the solution"', *The Edge*, 1 January 2006

such interests. Researchers at the Institute of Labor Economics found that both politician and corporate behaviour changed markedly as a result[174] – anticipated as stock returns for those companies with existing connections to MPs began increasing in the days leading up to 14 May. Donations to political parties reduced following the amendment too, as companies now enjoyed direct access to policymaking via their director or consultant MP lobbying for them. Some of the least surprising findings include the number of MPs with corporate affiliations grew, as did the number of appointments to select committees among these MPs. We now have a situation where only Russia and Thailand have a higher percentage of big corporations with links to serving MPs, likewise in terms of how this translates to market capitalisation. Among other notable outcomes is that companies with poor environmental records, lower regard for corporate social responsibility, and less transparent accounting practices were most likely to have political connections.

If you are part of 'the club' then you benefit in one way or another: usually via privileged access to government money (as noted already) or protection from wrongdoing. There is a long and disconcerting history of this; consider Patrick Rock, close friend of David Cameron who was appointed deputy director of the Downing Street Policy Unit in 2011. Rock resigned from this position after allegedly downloading and possessing images of underage girls, for which he was later convicted. Ironically, he had been responsible for developing policy that required filters on internet pornography to protect children during his tenure in this post. It later emerged that this news and an unrelated complaint about his inappropriate behaviour had been subject to an attempted cover-up by the government.

Cronyism hit the headlines across 2020–21 more than ever before due to the sheer scale of it as the government and their chums 'made hay' during the Covid pandemic. It began in March 2020 when the government put in place 'emergency procurement measures', meaning that contracts worth huge sums of taxpayer money could be awarded to companies without a competitive tender process. The principle of responding quickly to a crisis is clearly a sound one, especially after said government had presided over PPE stockpiles being diminished by over a third in the six years leading up to the

---

174 Institute of Labor Economics, 'Bringing Connections Onboard: The Value of Political Influence', June 2020

pandemic[175]. However, instead of securing the safest PPE at good value for the public in speedy fashion, it became a free-for-all among party donors and those with close connections in government. The National Audit Office, the UK's independent public spending watchdog, released a scathing report in November 2020 indicating that suppliers with political connections were ten times more likely to be awarded contracts[176] – leading to suggestions of a 'chumocracy' at the expense of the public whose civil liberties were all the while being restricted[177]. The result? What a Commons cross-party committee dubbed the 'worst public health failure ever'[178], although this would depend upon your perspective. Speaking during the pandemic about the issue of 'levelling up', Boris told BBC political correspondent Luke Walton 'I've given you the most important metric, which is – never mind life expectancy, never mind cancer outcomes, look at wage growth'[179]. A chilling insight into the value placed on the lives of others by an individual whose primary responsibility is to protect them.

Randox paid the Conservative MP for North Shropshire Owen Paterson £100k per year as a consultant and received £133 million on 30 March 2020 for Covid testing kits, around 750k of which were not fit for purpose. No issue for the government, who went on to award the company another £347 million again without other suppliers being invited to tender. Paterson eventually resigned, but only after public backlash following the Tories attempt to change the rules around ministerial standards, lobbying and MPs having second jobs (or in his case three jobs). He is but one. P14 Medical Limited was handed contracts worth £120 million in May 2020 to provide face shields to the Department of Health and Social Care, and then a further £152 million a few months later for isolation gowns. This small company making nearly half a million pounds worth of losses the prior year and being technically insolvent, with no track record in providing PPE, is owned by Conservative councillor for Shroud

---

175 *The Guardian*, 'Revealed: value of UK pandemic stockpile fell by 40% in six years', 12 April 2020

176 National Audit Office, 'Investigation into government procurement during the COVID-19 pandemic', 26 November 2020

177 And with good reason. In June 2021 the High Court ruled that a £500k+ (taxpayer-funded) contract awarded to Dominic Cumming's close friends at market research firm Public First was unlawful

178 House of Commons Health and Social Care, and Science and Technology Committees, 'Coronavirus: lessons learned to date', 21 September 2021

179 See video on *Independent*, 'Boris Johnson condemned for saying "never mind"' about cancer outcomes', 2 October 2021

Town Council (Gloucestershire) Steve Dechan, who stepped down from his role in-between the two contracts being awarded to his firm. Having gone from the helm of a company facing liquidation Steve, thanks to the taxpayer and pals in government, was able to upgrade to a £1.5 million mansion[180].

The money kept on coming. Take PPE Medro Limited, incorporated on 12 May 2020 (company number 12597000 for anyone wishing to see the details on Companies House), i.e. two months after the first national lockdown. It is registered to 85 Great Portland Street, London, which is home to over 8,000 other companies too. In effect, it does not have any staff or assets; in fact, it had a share capital of just £100 and is effectively a shell company created purely for one purpose. One month after being created, PPE Medro Limited received an untendered £122 million contract of taxpayers' money for protective clothing. There are two directors listed, Anthony Page and Voirrey Coole, who both work for Knox House Trust – whose Chairman Douglas Barrowman married Tory Baroness Michelle Mone just a few months earlier. As a final example, Ayanda Capital, owned by a company based in an offshore tax haven, received £252 million – over £150 million of which procured 43.5 million 'FFP2' medical masks with the wrong kind of straps, rendering them completely useless. The 'best' part? The deal was brokered by one Andrew Mills – a government advisor to the Board of Trade and International Trade Secretary Liz Truss – who also advises the company's board.

Alongside Tory party members their donors did very well during the pandemic too: a £350 million contract was handed to Medacs Healthcare plc., ultimately owned by long-time Tory donor Lord Ashcroft[181] being one example. The final qualification for government contracts is to either be related to the Health Secretary or run his favourite pub. Matt Hancock dished out £300k to Topwood Limited, a company owned by his sister that he, his mother, stepfather, and brother-in-law own shares in, to shred confidential NHS contracts. Meanwhile, former owner of the aptly named Cock Inn pub Alex Bourne offered his assistance to Hancock via WhatsApp and was given £30 million to supply Covid test vials – despite zero experience in the medical devices industry, something the Medicines and Healthcare products

180 *The Times*, 'Tory Steve Dechan's £276m in PPE contracts lands him a place in the country', 22 November 2020

181 OpenDemocracy, 'Tory donor Lord Ashcroft's outsourcing firm lands £350m vaccination contract', 20 January 2021

Regulatory Agency is investigating at time of writing[182]. Ultimately, existing codes of conduct that are supposed to limit legislators ability to also be lobbyists (thus undermining the whole notion of democracy and non-corruption) have proven no barrier to the procurement of equipment, largely from Chinese manufacturers, with a tidy profit on top – so long as you are well connected to the Tory party. No wonder Matt Hancock acted unlawfully in breaching his legal obligation to publish details of contracts awarded, which, as stated in the law, needs to be within 30 days for any amount worth more than £120k[183].

We already know how disastrously outsourcing public services to private interests typically ends, and the signs were already there early on. From the US healthcare company Movianto storing PPE in an under-staffed, smoke-damaged warehouse containing asbestos – requiring the British army to help disseminate PPE after delays to hospitals suffering shortages; NHS staff's attempted takeover of Deloitte's Covid testing operation at Chessington World of Adventures after lost and mishandled tests; and the continued circus that is Serco as targets were repeatedly missed on contracts worth over £400 million. If that was not enough, Tory party co-chair Ben Elliot was selling Covid tests to the super-rich via his company Quintessentially while his party simultaneously failed to get care home staff and residents tests, citing a national shortage[184]. At the very least, given the central importance of a fully functioning test and trace system to the pandemic response – a 'world-beating' one, as Boris Johnson promised[185] – you would imagine some semblance of a stringent recruitment process for the head of such a new, private body.

Yet the reigns were handed to Dido Harding, a communications executive with no medical experience whatsoever. Never mind the irony of people being asked to share sensitive information with the app given that Dido was in charge of TalkTalk during the data breach of 2015 that saw millions of customers bank details and personal information made public, for which they were fined £400k. She qualified on account of the fact that she is a Conservative peer. The result?

182 *The Guardian*, 'Matt Hancock's ex-neighbour under investigation by UK's medicine agency', 21 February 2021
183 *Metro*, 'Matt Hancock acted unlawfully over Covid contracts, judge rules', 19 February 2021
184 *The Times*, 'Ben Elliot's firm sold Covid tests to clients when NHS was struggling to increase capacity', 2 August 2021
185 Reuters, 'PM Johnson vows 'world-beating' track and trace COVID system by June 1', 20 May 2020

£40 billion of taxpayer money spent or committed[186] in what amounts to one of the most expensive public schemes ever undertaken, and yet, incredibly, the UK ran out of tests at the close of 2021. To put this into perspective, the successful Curiosity rover space landing on Mars in 2012 cost $2.5 billion. Construction of the underwater channel tunnel connecting Folkestone to Calais cost the equivalent of £12 billion in today's money[187]. The track-and-trace system has cost the same as approximately twenty-one Empire State Buildings, ten Disneyland theme parks, or 33,065 nurses – each employed for 40 years on a £31k salary[188]. Somewhat lost in the furore of the pandemic was the privatisation of Public Health England (PHE). One of the most catastrophic failures in history, both economically and in terms of loss of life, was not enough to dissuade the government to appoint Dido head of its replacement body, the National Institute for Health Protection. Incidentally, Dido is married to Tory MP John Penrose, who is part of the 1828 advisory board that had been calling for PHE to be scrapped (so too the NHS more broadly) and was also appointed as the Prime Minister's Anti-Corruption Champion; so one may question how much Dido will be held to account – by her husband.

At time of writing, with millions of Brits now vaccinated and society re-opening, Dido and co. were still paying consultants at Deloitte £900k *per day* to work on the failed programme. The unelected Lord Bethell, who is in charge of test and trace, founded his own private lobbying company for public contracts, Westbourne Communications, a decade before his peerage and subsequent appointment as Health Minister less than two years later. Among his clients, you guessed it, Deloitte (and also Ingeus, a company that is 50% owned by Deloitte) which worked on the heavily criticised Work Programme under the Tory-Lib Dem coalition. Bethell has shifted from fighting for Deloitte as a lobbyist to commissioning them as a minister, where again they are proving to be extraordinarily expensive and incompetent[189]. What the case with Deloitte highlights, as do the other issues outlined elsewhere (e.g. PFIs on hospitals,

---

186 *The Telegraph*, 'How Britain's Test and Trace system let coronavirus slip through its £40bn net', 3 January 2021

187 *The Telegraph*, '25 things you might not have known about the Channel Tunnel', 6 May 2019

188 Using the construction cost of the park built in Shanghai 2016; and the average UK nurse salary of £31k

189 Bethell was also found to be using private emails and WhatsApp messages when handing out multi-billion-pound contracts during Covid to the likes of Abingdon Health. After initially denying this, he went one step further and 'replaced' his phone once an inquiry was announced so that the messages could not be retrieved

housing, and so forth) is the 'false economy' when it comes to privatisation, beyond the eye-watering contracts and repayment plans. Hollowing out the civil service and other parts of government have stripped away vital bits of tacit knowledge and expertise, such that we now have to pay exorbitant prices for outside help as pools of senior civil servants capable of leading a response are now lacking.

Then there are the legal costs: take the £39 million of public money spent in 2016 alone by the DWP[190] defending, via various legal appeal processes, its (often wrong) decisions to strip benefits such as Employment and Support Allowance from sick and disabled people, largely due to the flawed nature of the Orwellian work assessments being used to 'test' just how sick or disabled people are. Who could forget Dawn Amos? Her letter from the DWP stating that she was fit to work and no longer entitled to sickness benefits arrived just hours before her life-support machine was turned off at Broomfield Hospital in Essex. We pay for this competence level of decision-making – money that could have been used to help those struggling was instead wasted in administrative and legal fees trying to force the sick and disabled into work, only to be proven wrong: costing the taxpayer more rather than actually saving money[191]. Step Change Debt Charity estimate that debt which is, in part, brought about by government economic mismanagement and practices exemplified by austerity cost the UK economy £8.3 billion for a multitude of reasons: children are more likely to be taken into care, the elderly into care homes prematurely, costs incurred due to mental and physical health repercussions, lost productivity at work, increased crime, and so forth[192]. Further evidence, as will be inspected below, that austerity was ideological rather than a necessity.

The government made poor decision after poor decision before and during the pandemic, and corruption was palpable – at great cost to everybody but those fortunate associates. The Department for Health's Annual Report estimates that £3.3 billion was spent on unusable PPE, £4.7 billion paying

---

190 *Independent*, 'DWP spends £39m defending decisions to strip benefits from sick and disabled people', 19 October 2017

191 The French outfit Atos, tasked with reducing the number of disability benefit claimants, saw 42% of the appeals against its decisions overturned in the quarter to September 2012 alone. Lost in the statistics is the real-life trauma and stress caused to those affected, with hundreds of thousands of old and disabled people losing their care support during the first five years of austerity, with the likes of Atos washing their hands of the work after pocketing millions in taxpayer money

192 Step Change Debt Charity, 'The social cost of problem debt in the UK' report

inflated prices for PPE that was not required, and that the government had 'written down' the value of over £1.2 billion in PPE that had not been delivered. The Good Law Project found via freedom of information requests that the storage of unusable PPE since April 2020 cost £1 million per day (comfortably in excess of £700 million – and counting) with more expense to be incurred contracting providers to recycle PPE, while that which is not recyclable would literally go up in smoke. We are talking about an effective transfer of around £10 billion from taxpayers to the wealthy for sub-par PPE alone. At the same time Rishi Sunak wrote off £4.3 billion of Covid fraud and the Tories voted to cut tax on bankers' profits from 8% to 3%, itself at a cost to the public purse of billions annually. Meanwhile, we were told that there was 'no money' to pay for care, despite the promise of a £350 million weekly Brexit bonus for the NHS, before a tax hike (for 'ordinary' people) constituting a 70-year high was duly enforced.

Privatisation is more concerned with efficiency than it is with concepts like resilience, which is entirely why stockpiles of PPE were considered 'waste' rather than resources, as was identified in a 2013 report by the Centre for Health and the Public Interest on whether the NHS was ready for the next pandemic[193]. Privatisation is more concerned with costs and competition, which is why (according to The Health Foundation) NHS money has been cut by £700 million in real terms over a five-year period, the natural consequence being tens of thousands fewer nurses, hospital beds, and so on. There is unlikely to be any organisation that can continue to operate effectively, let alone during a period of unprecedented demand.

At the one-year anniversary of the first national lockdown the Conservatives had presided over more deaths per capita than every other country on the planet except the Czech Republic with a similarly poor international showing in economic terms (more than double the national income drop of the likes of the US, Germany, and Japan). The papers may have fooled some into thinking 'they could not have seen this coming', but it is simply not true. As well as the CHPI report mentioned above, the government had run the exercise Cygnus to test the UK's response to a pandemic, which reported on many of the shortcomings we came to witness – which were simply not addressed. In mid-2019 two and a half million passengers arrived

---

193 CHPI, 'Getting behind the Curve? Is the new NHS ready for Pandemic Flu?', December 2013

into the UK every week, with the spread of virus extremely high here, not least due to the high levels of inequality compared to other OECD countries with spread more likely where people occupy overcrowded living spaces and so forth.

HOW THESE THREADS TIE TOGETHER

It is probably not a stretch to say that people do not enjoy paying tax. But most of us recognise its benefits or necessity. The evidence supports this: in *The Joy of Tax* Richard Murphy examines the correlation between tax rates and GDP per capita (oft used as a metric for assessing living standards), finding a strong relationship between higher tax rates and high GDP per capita. But taken into context, we are absolutely inundated with costs: from tax, to rent or mortgages, electricity, water, university, an endless list of compulsory costs. Thus, naturally, people would like to think they get value for money from their taxes and politicians preaching 'government as household' economics has proven to be a very powerful tool in their ability to maintain the status quo.

Given that the aforementioned costs are also a deliberate political ploy – for example, decisions are taken to *not* build more affordable homes and the privatisation of utilities has led to skyrocketing prices for something we now have no control over; moreover we are lied to constantly – including around how money is created; there are serious questions to be asked of our governing elites. Lest we forget, they are supposed to work for us! And despite our completely unequal position in society, not a great deal is done to change it. There can only be a small number of reasons for this: people do not understand the scale of their oppression? those in power are more deserving than we are, thus we are happy to be subordinated and continue working to liberate our masters? We are not happy about it but do not feel that there is any alternative way of life? We are unhappy about it but do not feel like we are able to change this state of affairs?

Beginning with the first rationale, there is certainly evidence that many 'ordinary' people do not understand the economy as well as would be optimal for a change in the status quo. As such, a considerable number of people therefore feel dependent upon 'the experts', whether government officials, think-tanks, or people rolled out for a soundbite on BBC News to guide financial thinking. This severely impedes our ability to open up economic decisions to wider participation and for people to buy into the alternatives, such as that money does not need to be created through debt. In March 2020 YouGov found that, on the eve of Rishi Sunak's budget, nearly a quarter of Brits did not know what the Chancellor of the Exchequer or the Treasury is[194]. Alarmingly, over a quarter did not know what austerity is, despite it ravaging swathes of the population for a full decade. This disparity in knowledge creates a huge power imbalance whereby those in powerful positions, with vested interests, are left to make decisions that often go without the level of scrutiny necessary. It is plausible that given a lack of specialised understanding of economic matters, austerity was an easy sell to the public based on the myths outlined in the next chapter. Likewise, the 'Vote Leave' campaign was able to tap into things that huge numbers of people do understand – that the current system is not working for them, and an influx of migrants could be a potential cause of a lack of jobs. Should people be more informed then things could be very different indeed. It is quite telling that UK graduates, i.e. those who have invested time, money and energy into their higher education, rank in the bottom percentile for both literacy and numeracy across the OECD countries. We know that schools are underfunded, but there needs to be serious conversations around changing what is taught to the next generation. Less algebraic formulas and more about how money is created, tax loopholes sustained, and a proper account of British history would be a start: and the fact that governments will not be willing to oversee such a change should reaffirm the main points being made here.

194 YouGov, 'Brits are confused by economic jargon', 11 March 2020. Sample size over 1.5k

THREE

POLITICS

There are numerous ways we can judge governments, but principally they are elected into office to represent and protect the public interest. It is therefore worth considering how Britain is faring as a nation under their watchful eye.

Beginning with the basics, life expectancy in the UK stalled in 2011 after a prolonged period of continuous growth, before plateauing in 2013. For women, life expectancy actually fell in 2012 and 2015[195], the first time this has happened since World War II. Furthermore, there are marked differences based upon income. For example, in the UK's 'richest' local authority area, the London Borough of Kensington and Chelsea, men can expect to live until 83. However, for their poorer neighbours (such as where the remains of Grenfell Tower stand), men can expect to live until just 69 years of age. At the other end of the spectrum, despite the government stating its intent to halve the stillbirth and infant mortality rates of 2010 (2.9 deaths per 1,000 births) this is largely unchanged (currently 2.8 deaths per 1,000 births), and actually increased between 2014–2017[196].

In terms of how our basic needs are being met during this stalled life course, the situation goes from bad to worse. The Joseph Rowntree Foundation found that over 1.5 million people (including 365,000 children) faced destitution at some point in 2018, defined as two or more of the following being true within a one month period: sleeping rough, having one or no meals for two

195 Office for National Statistics: 'Life Expectancies' statistical bulletins
196 Office for National Statistics: 'Child and infant mortality in England and Wales: 2018' statistical bulletin

or more days, being unable to heat or light your home for five or more days, going without weather-appropriate clothes or basic toiletries[197]. TUC statistics have child poverty in working households up by 800,000 over the course of 2010–2020 (the government's own statistics have the figure at 600,000), with considerably over half attributed directly to government policy[198]. This was before the Tories voted down the Labour motion (publicly backed by footballer Marcus Rashford) to provide food vouchers to disadvantaged children during school holidays, at a time when donors were smuggling £27,000 worth of takeaways into Downing Street for Boris Johnson. The Trussell Trust, with approx. two-thirds of the UK's food banks in its network, report a 73% increase in food bank use over the last five years, resulting in 1.6 million emergency food deliveries in the year up to April 2019[199].

The number of people officially recorded as homeless in the UK nearly tripled between 2010 (from 1,768) to 2017 (4,751), with hundreds of thousands of people suspected to be 'hidden homeless', for example sofa-surfing at friends' residencies[200]. For 'generation rent', despite the exorbitant prices they pay (effectively rendering saving for a house deposit unfeasible) one third of private rented homes contain safety hazards, such as unacceptable bathroom and/or kitchen facilities, inadequate heating, damp and mould, pests, improper electrical installations, dangerous chemicals, and so forth. Housing benefit no longer covers rent in many geographical areas, e.g. in November 2016 the maximum benefit offered for a room in shared accommodation in Manchester was £291/month; however, the Valuation Office Agency report that the lowest rent for a room in shared accommodation in Manchester is £325/month[201].

In terms of our general happiness: in 2005 there were approximately 29 million anti-depressant items prescribed in the UK. By 2015 this figure had more than doubled to 61 million[202]. The number of suicides in the UK was 6,507 in 2018, an increase of 10.9%, with a 23.7% increase in the rate of those

---

197 JRF (2018) 'Destitution in the UK', Fitzpatrick et al.
198 Examples include freezes to child benefit for five of these ten years that have equated to a real-term drop, and the two-child limit restriction in Universal Credit being introduced (itself resulting in a reduced income of more than £2k for already low-income households with approx. 1 million children). These compound pay freezes and other unfavourable trends for working parents during this period
199 Trusselltrust.org 'Record 1.6m food bank parcels given to people in past year', 25 April 2019
200 Danny Dorling (2018) *Peak Inequality: Britain's Ticking Time Bomb*, Policy Press
201 Dorling (*ibid*)
202 gov.uk website, 'Prescriptions dispensed in the community, England: 2005 to 2015', Health and Social Care Information Centre, 5 July 2016

aged under 25[203]. It is a similar story wherever one looks, be it how we perform in relation to health 'metrics' through to those pertaining to crime. It is genuinely difficult to find metrics that the UK is 'scoring' well in, whatever you consider to be an indication of a society that is cohesive and faring positively. According to the Prison Reform Trust 46% of our prisoners are re-convicted within a year of release; we have a higher divorce rate than all of the European Union countries (seventh highest in the world); it truly is an exhaustive list.

How much of this blame can we apportion to the government? After a 12-day visit in 2018 the United Nation's rapporteur on extreme poverty and human rights, Philip Alston, concluded that government policy is directly responsible – with his envoy's report stating that the government has inflicted 'great misery' on the population it was elected to serve, with 'punitive, mean-spirited, and often callous' austerity policies driven by political desire rather than economic necessity[204]. This last point is really significant – the suggestion that austerity was a deliberate choice and perhaps not wholly necessary. It seems strange that a government would pursue a strategy that results in so much misery for so many people. Similar ideas cropped up recently in the wake of the government's handling of the Covid pandemic, notably the delayed decisions to enter into lockdowns, how lax lockdown rules were, the Prime Minister himself declaring proudly that he had been shaking hands with Covid patients in March 2020 as we watched in horror at events unfolding in places like Italy. There are varying degrees of cynicism here. Major financial player PWC estimated that life expectancy changes in 2017 could cut a whopping £310 billion from British pension fund liabilities[205]; but if we are uncomfortable with the idea that our government will sacrifice lives for money then there are more concrete links to make.

The cuts to funding are undoubtedly central to the dismal picture painted above. For example, social services budgets were slashed by a third in real terms between 2010 and 2015. Before the pandemic ambulance response times hit record-high wait times, operations were routinely delayed, and a lack of hospital beds were available. As happens in any organisation, there comes a point where we can attribute cuts in funding to poorer service. Indeed, both

203 Samaritans, 'Samaritans Suicide Statistics' Report
204 'Statement on Visit to the United Kingdom, by Professor Philip Alston, United Nations Special Rapporteur on extreme poverty and human rights', London, 16 November 2018
205 As reported in the *Financial Times*, 4 May 2017: 'Life expectancy shift "could cut pension deficits by £310bn"'

the British Medical Association and the Royal College of Physicians have highlighted numerous times the very serious public health consequences of austerity and NHS under-funding. It is with our treasured health service that we begin.

NHS PLC

In many political debates it is contended that the government would never privatise the NHS as it would be tantamount to 'electoral suicide'. This view is understandable, but for the fact that NHS services have always been provided by a mixture of NHS and commercial suppliers (e.g. most GPs and dentists have never been employed by the NHS), and the proportion of care that has been provided by private, for-profit entities has been increasing for quite some time now. David Rowland, Director of the Centre for Health and the Public Interest, calculates from the Department of Health and Social Care's (DHSC) annual report and accounts that nearly one-fifth of NHS services have been privatised[206]. The dismantling of the NHS began with ancillary services such as cleaning, portering, catering, etc., followed by construction, maintenance and repairs, and finances, to core support services and beyond. Recent GP practice acquisitions by Operose Health, a subsidiary of US healthcare insurance giant Centene, now makes it the largest private supplier of GP services in the UK with 70 practices and over half a million patients. Even the *Daily Mail* has described Centene as 'profit-greedy'[207] as the firm faces legal action in the US for its poor service, typical of suppliers primarily focused on profit rather than quality of care. The number of people in the UK with private medical cover has oscillated but tends to be estimated at above 4 million. The reality is that this has been achieved via means less blatant than what people assume NHS privatisation might look like – and often not covered by the media in satisfactory detail. As former Tory MP and broadcaster Michael Portillo said on the BBC's *This Week* programme with Andrew Neil, the NHS is so important to the public that governments have to attempt to hide the changes they make to it in order to avoid election defeat.

206 'Flawed data? Why NHS spending on the independent sector may actually be much more than 7%' LSE blog, 1 October 2019
207 *Daily Mail*, 'A profit-greedy American health giant and why Connie, 89, and thousands like her in Britain, have suddenly lost their local GP', 12 May 2018

This viewpoint also ignores the huge precedent with which the elites prefer privatised healthcare provision, both from the viewpoint that healthcare (as a necessity) presents a huge business opportunity, and the fact that they typically do not need to use 'free' care themselves. The Tories and New Labour have wholeheartedly supported the market and thus an effective, popular public service goes against one of their most important doctrines. During its inception Aneurin Bevan, then-Labour Health Minister who ensured creation of the NHS, came up against much opposition – from both Churchill's Conservative Party, who voted down the bill 22 times before it was finally passed, and a range of other stakeholders, including the British Medical Association. Such was the opposition that Nye Bevan proclaimed, in the now-immortalised speech made on the eve of the first NHS hospital opening in Manchester[208]:

> *'That is why no amount of cajolery, and no attempts at ethical or social seduction, can eradicate from my heart a deep burning hatred for the Tory party... So far as I am concerned they are lower than vermin'* (4 July 1948, Bellevue Hotel Manchester)

Less than 40 years into its existence plans were afoot to increasingly privatise the service: notably the leaked cabinet office's Central Policy Review Staff's review of so-called 'longer-term options' in September 1982, showing that Thatcher and then-Chancellor Geoffrey Howe considered dismantling the NHS as a strategy[209].

Competition as opposed to co-operation became the order of the day when the Tories introduced the 'internal market' in 1990 and hospitals began bidding against each other to provide services[210]. It was Labour we have to thank for the NHS, but it was New labour who accelerated the trend towards increased competition and privatisation from 1997. Having been voted in on a number of promises, not least a commitment to avoid raising income tax and to keep public spending within the Tories' published spending plans for their first two years in office, New Labour's approach to reversing the financial starvation

---

208 One cannot help but see the irony that this same hospital – the iconic Trafford General Hospital – where the first NHS patient 13 year-old Sylvia Beckingham was treated for a liver condition, lost its A&E unit in 2013 under Tory 'reorganisation'

209 *Financial Times*, 'NHS privatisation leak damages Thatcher', 28 December 2012

210 When introducing competition, and promoting notions of 'fair' competition, you open yourselves up to lawsuits, as was the case in November 2017 when the NHS paid Richard Branson's Virgin Care £2 million

of the NHS inevitably led (alongside Blair and Brown's pro-business stance) to private providers accessing NHS services. John Major's Private Finance Initiative (PFI) was taken up with aplomb, ensuring that new hospitals were built without the need to raise taxes and effectively deferring public spending to a later time, but committing the public to long-term, expensive leases replete with other issues[211]. Whitehall's own spending watchdog, the National Audit Office, calculates the difference between what it would have cost to use public money to build new hospitals (£60 billion) as £139 billion *less* than what the eventual estimated cost is likely to be for the taxpayer – just for PFIs entered into at the time of their report's publication in 2018[212].

The Tory-Lib Dem coalition government pledged to increase NHS funding in each year they held office. However, in the first two years of their governance there was a dip in spending, before an 0.8% annual growth. Even with this growth, due to our ageing and growing population demand for services rose 4% per annum. Thus the service was effectively defunded by 3% annually and the trend set firmly in the wrong direction. The proportion of GDP spent on healthcare fell by nearly 1% in five years after 2010 to 7.3% – contrasted with 11% for Germany and France and continues on this trajectory. We spend 25% less as a percentage of GDP compared with the EU average and second lowest of the G7. Unsurprisingly, therefore, we witness a performance decline across practically every metric we could use for our health service[213]. As just one example, the rule that 95% of A&E patients should be seen within a maximum of four hours was almost met (94.9%) when Jeremy Hunt became Health Minister in 2012; however, it was 84% when he left in 2018[214]. In classic point-the-finger fashion, Hunt's response was to insinuate that too many people were trying to access the service and talks were underway to ban individuals from arriving at A&E without a referral. This being the same multi-millionaire, privately educated, fifth cousin to the Queen Jeremy Hunt, who in a failed Tory leadership bid described his pre-politician time as an entrepreneur as a 'daily grind to stay alive, to pay the bills'[215]. Bypassing how dangerous to people's health such a plan would be, this represented a continuation of trends

---

211 For an in-depth account of the NHS under New Labour, see *NHS PLC* by Allyson Pollock (2004) Verso

212 National Audit Office, 'PFI and PF2 Report', 18 January 2018

213 See england.nhs.uk website, 'Statistical work areas' offers all of the official statistics publications

214 See england.nhs.uk website, 'A&E Attendances and Emergency Admissions 2019–20'

215 YouTube video 'Jeremy Hunt releases official campaign video: 'I like to prove people wrong"

towards pushing people to the under-staffed and extensively privatised out of hours and 111 call service. The number of call handlers who are nurses has reduced significantly since the original NHSdirect phone service, which many top doctors – including the president of the College of Emergency Medicine Clifford Mann, health committee advisor to the House of Commons – cited as putting extra strain on resources with ambulances being called out for people who do not need them[216].

It is quite remarkable that things that are so important – cancer referral times, the number of hospital beds, postponed operations – every target missed and resources reduced yet we were told at the end of Hunt's reign as Health Secretary that funding had been unprecedented, and there was relatively underwhelming public outcry[217]. The strategy was clearly geared towards lowered expectations and soured attitudes towards the service, playing into the proclamations that the NHS needs reform, with the Tories portraying the service as under-performing, overly bureaucratic, and somewhat dysfunctional (arguments we still hear today). But the facts have never supported such claims; for example, a study in the RS of Medicine found that the NHS was second only to Ireland (out of 19 comparative countries) in terms of cost-effectiveness in reducing mortality[218]. One month prior to the white paper which set the wheels in motion for the Health and Social Care Act (HSCA) 2012, discussed below, which asserted the NHS was internationally poor across various performance metrics, the Commonwealth Fund scored the NHS as the best for both efficiency and effectiveness across Australia, Canada, Germany, the Netherlands, New Zealand, and the US[219]. If reducing public affection towards the NHS fails, creating a situation where people no longer want to work in the NHS could be a viable alternative to ensuring its reduced size. Even before the coronavirus pandemic, 60% of NHS staff responding to a UNISON survey reported morale to be low or very low, and in somewhat incomprehensible fashion, 88% had considered leaving the health service in the prior 12 months; with pay, work intensification and stress the key reasons[220].

216 *Financial Times*, 'Top doctor links A&E chaos to NHS advice line', 14 January 2015
217 According to OpenDemocracy Hunt oversaw years of historically low funding increases (around 1%, compared to an average of 6% in the years between 1997 and 2010, and compared to the 4.3% recommended by the Office of Budget Responsibility as the minimum to keep up with health inflation and increasing demand)
218 Pritcherd and Wallace, 2011
219 Davis K, Schoen C and Stremikis K (2010) 'Mirror, Mirror on the Wall: How the Performance of the U.S. Health Care System Compares Internationally.' The Commonwealth Fund
220 IPA, 'Working Well: Perspectives on Good Work and why it matters', bulletin 8 February 2018

The HSCA cemented what we are continually told will never happen, with all NHS contracts opened up to any 'qualified' private provider (underwriting in legislation, and therefore formalising the relationship between the health service and private providers). All parts of the NHS became Foundation Trusts and could earn up to half of their income from private patients; what one would interpret to be the first step in a system that will eventually increase to 100% and create a US-style insurance system. Perhaps most importantly, the formal commitment of the Secretary of State for Health to *provide* comprehensive universal healthcare was changed simply to *promote*, thus signalling a move away from the founding principle of the NHS that healthcare should be free at the point of service to all. The dismantling of the NHS in this fashion is close to completion with the Tories voting through the Health and Care Bill 2021–22. This enables private companies onto NHS boards for the first time in history via the introduction of 'integrated care system boards', with the likes of Operose already accredited to be involved, and ends the requirement for compulsory competitive tendering of NHS services. This effectively means that the dodgy PPE contracting processes during the Covid pandemic will become standard practice, as the NHS becomes little more than a logo attached to a system operated by private providers.

Most of us have little idea how much operations and treatment costs as our national insurance contributions and taxes often cover such things. Effectively, GPs and hospitals are paid for the care they provide based on an NHS tariff system, which sets the prices for each treatment. According to the independent fact-checking charity Full Fact, under the HSCA the government have set the NHS tariff at 'maximum', i.e. other providers can charge less. This naturally opens the floodgates for providers who a) may not have the experience and expertise of the NHS to provide care, and b) competition based on price almost certainly leads to reductions in the quality of care. Opposition to it within the medical profession was unanimous with 98% of the Royal College of General Practitioners calling for its withdrawal, as did the Royal College of Nursing and the Royal College of Midwives. Former Tory Health Secretary Stephen Durrell proclaimed it 'our biggest mistake in this parliament'[221], although that did not perturb him from voting for it.

No less than 225 politicians and 145 members of the House of Lords had financial connections with private healthcare providers. Unite published a

---

221 *The Observer*, 'Health reform is our biggest mistake in this parliament, says Tory ex-minister', 31 January 2015

list implicating 71 MPs of such links, with a few household names[222]. David Cameron gave a peerage to (nursing and care home tycoon) Dolar Popat in 2010, who had donated over £200k to the party at the time[223]. Then-Health Secretary Andrew Lansley, responsible for a number of contentious health reforms aside from driving the HSCA through parliament, received a personal donation of £21k from John Nash, former chairman of Care UK[224], the company that took over most of the NHS 111 contracts after Lansley privatised the helpline. Iain Duncan Smith bought 65,000 shares in Byotrol PLC in 2009, which sells products to the NHS. Jacob Rees-Mogg, Priti Patel, Jeremy Hunt, Philip Hammond, Sajid Javid, and George Osborne are among the past and present front-benchers to have vested interests in private healthcare companies, i.e. parties who stand to directly benefit from the privatisation of the NHS. They were not alone: prominent Lib Dems Nick Clegg and Vince Cable also shared these interests, ensuring that our unelected coalition were able to introduce changes that stood in direct contrast to the will of most of the population. But it was in the interest of the few: Unite went on to claim that 15 such companies won NHS contracts worth £1.5 billion over the following two years.

These interests diverging from those of the public was evidenced once again in July 2020 with 'New Clause 17', a hugely important (non) piece of legislation that you may have missed, given that most sections of the media chose not to cover it, and rather suspiciously the UK House of Commons Twitter account almost immediately deleted the tweet that offered details of it. This was effectively a proposal put forward by Caroline Lucas of the Green Party to ensure that the NHS would be exempt from any future post-Brexit trade agreement. It was to be added on to the Tories' trade bill, which provided the foundation for the UK's post-Brexit trade deals and did not have any such clause. Every single member of the Tory party voted against it, while all members of every other party who voted (bar Julian Lewis, who had just been stripped of his Tory whip), all voted 'yes'[225]. The Tories also rejected 'New clause

---

222 Unite, 'Unite investigates: government links to private healthcare', 2014. See also 'Compilation of Parliamentary Financial Links to Private Healthcare' on the Social Investigations blog for a comprehensive run-down of all the politicians who have private interests in the NHS rather than those of their constituents
223 *The Telegraph*, 'Two major Conservative donors appointed to government', 11 January 2013
224 Electoral Commission records show John Nash and wife gave <£300k in total, with the enthusiastic sponsor of education academies, i.e. privatised schools, appointed as an education minister by Michael Gove in 2013
225 https://votes.parliament.uk/Votes/Commons/Division/822

4', which stipulated that all trade deals should be debated in parliament before being signed. This effectively frees them up to sign trade deals in secret, without debate, and there is nothing that parliament can do about it. The party that has managed to convince swathes of people that Britain was 'taking back control' after Brexit, is effectively giving this control, and the jewel in Britain's crown, away.

At one time it would have been unfathomable that a prime minister, who could not express his gratitude enough to NHS staff after recovering from Covid, can then vote down a pay rise soon after and continue to preside over its demise. Who better placed to tell us what Tory MPs really think about the NHS (and 'poor people', while we are at it) than Boris's chief advisor Dominic Cummings? He has not been shy in offering his view that many do not care about either[226]. All of this collectively should worry us a great deal: profit before health is unacceptable. Access to quality healthcare should be a basic human right and there is absolutely sufficient funding for this. Yet, it is sacrificed by governments ideologically opposed to a universal, publicly funded health service. Billions of pounds have been, and are being, wasted on NHS privatisation and what do we have to show for it? Treatments once available on the NHS are now prey to private providers, there are tighter eligibility criteria for certain procedures (e.g. a hip replacement is only granted once a certain pain threshold is reached, cataract operations only granted once sight becomes extremely limited, and so forth), and the most serious of things like missed diagnoses and deteriorating health during prolonged waiting lists are the result.

OUR MASTERS

'It is not easy to make the best of both worlds when one of the worlds is preaching a Class War, and the other vigorously practising it' (George Bernard Shaw, Back to Methuselah)

Why does the government persist in maintaining such inequality? Why are they telling us the NHS is not for sale while outsourcing it piece by piece?

---

226 YouTube video, '"Tory MPs don't care about NHS or poor people", Dominic Cummings, Boris Johnson's special adviser'

Is it deliberate, or is the job beyond their levels of competence? Indeed, is it unavoidable? To answer these hugely important questions, firstly we need to identify where our rulers generally come from, i.e. are there any patterns in terms of education, geographical location, family background, prior occupation, and so on? The 'closed shop' that is our political arena was well surmised by Andy Beckett – himself Oxford University alumni:

> *Monday, 13 April 2015 was a typical day in modern British politics. An* **Oxford** *University graduate in philosophy, politics and economics (***PPE***), Ed Miliband, launched the Labour Party's general election manifesto. It was examined by the BBC's political editor,* **Oxford PPE** *graduate Nick Robinson, by the BBC's economics editor,* **Oxford PPE** *graduate Robert Peston, and by the director of the Institute for Fiscal Studies,* **Oxford PPE** *graduate Paul Johnson. It was criticised by the prime minister,* **Oxford PPE** *graduate David Cameron. It was defended by the Labour shadow chancellor,* **Oxford PPE** *graduate Ed Balls.*
>
> *Elsewhere in the country, with the election three weeks away, the Liberal Democrat chief secretary to the Treasury,* **Oxford PPE** *graduate Danny Alexander, was preparing to visit Kingston and Surbiton, a vulnerable London seat held by a fellow Lib Dem minister,* **Oxford PPE** *graduate Ed Davey. In Kent, one of Ukip's two MPs,* **Oxford PPE** *graduate Mark Reckless, was campaigning in his constituency, Rochester and Strood. Comments on the day's developments were being posted online by Michael Crick,* **Oxford PPE** *graduate and political correspondent of Channel 4 News.*
>
> *On the BBC Radio 4 website, the* Financial Times *statistics expert and* **Oxford PPE** *graduate Tim Harford presented his first election podcast. On BBC1,* **Oxford PPE** *graduate and* Newsnight *presenter Evan Davies conducted the first of a series of interviews with party leaders. In the print media, there was an election special in the* Economist *magazine, edited by* **Oxford PPE** *graduate Zanny Minton-Beddoes; a clutch of election articles in the political magazine* Prospect, *edited by* **Oxford PPE** *graduate Bronwen Maddox; an election column in* The Guardian *by* **Oxford PPE** *graduate Simon Jenkins; and more election coverage in* The Times *and* The Sun, *whose proprietor, Rupert Murdoch, studied* **PPE** *at* **Oxford**[227].

---

227 *The Guardian*, 'PPE: the Oxford degree that runs Britain', 23 February 2017

If we believe that the elites want the best for us then we have very short memories – the battle to win the right simply to vote should demonstrate this. The Peterloo Massacre in Manchester 1819, when a peaceful rally aimed at male suffrage saw yeomanry on horseback kill 18 people and injure 500[228]; the attempts just over a decade later of the Chartists; and of course the Suffragettes at the start of the twentieth century. At each turn, when public pressure was too great the elites were forced to make concessions – propertied men of a certain value in 1832 were granted the vote, all propertied men in 1884, latterly women of a certain age – before full suffrage was finally won with Representation of the People (Equal Franchise) Act in 1928. Since then, every attempt has been taken to ensure that we the people do not meddle in the affairs of the rich and powerful despite the ability to vote, i.e. ways have been found by the elites to insulate themselves from us and our interests, which stand in stark contrast to theirs[229]. This has involved concessions from time to time: for example, the working majority has been responsible for the demise of governments; notably Ted Heath's Conservatives in 1974 and to a large extent James Callaghan's Labour government 1976–79. Opposition to the poll tax led to rioting and signalled the end of Thatcher's reign. There have been a range of token gestures at reform, the National Minimum Wage being one example, and undoubtedly the NHS would have been privatised much more quickly had the public not had to be appeased to an extent.

It has of course been done by trail-blazing working-class types, but just being able to stand as an MP for one of the main political parties, even in a backwater constituency with little chance of winning, has become ever more difficult in recent times. In *Why We Get the Wrong Politicians* Isabel Hardman notes that someone needs to be in the financial position to campaign tirelessly without pay, using much of their own money, from transport, to accommodation, perhaps even relocation, glossy leaflets, and so forth. This begins even before you'll be considered for your backwater constituency, with political parties expecting to see evidence of your commitment to the cause, which usually requires hundreds of pounds attending party conferences and fund-raising dinners. According to a study conducted by Hardman, the average *personal* cost for a Tory who won in a marginal seat in the 2015 election was £121,467.

---

228 The yeomanry was composed of mill-owner and shopkeeper volunteers, alongside war veterans at the behest of the state

229 Paul Foot's (2005) *The Vote* comprehensively outlines how democracy in Britain has been undermined throughout history in this fashion

Safe to say that there is plenty of risk given that not winning a seat can result in an abrupt end to your unpaid, time-consuming career. Naturally, having contacts in the Westminster bubble helps, but putting such factors together demonstrates that potentially good candidates simply cannot see politics as a legitimate career for them. As is discussed elsewhere, there are many in working-class communities who respond to polls indicating that they do not think politicians 'are people like me', and with trade unions no longer the route into politics they used to be, no wonder that the Labour Party has seen an increased number of metropolitan types standing for them. Even the selection processes for choosing who will stand as an MP is usually overseen by a small number of party members, themselves often from a narrow sub-section (thus unrepresentative) of society. Those MPs that are working class are therefore likely to have embarked on a successful career doing something else first (such as in the legal profession) and their perspectives may have changed somewhat from their earlier roots.

ETON MESS

Most of us do not grow up being told that we will become Prime Minster or even perceive it to be a possible career option. It just isn't positioned as a job for *us*. This is partly because the system is gamed so that people from similar backgrounds with similar interests are in positions of power to ensure the status quo is maintained. Boris Johnson became the fifth Prime Minister since the Second World War to have attended Eton, the independent boarding school for privileged 13- to 18-year-old boys in Windsor, and the twentieth overall (all of whom have been in the Conservative Party). Fees to attend Eton are £42k per year, comfortably more than the average UK salary. No wonder Boris described the £260k per year he was paid by *The Telegraph* for his Sunday column (on top of his £140k-per-year Mayor of London job) as 'chickenfeed', with typically discernible lack of real-world awareness[230]. What exactly is so special about this 'college'? It is certainly not the exam results, despite the amount of money thrown at the education by parents. Eton was established by King Henry IV, originally with the admirable aim of providing a free education to under-privileged children, but this royal connection proved to be a source of attractiveness to gentry and nobility thereafter.

---

230 Snippet taken from the BBC HARDtalk interview on YouTube: 'Boris Johnson: "£250,000 is Chickenfeed"' video

According to old Etonian Palash Dave, 'Kids arrived there with this extraordinary sense that they knew they were going to run the country[231]' and this feeling was fuelled by mixing with aristocratic schoolboys night and day and receiving a political education not offered elsewhere. In the BBC programme *Posh and Posher* aired in 2011, Andrew Neil sat in to watch Eton's own version of the House of Commons, with students debating amidst visits from present and former political heavyweights and newspaper political editors who provide constructive advice. In effect, the ruling class groom their heirs to continue their domination over UK politics. This is apparent time and again, with a recent example being Boris's fellow Bullingdon Club chum Ewen Fergusson being appointed to the Committee on Standards in Public Life, whose job it is to advise Boris on ethical standards[232]. The 2011 entrance exam created controversy for a number of reasons, but certainly offers us an insight into the type of 'training' Eton children receive:

The year is 2040. There have been riots in the streets of London after Britain has run out of petrol because of an oil crisis in the Middle East. Protesters have attacked public buildings. Several policemen have died. Consequently, the Government has deployed the Army to curb the protests. After two days the protests have been stopped but twenty-five protesters have been killed by the Army. You are the Prime Minister. Write the script for a speech to be broadcast to the nation in which you explain why employing the Army against violent protesters was the only option available to you and one which was both necessary and moral[233].

Old Etonians are not always difficult to spot, as well illustrated by Jacob Rees-Mogg. It is difficult to imagine what proportion of the British population he actually represents in views or mannerisms, yet he has managed to remain an elected MP for over a decade. Is it that he epitomises what we think an MP should be or look like – posh? So posh that despite having six children he revealed in an LBC interview with Nigel Farage that he has never changed a nappy, a

---

231 BBC News, 'Why has Eton produced so many prime ministers?', 12 May 2010
232 This being the elitist club infamous for hiring prostitutes, wearing Nazi uniforms, and burning £50 notes in front of homeless people. Boris flaunted the rules of secrecy around their activities, see YouTube video: 'Boris Johnson, David Cameron & The Bullingdon Club'
233 *Indy*, 'Eton College exam question asking students to justify the Army killing protesters resurfaces', 3 September 2019

job that is reserved for the family's hired nanny. Is it his use of polysyllabic holophrastic verbalism? He does, after all, hold the record for the longest word ever used in parliament (that everyday one, 'floccinaucinihilipilification'). Or presumably it was a fairly natural progression for him given that his father was a member of the House of Lords.

This is indicative of a wider issue, whereby privately educated millionaires who represent <1% of the population, dominate positions that are meant to represent the majority. The issue of an over-representation of millionaires among MPs re-emerged in 2010 when the Tory-Lib Dem coalition cabinet, made up of 29 ministers, contained 23 millionaires. More recently *Business Insider* used the register of parliament's financial interest to calculate yearly earnings among MPs, based on their annual salary and additional non-parliamentary jobs[234]. Those doing particularly well included Torridge and West Devon MP Conservative Geoffrey Cox, whose provision of private legal services raked him in over £650k per year. Second was Stratford-upon-Avon MP Nadhim Zahawi, whose directorships, including for an Iraqi oil company, netted him £530k+, also a Conservative. In fact, the entire list was made up of Conservative MPs doing very well for themselves alongside what is supposedly the primary role of representing their constituents.

The dynamic is quite straight-forward: in exchange for party donations (then used for election campaigns and such) and/or the promise of lucrative positions in the private sector, MPs conduct the will of wealthy individuals. As MPs are largely from wealthy stock themselves, groomed in places like Eton, their interests are pretty much aligned anyway, but the money secures their services. Once elected, said governments ensure tax breaks and minimal pieces of unfavourable legislation for their wealthy bankrollers and associates, who then formalise the relationship with advisory or directorship positions in their companies – useful for insider information too. And this is how democracy is managed by the rich, for the rich, so the pesky non-millionaires do not get their grubby hands on too much wealth and are denied opportunities to join their ranks. An additional problem here is that with other MPs acting this way, there is a heightened incentive for other MPs to follow suit, even those not schooled at places like Eton. Apart from having one eye on a nice big contract at a private firm either during or once their days in parliament are over, ultimately the parties serve the big businesses and so those who are demonstrating their

---

234 *Business Insider*, 'The richest MPs in Britain based on income', 3 August 2017

willingness to be co-opted will be the ones receiving donations, creating a buzz for themselves by attending conferences, corporate dinners, and the like, and thus more likely to stand for their party in a constituency.

Again, questions arise regarding the legitimacy of meritocracy. I am sure that intelligence and hard work are required to complement the networking and exclusive doors that become opened to Etonians and the like, but it is clear that someone who does not attend such institutions has to work a damn sight harder than someone who does. And those types of advantages are exactly how the same types of people come to dominate politics, rather than people who understand what everyday life is like for ordinary Brits, and thus a foundational knowledge of how to represent them accordingly. The accounts of old Etonians[235] tell us that the college operates a culture that provides a degree of shielding from the rest of society. Maintenance of these networks into Oxbridge and beyond serve to ensure positions of authority and protection in them that others are not provided. It is hard to imagine that someone without Boris's background and connections could survive in their job after a series of such catastrophic and calamitous actions. Etonians are given as many chances as they like: was Jacob Rees-Mogg remotely worried about his position after alluding that the victims of the Grenfell tragedy lacked common sense when following fire service advice? It is highly unlikely.

It is not just their schooling that creates this image to future Tories that they are superior to everybody else; people in the elitist class genuinely believe this to be genetically true. Dominic Cummings' father-in-law, Sir Humphry Wakefield, revealed himself to be a eugenicist when rambling on at a group of working-class individuals in a 2012 documentary entitled *The Guest Wing*. He states that he would not wish for any of his children to become romantically involved with someone from a lower socio-economic group because they do not have 'winning genes'. Dominic himself has written extensively on the subject, claiming that 70% of a child's attainment is pre-determined by their genes[236], eschewing all scientific evidence. Hardly the views of individuals we could therefore expect to 'level up' education given that those from lower-income backgrounds are essentially viewed as genetic lost causes. Much more feasible is the level of opportunity one is exposed to: despite only 7% of the general population attending fee-paying schools, 41% of Conservative MPs,

---

235 Many of the Etonians in politics prefer to play this part of their lives down for fear of being viewed as 'out of touch' but there are other accounts, e.g. *The Importance of being Eton* by Nick Fraser (2008), that offer some
236 'Some Thoughts on Education and Political Priorities'

30% of Liberal Democrat MPs, 14% of Labour MPs, and 7% of SNP MPs did[237]. In recent governments these figures are 65% of Boris's cabinet, 50% of David Cameron's cabinet and 62% of the coalition cabinet.

Is it any surprise therefore that governments whose cabinet ministers largely attend fee-paying schools are mis-managing and underfunding state schools? A clear indictment of the state of our schools is revealed in the fact that Ofsted Chief Inspector Amanda Spielman, whose job is to instruct and help school heads effectively run schools, sends her two daughters to a private school[238]. Clearly a commitment to state education is not a prerequisite for the job. The Education Policy Institute estimate that it would take 50 years to reach an equitable education system, at the rate of current attempts to close the attainment gap for disadvantaged children by age 16, with the most disadvantaged children actually falling even further behind than before[239]. It is hardly surprising that this government oversaw an algorithm that inflated the grades of fee-paying students and downgraded those who do not during the Coronavirus pandemic. The following year, instead of celebrating record numbers of A and A* A-level grades, the Tories' response was to contemplate scrapping the traditional grading system as in their view too many working-class children were having their grades inflated by teachers. This reveals the true purpose of exams – to stratify students rather than objectively assess their abilities. Likewise, when around one-quarter of cabinet ministers (Boris included) are buy-to-let landlords, as are one-fifth of MPs in Parliament, can we really expect anything other than unfavourable policies for tenants? Exorbitant rent prices and a lack of protections for those who rent are just some of the problems. 24% of Tories are landlords, 15% of which (again Boris included) rent out more than one property. 8% of Labour MPs are landlords, 2 of 11 Lib Dem MPs, and 4 of 47 SNP MPs[240]. As one would expect, this is much more than the general population, where approximately 5% of people are landlords.

This chapter started with some stark statistics about poverty levels, recourse to food-bank use and the like. It may be a tad optimistic to expect poverty to be tackled in any meaningful way when it is just an abstract concept to the people in

---

237 House of Commons Library, 'Social background of MPs 1979–2019', briefing paper, 27 March 2020

238 For this and a comprehensive history of public schools in Britain, see *Posh Boys: How the English Public Schools Run Britain* by Robert Verkaik (2018), Oneworld Publications Ltd.

239 Education Policy Institute, 'Closing the Gap? Trends in Educational Attainment and Disadvantage' report

240 *Tribune*, 'Government by Landlord', 20 May 2020

office. At the risk of bestowing far too much faith in humanity, I cannot believe that politicians as human beings would make decisions that are so damaging (often life-threatening) to huge numbers of people if they truly knew the effect of those decisions, rather than being far removed from them. Yet they do their best to demonstrate that they do have nothing but contempt for the 'ordinary' people they purport to serve. When Labour MP Hugh Gaffney won a seat in Parliament at the 2017 election he wore his former postal uniform 'to say that the working man has arrived' and was met with scorn from Tory MPs over both his accent and appearance[241]. In a truly democratic society we would be pushing for more equal representation of all citizens: an according proportion of MPs of different ethnicities, working-class background, and so forth, rather than business folk who are likely to look after the interests of said big business.

This does not mean that people are being 'given the job' on the grounds of their demographic characteristics rather than merit. We have already established that the meritocracy argument is deeply flawed: people from any walk of life cannot become whatever they want to be by working hard, because the infrastructure is not there to facilitate it. Yet elites have an easy fall-back argument, that such a view is too pessimistic and doing a disservice to hard-working individuals from lower-income families. Regardless, if the yardstick for an MP relates to how effectively they can represent the interests of the people, it is hard to imagine that they would do a much worse job than we currently have for large sections of society. We have enough bankers and lawyers in politics; where are the people with a passion for social justice? A track record of fighting social causes that are important to the well-being and fabric of society? There are enough advisors to help with those more technical matters. For example, Boris Johnson appointed 44 special advisors in Downing Street (at a pretty cost to the taxpayer, with the man effectively running the operation, Dominic Cummings, paid a six-figure salary alone) making it a total of 108 advisors across the different government departments.

Politicians genuinely passionate about learning would encourage a drive for a proper political, economic, and real-world education for all people rather than under-funded schools teaching to uninspiring curriculums determined by Michael Gove. Even a cross-party House of Commons Education Select

241 BBC News, 'Scottish Labour MP Hugh Gaffney "heckled over weight and accent"', 15 January 2018

Committee[242] warned that high-stakes frequent testing was leading to teachers being forced to 'teach to the test', with the more creative aspects of the curriculum often first to go too, leading to a narrowing of the curriculum. This is a far cry from the experience of those heading towards the study of PPE at Oxbridge. A great deal of research tells us that the wealth and inclination of parents are key determinants of a child's educational progress, and even where schools are mixed working-class children are often 'sorted' into bottom sets, which creates a ceiling to which they are implicitly told their potential lies – with all of these factors contributing to fewer children from lower-income families attending university (close to 90% of MPs are university graduates, to put this into context)[243]. In sum, politics would become for the people, rather than an inconvenient management exercise for the rich and powerful.

Trade unions as the typical route for working-class people into politics became less influential under New Labour as they attempted to increase their perceived electability to former Lib Dem and Tory voters by standing more middle-class candidates. Such middle-class career politicians or those from related professions naturally favour more centrist policies (notably around welfare) or those that may attract swing voters, rather than policies that benefit the working classes[244]. In fact, the 'left' of the Labour Party has long experienced a fractious relationship with the centre and right of the party in a tussle for more socialist policies that would transform the lives of the working classes, as is well documented[245]. This should worry us all – Nye Bevan, architect of the NHS, was propelled to a top political position by virtue of his being General Secretary of the Transport Union. Despite its many limitations the Labour Party remains the most effective vehicle for working-class people to be represented in parliament as things stand. The Tories especially, Lib Dems also, will never be a party populated by working-class MPs, nor will they transform society for the betterment of working-class people because this goes against the interests of their donors and own life situations (as landlords, often with links to the financial services sector,

---

242 House of Commons Education Committee, 'Primary assessment: Eleventh Report of Session 2016–17' 1 May 2017

243 Diane Reay (2017) *Miseducation: Inequality, Education and the Working Classes*, Policy Press

244 Tom O'Grady, 'Careerists Versus Coal-Miners: Welfare Reforms and the Substantive Representation of Social Groups in the British Labour Party'. Comparative Political Studies 52 (4) 544–578

245 See *Searching for Socialism* by Leo Panitch and Colin Leys (2020, Verso) as one example, or Tony Cliff and Donny Gluckstein's (1996, Bookmarks) *The Labour Party: A Marxist History* for a more scathing assessment

etc.). We might see a working-class Tory candidate shoved into the limelight at some point as part of the pantomime that is contemporary British politics, but that is all it will be – a disingenuous act to retain working-class votes.

What the recent pandemic has re-illustrated is that public school boys are not receiving the education or life experience required to ensure that all members of a society are represented, protected, and given opportunity. I should know – I am one. Many public schools teach bluster, ignorance, and Latin. In a classic case of the powerful rewriting history in ways that fit their narrative, Winston Churchill has perhaps been the most mythologised person in British history. There is a case to be made that such unwavering self-entitlement to personal victory imparted into young Winston during his days at Harrow, a public school, helped Britain overcome seemingly insurmountable odds. Yet, reckless self-belief breeds reckless decision-making that came at a heavy cost to British troops certainly in the earlier stages of the war effort, and American intervention was critical to Churchill overturning our fortunes. It was working-class endeavour and sacrifice that upheld the war effort, state-educated men who developed innovations like the radar, and the working-class public that overwhelmingly rejected Churchill following victory – handing Labour a whopping 146-seat majority in 1945[246]. It was this Labour government under PM Clement Attlee, with the fewest number of privately educated cabinet ministers in history (circa 25%), that created the NHS and nationalised a fifth of the economy (including heavy industries, the railways, and the Bank of England). We have seen the same bluster and recklessness from current PM Boris Johnson during the pandemic whose hero is, of course, Churchill.

AUSTERITY: WHO CAN BE TRUSTED WITH THE ECONOMY?

Austerity is a perfect illustration of governments subordinating the interests of the majority to the 'few', and at untold cost. Austerity was a classist project. Within a decade of the Tories first coming to power in 2010 there were 20,600

---

246 Lest we forget, the immortalised Duke of Wellington defeated Napoleon at Waterloo with 'common' soldiers he referred to as 'scum of the earth' in notes dated 4 November 1813. In most armies it is the poorer classes that do the fighting, and the wealthy who enjoy ruling over the ensuing empires

fewer police officers[247] and 600 fewer police stations[248]; 728 fewer schools[249] and spending on pupils reduced by nearly 10% per child[250]; 773 libraries were shut[251]; a 70% real-terms cut in youth services, including 763 youth centres closed[252]; 9,668 firefighters axed by 2016[253]; 18,000 fewer hospital beds[254] and over 100 A&Es closed. The figures are shocking. They also tend to elicit a number of responses. One is the feeling that we still fare relatively well by way of international comparison, but this is simply not true. As one illustration, there are 34 countries with a better hospital bed to population ratio than us[255] and we have one of the lowest number of doctors per-person ratios across all OECD countries[256].

Another common response centres on the fact that we were told these cuts were necessary because the previous Labour governments had recklessly amassed debt and that the Tories have been getting the nation's finances back under control. However, as we will see in the section below, the government's own figures reveal that each New Labour government spent and borrowed *less* money than Conservative governments did, and repaid back more of the national debt. The truth? The aforementioned cuts were implemented in order to further lessen the tax burden of the wealthiest in our society. At the onset of the Covid pandemic, government savings from the welfare cuts (estimated at £35 billion per year) were vastly outweighed by how much money has been lost due to tax cuts introduced by the same government which equate to approximately £47 billion per year[257].

Austerity is a very harsh fiscal programme that centres on significant cuts to public spending, supposedly to create more opportunities for private-sector investment and freeing up such wealth by cutting the tax burden to stimulate

247 FullFact, 'Police officer numbers in England and Wales', 8 November 2019
248 *The Times*, '600 police stations shut in eight years', 2 September 2018 (via FOI requests)
249 Statista, 'Number of schools in the United Kingdom from 2010/11 to 2019/20', November 2020
250 Institute for Fiscal Studies, 'School funding per pupil falls faster in England than in Wales', 12 July 2018
251 *The Guardian*, 'Britain has closed almost 800 libraries since 2010, figures show', 6 December 2019
252 YMCA, 'Out of Service Report', January 2020
253 Fire Brigades Union, 'Fire and Rescue Service Matters – September 2016', 12 September 2016
254 The NHS website publishes annual data series on bed availability
255 OECD data website, 'Hospital beds' (see https://data.oecd.org/healtheqt/hospital-beds.htm)
256 *The British Medical Journal* (2017) 'UK has fewer doctors per person than most other OECD countries'
257 Frances Ryan (2020) *Crippled: Austerity and the Demonization of Disabled People*, Verso

investor confidence. It has a long history of failure, largely because cutting public spending at a time of economic weakness merely reduces consumer spending power, which leads to lower levels of economic growth. Where there is lower growth, the state receives less 'revenue' to pay its already high debts, and resultantly the deficit goes up. There is a knock-on effect, as then there is less confidence from borrowers that the state can pay its debts and thus the cost of borrowing goes up too, which means that a new round of cuts are required to keep up with repayments. The early signs were there for the UK too, with the Office for Budget Responsibility reporting that growth reduced by approximately 1.4% over the course of 2011–12 after austerity was implemented.

People are aware that they continue to pay increasing levels of tax despite public services being turned over to private providers and/or a reduction in both the availability and quality of such services. The government must therefore propagate a series of myths[258] in order to sell austerity to the people they are about to afflict with great misery, be they cuts to disability support, social care, healthcare facilities, and schools. The inevitable consequence of these cuts has been premature deaths – as many as 120,000 in what has been termed 'economic murder' by researchers based in Oxbridge and further afield[259]. The evidence shows that the working class were targeted and the elites were protected: over one million sanctions were applied to people claiming employment-related benefits, through to cuts to the NHS affecting those who cannot afford private healthcare and to community centres that affect low-income children the most. Alongside the many elderly who died prematurely, thousands of working-age people died in the days and weeks after their benefits had been withdrawn – take thirty-two-year-old pregnant Christelle Pardo, who, clutching her five-month-old son Kayjah, jumped from her third-floor balcony after her benefits were stopped[260].

One of the myths we were sold by the Tory-led coalition in 2010 was that austerity was our only choice, which is completely untrue. Take Iceland as a comparison, which abandoned austerity and allowed the losses of the crisis to fall more directly on the shoulders of bank shareholders and the financial elite.

---

258 For a powerful account of these myths see Cooper and Whyte (2017) *The Violence of Austerity*, Pluto Press
259 *BMJ* Open, 'Effects of health and social care spending constraints on mortality in England: a time trend analysis', 15 November 2017
260 Danny Dorling (2019) *Inequality and the 1%*, Verso

This makes sense to any government who is not effectively in the pockets of said individuals, given that they were the architects of the crisis and represent where much wealth is concentrated. As a consequence, Iceland was one of the first countries to surpass their pre-crisis economic output following the crash.

The second myth propagated by the Tories was that we were 'all in this together', a phrase uttered by then-Shadow Chancellor George Osborne at the Conservative Party conference 6 October 2009 and then repeated many times. The reality is that the burden of cuts was split roughly 80% on reduced benefits and services, and only 20% on higher taxes. In fact, the tax rate was lowered from 50% to 45% for those earning £150k per year or more. Average real wages have fallen while the richest 1,000 have doubled their wealth to over £½ trillion, at a time when living costs had been rising. To illustrate this point with reference to the utilities that were taken out of public ownership (to go with those examples in the previous chapter) the price of domestic energy between 2003–2013 went up 150%, water 70%, and in the latter stage of that period food prices up 28%. The Bank of England calculated that the money created to bail out the banks equated to the biggest transfer of wealth from government to the rich ever known: with the poorest 10% of Britons losing approx. £779 each out of the deal, while the richest 10% saw a £322k jump in the value of their assets[261].

The result of the above deceptions was to successfully shift a private-sector problem into a public-sector one, i.e. a problem of public debt. The debt owed to the taxpayer by the banks peaked at £1.162 trillion according to the National Audit Office in 2011, with much of the public shareholding in banks being sold off at a loss, and a significant proportion of the subsidy will never be repaid. And so it became our problem, and an assault on benefit claimants began in earnest. In short, austerity was never about balancing any books. Coalition partner Nick Clegg indicated that David Cameron and Chancellor George Osborne 'had very little sympathy or understanding of people on very low incomes and were inclined to write them off politically as "not our voters"'[262].

The third myth regarding austerity was that we all played a part in the crisis, particularly playing on a perception that Labour cannot be trusted with the economy. Each of these justifications were effectively mistruths to mask the reality of the situation, that those chiefly responsible for the financial crisis

---

261 *The Spectator*, 'QE – the ultimate subsidy for the rich', 23 August 2012
262 *Tribune*, 'How Tory cuts created the child hunger crisis', 11 March 2021

were able to accumulate more wealth while those not responsible bore the brunt, to great devastation. There are really important lessons for us to learn from this as the word 'austerity' begins to reappear as politicians look towards recovery from the Covid pandemic in 2022 and beyond.

THE TORIES AS THE PARTY OF FISCAL RESPONSIBILITY

We were told by David Cameron that the chief causes of the global financial crisis were reckless spending from previous Labour governments and debt-fuelled personal consumption that was untenable. This was of course aided by an incredibly poor attempt at humour when treasurer Liam Byrne left the infamous 'I'm afraid there is no money' note for incumbent David Cameron[263]. One cannot help but feel that giving Tony Blair and Gordon Brown credit for a *global* financial crisis is a bit of a stretch, but what does the evidence suggest?

The Conservatives have actually borrowed more money in total (naturally, as they have been in power for more time) but also on average, per year in office, than Labour – even pre the Coronavirus pandemic. The average yearly borrow for the former is £23 billion, and for the latter £17.5 billion[264]. Political economist and author Richard Murphy recalculated these amounts into 2021 monetary values for consistency (as naturally prices change over time), and the figures remain wide apart, respectively £45.9 billion and £33.9 billion[265]. Public sector net debt was down under Labour, who have repaid more than the Tories have (at c36% of GDP in 2007–08, compared to 40.4% when they took office in 1997–98) until a huge jump at the onset of the crisis in 2008–09[266]. This was despite a huge increase in government spending (£338,578,000 in 1999–00 to £588,934,000 in 2007–08)[267]. The chief beneficiaries of this increase in spending were the likes of our NHS, with spending on healthcare practically doubling in real terms between 1999 and 2007[268].

One thing that is truly baffling is this notion that the Conservatives are the party of fiscal responsibility. From the billions wasted on bad privatisation deals, to the billions wasted on inadequate PPE and a failed track-and-trace

---

263 See Liam's apology and explanation in *The Guardian* Opinion column, '"I'm afraid there is no money." The letter I will regret for ever, Liam Byrne', 9 May 2015

264 Calculated from data in the House of Commons library, 'Government borrowing, debt and debt interest: statistics'

265 Tax Research UK, 'The Tories have always borrowed more than Labour, and always repaid less: they are the party of big deficit spending', 24 June 2021

266 Office for Budget Responsibility, 'Public finances databank'

267 Office for National Statistics archive, 'Public Sector Finances'

268 Institute for Fiscal Studies, 'UK health spending', 3 May 2017

system, such escapades as Chris Grayling's £56 million ferry debacle[269]; a truly endless list. Apart from spending less than Tory governments when in power, at least the public generally has something to show for the spending: under New Labour investment in public services hit record levels and Britain had the largest growth in social mobility of any developed nation. This is not to say that Labour have a perfect fiscal record, but the evidence does not put them in the same league as the wasted money that the Tories have presided over.

My wish is not to dissolve Labour of all responsibility for the economic crash; it is certainly true that their commitment to making London a global financial power enabled the kind of trading activity that contributed to the crisis (e.g. subprime mortgage lending, hedge funding, toxic asset trading, and so forth[270]). It is also difficult to reconcile Treasurer Alistair Darling's decision to thrash out a £550 billion bank bail-out 'over a Balti takeaway' with senior members of the banks, and little by way of democratic say for the millions affected, or even debate in parliament by those elected by said millions. But the coalition, in wanting to be elected and needing justification for harsh austerity measures, proclaimed that Labour governments had overspent for a (factually incorrect, but) easy win. With the odd scapegoat in the banking sector, such as Fred Godwin of RBS and Bob Diamond of Barclays, and this positioned as rogue practice, corporate capitalism was able to avoid meaningful scrutiny, as did the dominant political and financial class that was chiefly responsible for the crash. In effect, we have not learnt the lessons from this crisis nor sought to change a system that is doomed to fail repeatedly.

THE HOUSING CRISES (PLURAL)

If we want to think about how much long-term progress our governments have made, we could begin with one of our most basic needs – a roof overhead. To

---

269 Grayling awarded £13.8 million to Seaborne Freight to operate ferries between Ramsgate (Kent) and Ostend (Belgium) in the event of a no-deal Brexit. This, despite the company having no ferries, no history of ever operating a ferry service, and, with assets of only £35,000, no means to acquire any vessels. But that wasn't all – Grayling then paid out nearly £20 million more of taxpayers' money to Eurotunnel to stop it pursuing a legal battle with the government over a 'secretive and flawed procurement process'

270 Evidence of how poorly regulated the banks were throughout this period can be seen in the fact that, after bankrupting themselves and the nation, the City's 'bonus pot' in 2010 was still estimated at around £7 billion

build more housing is often a pledge of parties vying for election, including that of Boris Johnson's Conservative Party in power at the time of writing. Thatcher's 'Right to Buy' council houses scheme in 1980 was intended to increase home ownership: offering incredibly favourable terms for residents to do so. This was perfectly crafted to the ideological shift Thatcher's government was attempting to generate among the working classes, as aspirational 'we're all middle-class aren't we?' individuals who would want to move on from paternalism, welfarism, and trade unionism associated with the Labour Party. Problems with this included the fact that it was feigned egalitarianism, with a hugely disproportionate number of the sales recorded being semi-detached houses (rather than terraced or high-rise flats) with gardens and garages, often in suburbia, to middle-aged 'better-off' individuals[271], i.e. relatively assured Conservative voting groups.

If we fast forward to the present day, we have already pointed out that home-ownership rates are rapidly falling, with exorbitant house prices, private-sector tenancy rates, unprecedented levels of homelessness, and so on. The selling-off of public assets at grossly under-valued sums is not intrinsically problematic when it is the public that benefits (albeit just some of the public), yet it has proved to hugely distort house prices ever since. For example, the first 'Right to Buy' sale, 39 Amersham Road in Romford (famed for pictures of Thatcher drinking tea there after handing over the keys), was bought in 1980 for £8,315; sold in 1996 for £57,000; sold again in 2001 for £101,000; again in 2004 for £131,000; and just three years later for £183,000: a whopping 22 times its original sale price in just 27 years[272]. House prices relative to average household disposable income and indeed modest income gains have risen highest since the 1970s in the UK among all OECD countries, effectively making it almost impossible for low- and middle-income households to improve their living standards[273].

The result has been thus: those unable to take advantage of Thatcher's scheme have found themselves somewhat perpetually worse off when accounting for the capital gains increases property buyers have reaped in the time since, plus the leverage that owning property gives one in a society such as ours. These

---

271 Social and Community Planning Research, on behalf of the Department of the Environment (1988) 'The Right to Buy: National Survey of Tenants and Buyers of Council Homes'

272 *The Telegraph*, 'What happened to Margaret Thatcher's first Right to Buy council house?', 14 April 2015

273 *The Sunday Times* reported on 30 January 2021 that in the past year nearly 40,000 new millionaires had been created by virtue of their properties increasing above the £1 million threshold

beneficiaries are more likely to be in a position to buy housing in high-cost areas, which are usually indicative of good schools, economic opportunities, and amenities further safeguarding the privileged classes. Karagiannaki (2011) estimates that most of the growth in inheritance value (approx. £56 billion in 2005, from £22 billion in 1984) has been driven by the increased value of property further dividing those who 'have' and those who 'have not'.

We have seen a mirroring of the same issues with David Cameron's £7 billion 'Help to Buy' scheme, touted as a helping hand to first-time buyers, which has been shown to have benefitted the wealthy too. Over 5.5k homeowners earning above £100k per year made use of these taxpayer-funded loans between 2013–18 (amounting to more than £280 million), of which nearly 1.3k already owned at least one other property. This effectively pushed house prices up even further than the astronomical growth demonstrated by the original Romford abode[274]. That is not all: the scheme was tantamount to pumping public money into the hands of the very same private construction corporations that had been starving Britain of affordable housing in the first place. As two examples, after just one year of the 'Help to Buy' scheme, Persimmon's Jeff Fairburn saw his bonus increase from £540k to over £832k; and Taylor Wimpey's Peter Redfern's to over £1 million[275].

It is entirely plausible that supply has deliberately not kept up with demand to ensure that those early property owners have been able to secure such gains and rentier opportunities. Particularly as demand was supported by policy such as the deregulation of mortgage finance, reductions in relative property taxes, and so forth. Nye Bevan was not only chiefly responsible for the creation of the NHS; housing was considered key to health during his time in office and in his position as Minister for Health and Housing 800,000 council homes were built. Not bad after the bankruptcy of the most destructive war the modern world has ever known, putting into perspective recent failings on the affordable housing front for one of the world's largest economies which increasingly looks like a political choice.

There has been a growing propensity in our society since the 1970s to see people's misfortune as being brought about by their own poor choices or wrongdoing, and the homeless do not escape this view. Naturally one can apportion responsibility for things like alcohol or substance abuse to the individual in question, although there are serious discussions needed around the

274 Shelter, 'No Help to Buy', 2 September 2019
275 *Independent*, 'Thanks to Help to buy, builders are the new bankers', 20 May 2014

criminal – rather than health – interventionist consequences of drug use in this country. But what about the increasingly unequal distribution of housing? The exorbitant prices? Years of reduced government spending on affordable housing? Likewise on hostels and support services for those at risk of sleeping rough.

Government policy on housing (aside from lack of spending) has been abysmal at best. As was suggested when examining the types of people who enter parliament, given that they represent a narrow section of society even issues that are glaringly obvious as real, immediate needs, can be delayed or even ignored. The Grenfell Tower tragedy is a sombre reminder that when you have decision-makers economically and socially far removed from other people, the pressing concerns of such people may not be addressed until it is too late. Refurbishment at Grenfell Tower between 2014–16 saw the non-combustible cladding originally selected passed up in favour of the cheaper, flammable substitute as part of wider cost-cutting measures on the local authority during the Tory-Lib Dem coalition's austerity programme. The infrastructure was meant to contain fires within separate flats, prompting calls for residents to 'stay put', but due to this familiar story of profit before people, those who did as they were told were left in an inferno burning four times more quickly than was expected. This negligence – by the construction firms in question, central government by way of their refusal to properly regulate the industry, and the local authority who inspected and approved the remediation works – led to the loss of 72 lives, and unquantifiable pain for their families and the survivors.

Residents in the Grenfell Action Group chillingly predicted in November 2016 that only a fire would allow their plight to be heard, after continued alarm-raising about fire safety (not least relating to the standard of work of the main private contractor Rydon Maintenance Ltd) to the landlord, Kensington and Chelsea Tenant Management Organisation, which has since passed social housing management back to the council. Despite the usual PR stunts from the government, it has taken three and a half years for a serious inquiry into the 72 deaths to commence; at which point not all survivors had even been permanently rehoused, and an embarrassingly laboured approach to the hundreds of thousands of flats up and down the country saddled with the same combustible cladding.

There is quite a lot to unpack here: but to illustrate how incompetent and perceptibly unmoved the government has been, anywhere between 1–3 million people remain in unsafe buildings like Grenfell four years after the tragedy.

Innocent leaseholders who do not own the buildings that require remediation, nor were responsible for the sub-standard construction works, have been footing bills for 24-hour fire marshal patrols, and unscrupulous insurance companies hiking premiums (on exactly the same buildings) as much as 1,400% in some cases. As the properties were rendered worthless until works were undertaken, these people were trapped in unsafe homes, during a national lockdown with the heightened potential for fire risk. To make matters worse, as the costs of these remediation works began to filter in, each individual leaseholder was facing bills of anywhere between £30–140k, sometimes almost the same value of the property itself. Bankruptcies and even suicides were only enough to encourage the government – kicking and screaming – to offer financial support for just the removal of unsafe cladding on buildings over 18 metres in height: this particular measure because, according to top civil servants, ministers did not have time to 'come up with a better number'[276]. The government very carefully selected their words in offering up money for 'cladding', given that the extent of the fire safety issues were innumerable – timber balconies and missing or sub-standard firebreaks (that councils themselves had signed off on as safe) meant that the dent to leaseholder bills by government funding was relatively trivial if anything at all.

This whole fiasco constitutes what Hodkinson, borrowing from Friedrich Engels, terms 'social murder', when people die prematurely due to unregulated private greed and the ruling class ignoring their cries for help[277]. To put matters into perspective, of the wildly insufficient £5 billion funding offered up to 'resolve' the fire safety crisis, only £3 billion was being fronted by the government. At the same time this scandal was unravelling, £3.1 billion was dished out to those buying homes worth £500k or more via the stamp duty holiday[278]. The former figure is also misleading: the estimated cost of the fire safety crisis is in excess of £15 billion. With the government forcing innocent leaseholders to pay VAT on remediation works, this equates to £2.5 billion. With £2 billion being levied on the profits of the leading property developers over a ten-year period (an idea actually proposed by the developers themselves, according to Rishi Sunak), the actual taxpayer contribution is

---

276 *Daily Mail*, 'Backlash over "18-metre rule" to qualify for cladding cash as civil servant admits officials 'didn't have time to pick a better number', 17 February 2021

277 This text, *Safe As Houses: Private Greed, Political Negligence and Housing Policy after Grenfell* is a valuable resource

278 *Financial Times*, 'Homebuyers in England gain £6bn tax break from Covid stamp duty holiday', 23 November 2021

closer to £500 million. As such leaseholders, themselves taxpayers and stamp-duty payers, were picking up circa 85% of the tab despite being the only party with no culpability. It again testifies to the problems of neoliberalism: privatise something as important as housing to companies interested solely in profit, de-regulate to help such corporations on their merry way, and leave innocent taxpayers and members outside the elitist class to pick up the cheque when things go (in this case, very very) badly wrong. In 2016 Conservative MPs voted against tackling unsafe housing conditions, saying '[new clause 52] will result in unnecessary regulation and cost to landlords'[279].

The solution was clear to everyone – the property developers responsible for cutting corners should foot the bill: not innocent leaseholders nor the taxpayer. When a fire spread across ACM cladding (that used on Grenfell) in Melbourne Australia in 2014, the entire state of Victoria immediately underwent evaluation of fire safety issues and all unsafe accommodation were remediated – with those responsible held accountable. Why has it taken so long for the government to act, and why have they both ignored opposition within their own party and rejected House of Lords amendments an unprecedented four times that stipulated leaseholders should not have to pay? The reasoning is a very familiar one: *The Telegraph* reported that property developers who built flats using dangerous, flammable cladding donated at least £2.5 million to the Tories since the fire in 2017, including brothers David and Simon Reuben[280], worth an estimated £16 billion, and money was donated to Boris Johnson personally[281]. *Private Eye* has the figure of donations much higher, with suggestions that as much as 37% of Tory donations after the 2019 general election came from those guilty looking to shirk their responsibilities. These are the same developers who were simultaneously making billions from the government's Help to Buy scheme; for example, Barratt pocketed £1.2 billion, and Permission similarly £1.2 billion with help from the government's stamp-duty holiday. No criminal charges for putting millions of lives in danger, a tiny token gesture financially with a small levy on developers' profits over ten years, and truckloads more of

279 UK Parliament website, 'Housing and Planning Bill, Volume 604: debated on Tuesday 12 January 2016', column 785
280 David's son Jamie, now co-owner of Newcastle United FC, makes up part of a secretive advisory board that has donated over £22 million to the Tories in exchange for direct access to lobby ministers, public contracts, and peerages. Created by the Tories, it is not subject to the usual government monitoring and accountability laws, enabling the rich to continue ruling for the rich
281 *The Telegraph*, 'Builders who use Grenfell cladding give Tories £2.5m', 13 February 2021

taxpayer money. In Stalin-esque fashion, the Conservatives attempted to ban flat owners applying for government funding from speaking to the press about their nightmare experiences without government approval[282].

There are now more than 300 community land trusts (CLT) in England where people are taking the initiative to resolve the housing mess themselves. A CLT is typically non-profit, community-focused, and democratic – ensuring that local people are part of the key decisions being made. Once land is bought or gifted, the CLT builds affordable homes that people in the community can rent or buy, with the CLT retaining long-term 'steward' of the land and properties. It is not uncommon for such communities to work towards a sustainable and localised way of life; for example, if enough members wish to progress towards self-sufficiency of food, land can be allocated for allotments or farming co-operatives. Another example is greater renewable energy initiatives and usage, right through to a range of community enterprises (one can take over the local pub if that's their wish)[283]. For as long as shelter is driven first and foremost by profit rather than basic human need, we are unlikely to see the wholesale change required in this state of affairs.

WHAT BREXIT SIGNIFIES ABOUT BRITISH POLITICS

Brexit confirmed one of the worst-kept secrets in politics; namely that the Labour Party has continued to neglect the working classes. A common perception during the 1990s through to circa 2015 was that the Tories, Lib Dems, and Labour are 'three cheeks of the same arse', i.e. there was not a great deal of difference between them. Statistics show us that 38% fewer people in the lowest socio-economic grades (C2 and DE) voted Labour by 2019 as compared to 1997, compared to 6% fewer in grades AB and C1, with many of the former opting not to vote at all[284]. Panitch and Leys (*ibid*) offer a meticulous account of how those on 'the left' have long been subordinated in the Labour Party, and that policy differences between Blair's 1997 government and

---

282 BBC News, 'Cladding building owners told not to talk to press', 10 January 2021
283 The National Community Land Trust Network website provides a number of 'success stories'
284 See IPSOS MORI 'How Britain Voted', 1997, 2001, 2005, 2010, 2015, 2017, and 2019; and Oliver Heath (2018) 'Policy Alienation, Social Alienation and Working-Class Abstention in Britain, 1964–2010', *British Journal of Political Science*, Vol. 48, Issue 4

those of the Tories had grown increasingly narrow. New Labour made token gestures to spread some of the wealth to their heartlands in the Midlands and Northern areas, with some public-sector jobs relocated, but largely relied on tax credits to top up menial (often service) roles, while simultaneously facilitating the stigmatisation of those on benefits. The result was prolonged political 'mismanagement' that did not do enough to bring pride or self-sufficiency back into areas such as the former industrial communities. This idea that such people could 'take back control' after decades of feeling ignored clearly resonated, and with good reason. The Brexit result was not as big a surprise to those of us outside of the metropolitan bubble in London who run politics and the media in this country as it was to them – Brexit was a chance to be heard by groups neglected by all mainstream parties, including Labour, whom some had continued to vote for. 58 of the 60 seats Labour lost in the 2019 election were in leave-voting areas, Stroud and Kensington being the outliers.

Lord Mandelson's assertion that such people had nowhere else to go proved dated as these people were not willing to be ignored another time; indeed, the signs were there at previous elections where Scotland began opting for the SNP. Failure to adhere to the referendum result, warts and all, would be the nail in the coffin for these 'left-behind' individuals, located what can often seem a million miles from Westminster and where decision-making power lies, some of whom are represented by MPs either from, or living, in the South, increasingly from middle-class and professional political backgrounds. London is where the finance is and foreign investment was attracted to; as we had the huge drive towards 'Global Britain', that is where much of the resources go. The Institute for Public Policy Research shows that current and planned spending on infrastructure and overall spending has fallen by over £6 billion in real terms, yet spending in the South increased by over £3 billion[285], illustrating clearly where the spending shortfall has been.

We gain a better understanding of who these people are by considering the demographic patterns among 'leave' voters, who were notably older, low income and with fewer qualifications[286]. It is telling that 'leavers' were less

---

285 IPPR, 'Amid the Brexit Chaos: A Plan for the Northern Powerhouse'
286 Social Mobility Commission (2016) 'State of the nation 2016: social mobility in Great Britain'

satisfied with life pre-referendum[287] and occupied many areas particularly hard-hit by austerity cuts. Both the government and opposition parties were simply not paying attention to this large, disenfranchised demographic, as the signs of discontent were clearly there. For example, people on lower incomes are less likely to trust politicians to tell the truth; more likely to report that 'public officials don't much care about what people like me think', and similarly 'people like me don't have any say in what the government does'[288]. Clearly, anyone refusing to vote for Labour because they do not represent the working class cannot logically then vote for Eton and Bullingdon Club alumni Boris Johnson and company. Yet the Tories have been very effective at mopping up votes from people whose interests they do not serve in a number of ways, not least positioning themselves as the patriotic party.

This is partly because they do hold the bizarre beliefs about gene superiority we have already touched upon, where perhaps they do genuinely think that 'empire' brought civility and democracy to parts of the world that they are convinced needed it. Some are linked directly to 'empire' and have land appropriation, enslavement, and other such endeavours abroad to thank for their positions of privilege today, with David Cameron one former PM of slave-owning lineage[289]. But this is really as far as it goes. In the same way that the Tories have successfully painted themselves out to be the party of fiscal responsibility, it has been a similarly impressive feat that they are the party for those who want Britain to be 'great'. A patriotic government would surely be one that properly funds its institutions, renationalises key industries as a real 'taking back control', does not inflict austerity and thus misery on much of the population, continually impinges on the rights of its citizens to a decent life (stripping employment protections, the right to protest, etc.), and basically everything else that would protect and improve the lives of British people. Would a patriotic PM lie to the queen in order to unlawfully prorogue parliament, and host multiple parties on the eve of her husband Prince Philip's funeral? Given that they have chosen not to provide affordable housing to

---

287 Powdthavee and colleagues (2019) 'Who Got the Brexit Blues? The Effect of Brexit on Subjective Wellbeing in the UK'. Economica 86 (343) 471–494

288 Joseph Rowntree Foundation (2016) 'Leave voters felt ignored and left behind as post-Brexit poll reveals extent of economic division across UK', 15 July 2016

289 *The Guardian*, 'How do we know David Cameron has slave owners in family background?', 29 September 2015. South Dorset MP Richard Drax is another, owning a 621-acre sugar plantation estate in Barbados that was operated by slave labour for nearly 200 years, the profits of which helped procure 15,000 acres of land in Dorset

everyone, nor sufficient care for the sick or disabled, how exactly are they the party for the British? An objective assessment of their time in office would suggest that they are the party for themselves, taking as much as possible from the public while giving as little as possible in return.

Conveniently for the Tories, this patriotism serves as a useful ploy to acquire votes in areas that have been decimated by their own party's actions. Thatcher was the architect of deindustrialisation and the decline in trade union influence; more recently Cameron and company were responsible for the harsh austerity that ravaged many of the same areas; and current PM Boris Johnson might talk a good game about 'levelling up' these hard-hit, traditionally Labour-voting constituencies, but is facing High Court legal proceedings over billions of pounds of Levelling Up Funding being diverted to wealthier Tory areas[290]. The Health Foundation found that mortality rates for those living in deprived areas were 3.7 times higher[291], so too unemployment, with many opportunities incompatible with home-working. People are also more likely to be employed on bogus self-employed contracts and fear unemployment if they take time off work, and pre-existing health inequalities have been hugely accelerated by austerity measures over the previous decade. Government support for those in the former industrial towns has been described as 'reluctant' at best[292]. Those among the most deprived areas that also had above average Covid infection rates stripped of money included Sunderland, Blackpool, and Sheffield, with big winners including the top 10 richest areas (which happen to be Tory-controlled), such as Buckinghamshire, Windsor, and Surrey.

This is part of a longer trend, with analysis undertaken by *The Guardian* and Sigoma showing that poorer, Labour-held areas lost more spending power (local councils saw their budgets reduced by 34% on average) under austerity than Tory areas (24% on average) over the period 2010–19[293]. 28 of the 50 councils worst hit by austerity belonging Labour, compared to just six run by the Tories, figures that became 38 in comparison to five by the end of the

290 *Independent*, 'Boris Johnson facing corruption legal battle over £4.8bn "levelling-up fund" that sent cash to Tory areas', 24 August 2021

291 The Health Foundation, 'What geographic inequalities in COVID-19 mortality rates and health can tell us about levelling up', 17 July 2021

292 Centre for Regional Economic and Social Research, 'The Impact of the Coronavirus Crisis on Older Industrial Britain', January 2021

293 *The Guardian*, 'Labour councils in England hit harder by austerity than Tory areas', 21 June 2020

decade. Surrey County Council hit the headlines in 2017 over such supposed 'sweetheart deals', but this is endemic, as illustrated by the 'Towns Fund' – a scheme to provide additional support to areas with high levels of income deprivation. Of the 101 towns drawn up by housing ministers in September 2019 (in the run-up to the general election) and thus subsequently successful, journalists and the National Audit Office found Tory marginals were the most likely[294].

This scheme, literally designed for direct 'levelling up' subsequently awarded a share of the near £5 billion spoils to 45 towns, 40 of which are held by the Tories: including the money man himself Rishi Sunak's Richmond local authority being placed in the highest priority category. According to the government's own Indices of Deprivation Richmond ranks 251st (out of 317), compared to, say, Salford, which sits at 19th[295]. Is it possible that a government would consistently, willingly, make life worse in already deprived areas to better increase their chances of swinging the vote at the next election? While simultaneously rewarding areas that voted in their favour, as opposed to genuine need and principles of fairness? These more deprived areas are already losing over £1 billion a year from EU Structural Funds following Brexit, with the Tories stopgap Community Renewal Fund only amounting to £220 million. Most of this fund has not actually been allocated halfway through the year (at time of writing), and yet again cabinet minister constituencies have been categorised as 'priority' areas[296].

We entered 2022 with the Bank of England warning the public to brace themselves for the biggest drop in living standards since records began[297]. But this is far from unavoidable: on the same day it was announced that energy bills would soar 54% in April, serial climate-polluters Shell announced a 14-fold increase in annual profits to $20 billion and promised shareholders $8.5 billion. Despite Shell (and BP) paying zero corporation tax on oil and gas production in the North Sea the Tories refused to vote in favour of a windfall tax on the big fossil fuel

---

294 LSE British Politics and Policy, 'The pork barrel politics of the Towns Fund: funding decisions were driven by party-political considerations, not by need', 2 October 2020
295 Ministry of Housing, Communities and Local Government, 'The English Indices of Deprivation' statistical release, 26 September 2019
296 *Independent*, '"Red Wall" and other poorer areas lose £1bn of development cash after Brexit, despite "level up" pledge', 15 August 2021
297 Despite all costs (housing, transport, food, etc.) going up but wages effectively going down, the bank's governor Andrew Bailey stated people should not ask for a pay rise. This is very typical of an establishment that often calls for people's acquiescence to hardship while, in Bailey's case, he takes home £575k per year

companies, partly because the energy industry donated £1.5 million to Boris Johnson's government. Meanwhile, the French government capped rocketing energy bills at 4%, forcing (state-owned) EDF to take a financial hit rather than households, demonstrating the control that can be exercised when things are kept under public ownership. To be clear, this is not a failed attempt at 'levelling up'. There was never any real intent to do so and talk of doing so was merely rhetoric.

All metrics lead to the same conclusion; for example, the National Audit Office found that of the increased funding allocated to schools during 2020–21 the poorest fifth got nothing, while nearly 40% of the least-deprived fifth saw an increase[298]. Many of these areas, neglected by politicians or directly targeted with adverse policy are breeding grounds for those whose sense of community has been lost, and look for a sense of pride in notions of greatness at the national level[299]. In my own research among former steelworkers and their sons in Sheffield, they are very blunt in being proud of where they come from but equally describing it as 'a bit of a shithole'. Many of them look to the idea of Great Britain (with Sheffield the only of the north's five biggest cities to vote Leave) to restore a sense of pride now that their once fabled 'steel city' employs just a fraction of what gave past generations great occupational pride[300]. The Tories rely on mythologising Britain's past to keep people voting for them as they fail to deliver on practically every promise made. This is all perfectly illustrated in the furore created around centurion Captain Tom Moore as the nation celebrated him completing 100 laps of his garden to raise money for the NHS – a service his comrades voted a Labour government in to create in 1945, to whom his charity is only needed in one of the world's wealthiest nations due to government cuts.

The Tories as the party of patriotism further drums up support by pitting Labour as the party of immigrants and supposed 'vocal minorities' rather than the so-called 'left-behinds'. The reality is that all of the political parties have been culpable in allowing resentment to fester towards migrants. Yet, Labour have more often been caught between voters who recognise the social justice case for immigration or the benefits that immigration brings, while also wanting to appease Leave-voting areas, thus they have erred into often ambiguous or

298 National Audit Office, 'School funding in England', 2 July 2021
299 Which is somewhat equally admirable given that by all international metrics we fare pretty poorly in terms of inequality and so forth
300 For a more comprehensive exploration of white, male working-class identity see *A Small Man's England* by Tommy Sissons (2021), Repeater Books

contradictory messages. It comes as no surprise that in July 2020 the Tory government rejected out of hand a letter written by 30 cross-party politicians asking for greater input into the student syllabus by non-whites, presumably because the 'dark side' of British history might dispel a few myths the Tories rely on for the patriotic working-class vote[301]. Heaven forbid such children learn of the inextricable link between colonialism and the system that went on to kick their ancestors off common land and forms the exploitative wage system that will subordinate them personally post-school. People's ignorance on these matters is part of the Tories' election strategy.

Yet we know that Leave voters are not a bunch of racist northerners; these people have agency and they are not guided by simple laws of behaviour, easily manipulated by government and media. As already noted, they have plenty of reasons to be unhappy with Labour and the establishment more generally. Working-class communities in the North, Midlands, and other political 'backwaters' often have proud histories of fighting fascism, protesting for equality, and so forth. As one example, folk in nineteenth-century Manchester, who made livelihoods in the mills of 'Cottonopolis', knew of their employers' reliance on American slavery. Prior to the American Civil War locals in Manchester had established an anti-slavery committee raising money for the underground railway through which slaves could escape to free states[302]. History is replete with such examples, including those who left their working-class families in the North East to fight Franco in the Spanish Civil War circa 1937, through to regular fighting against the British Union of Fascists in Yorkshire and other areas[303]. Recently, thousands of working-class people of all ethnicities staged a funeral procession to the gates of a BAE systems factory in Lancashire that makes parts for F-35 fighter jets used in the May 2021 bombardment of Gaza that left over 250 Palestinians dead, including 60 children[304]. Around the same time members of the Leicestershire Fire Brigades Union withdrew from assisting the police attempting to disperse protestors at the UAV Tactical Systems Factory, owned by Israeli weapons manufacturer Elbit and Thales UK, where combat drones are built. Elbit were

301 This months before the government voted against a United Nations call for concrete action to eliminate racism and xenophobia. See UN digital library, 31 December 2020

302 *Morning Star*, 'The Co-op, anti-slavery and the Lancashire cotton famine', Nick Matthews

303 See Paul Salveson (2012) *Socialism with a Northern Accent*, Lawrence and Wishart; and Richard Baxell (2012) *Unlikely Warriors: The British in the Spanish Civil War*, Aurum Press Ltd

304 *Morning Star*, 'Gazan children remembered at arms firm's gate', 4 June 2021

forced to close their Ferranti factory in Oldham after a sustained campaign of protests and occupations by activists – a reminder that direct action remains the most potent weapon for the masses.

DIVIDE AND CONQUER

> *'This is typical, trying to treat history as though it is the property of the ruling class, which will dispense however much of it they want to dispense at any given point in time'* (Walter Rodney)

We know the centrality of immigration to the Brexit vote. Ipsos Mori opinion polls conducted in the week leading up to the June 2016 Referendum vote found it to be the most important factor in people's decision-making[305]. The context for this is relatively clear: the UK has the fifth largest immigrant population in the world, comprising approximately 8.5 million migrants[306]. This doubled between 1990 and 2015, equating to around 13% of the UK population being foreign-born. It is perfectly valid in a society like ours that is so work-focused to worry about an influx of able-bodied people, many here specifically with the intention to work, to increase the competition for jobs that may already be sparse. It does not automatically follow that someone espousing these views is xenophobic, although 40% of leave voters responding to one poll stated that they would be willing to experience a drop in personal income in exchange for a reduction in immigration, signalling that anti-immigrant views cannot always be passed off as economic anxiety[307]. Typically, there are two concerns regarding an influx of migrants: the effects that this has on competition for jobs and thus potentially unemployment, and also potentially stagnating wages as migrants may offer a cheaper substitute for British-born labour.

What becomes apparent quite quickly when reviewing research on these hypotheses, is that they are largely unsubstantiated. For example, in a study

---

305 Ipsos Mori, 'Immigration is now the top issue for voters in the EU referendum', 16 June 2016

306 David Blanchflower (2019) *Not Working: Where Have All the Good Jobs Gone?*, Princeton University Press

307 See via *Hostile Environment* by Maya Goodfellow how successive governments have facilitated a climate that is unfavourable to migrants in both rhetoric and policy (while simultaneously recognising the need for migrants to continue fulfilling labour shortages and thus subjecting those who aren't deported to said climate)

conducted by the London School of Economics, Wadsworth et al. (2016) found that UK areas with large increases in EU migration did not suffer greater declines in the number of available jobs, or wage levels, of UK-born workers. In actual fact, while a many great other studies find only negligible difference on the job prospects or wages of British-born workers (e.g. the Migration Observatory at Oxford University and the National Institute of Economic and Social Research being two[308]), the International Longevity Centre think-tank found that areas with higher employment rates for immigrants also tended to have more of the white UK-born population in work on average[309]. There is also a consensus that European migrants make a net contribution to the UK economy. According to the government's own commissioned report, European migrants contribute £2,300 more per year than the average adult (effectively £78,000 over their lifespan in the UK) via paying more in taxes than they 'cost' via use of public services or welfare; resulting in a total net contribution of approximately £4.7 billion[310]. Not to mention supporting UK businesses while here, thus creating demand for products and services alongside providing them. They are absolutely crucial to the nation's health, fulfilling nearly one-third of positions in NHS hospitals[311]. Highly skilled migrants boost our innovation, particularly in sectors such as the sciences, and they populate sectors where there are huge labour shortfalls such as agriculture, food production and hospitality.

If people truly want to have frank discussions about immigration, they would be well served to consider the role Britain's foreign policy plays in creating economic migrants and asylum seekers, and how seriously they are taking climate change (with those displaced due to environmental factors double the amount of those migrating due to conflict in the first half of 2020 – approx. 10 million globally[312]). We would also do well to offer people a proper history lesson of Britain to dispel this myth that immigration only began happening after the Second World War and threatens the fabric of society when

308 The Migration Observatory, 'The Labour Market Effects of Immigration', 18 February 2020; National Institute of Economic and Social Research, 'Immigration, Free Movement and the EU Referendum', May 2016

309 The International Longevity Centre, 'Immigration: Encourage or Deter', 20 June 2016

310 Migration Advisory Committee, 'EEA migration in the UK: Final report', September 2018

311 Office for National Statistics, 'International migration and the healthcare workforce', 15 August 2019

312 Internal displacement monitoring centre, 'Internal displacement 2020: mid-year update'

it *is* that very fabric[313]. Even before the mass migrations we do know about, for example the Romans in the year 43 (themselves a broad mix of people due to the Roman Empire's size), the English were already a mix of languages and cultures, with the first inhabitants from Southern Europe[314]. As the statues of slave owners like Edward Colston were toppled, the more conservative-minded invoked Churchill when suggesting that such actions were wrong as 'a nation that forgets its past has no future'. Yet we know that records of British colonial crimes were not only hidden but many destroyed, including details of the torture and killing of Mau Mau insurgents in Kenya[315].

Part of this history lesson would reveal just how much work it takes to keep the majority divided, in what is a completely manufactured state of affairs that has harmed us all. Taking 'race' as one example, historian Theodore W. Allen mused, 'When the first Africans arrived in Virginia in 1619, there were no "white" people there; nor, according to the colonial records, would there be for another sixty years', having found no official record of the word 'white' used in any way connected to social status before the year 1691[316]. The first colonisers to arrive in what became Jamestown considered themselves to be English, their children too. This all changed due to solidarity between the white, European-indentured servants brought over to the US with their masters, often serving between five and ten years on the islands before returning home, and the Africans.

Fear of uprising was rife due to how outnumbered the colonisers were, and earlier attempts had been made to create division between the two groups in servitude who ate, slept, and indeed engaged in acts of rebellion together. For example, the 1661 Act of Better Ordering and Governing of Negroes banned sex between the two races and created a number of white privileges for the servants over the slaves and race began to become more salient. This all came to a head during the 'Bacon rebellion' and the ruling class deliberately invented a system of racial privileges that defined the 'white' race, simultaneously solidifying

---

313 Such a lesson requires the perspectives of both Brits – e.g. Robin Blackburn, Richard Gott, John Newsinger, and Dave Sherry – and non-Brits from whom we have much to learn about ourselves and Europe more widely – e.g. Walter Rodney, CLR James, Frantz Fanon, Sven Lindqvist, Olivette Otélé, Eric Eustace Williams, and Howard Zinn. Also, those who draw attention to how history becomes distorted, e.g. Michel-Rolph Trouillot, Michael Parenti, David Graeber, and David Wengrow. There are many more

314 An accessible and free resource for such information is Our Migration Story (ourmigrationstory.org.uk)

315 *The Guardian*, 'Britain destroyed records of colonial crimes', 18 April 2012

316 *The Invention of the White Race, Volume I* (1994) by Theodore W. Allen, Verso

the racial division of slavery that came to be (formally via the Virginia Slave Codes of 1705). This was partly to prevent further united uprisings between the European and African servants, but created a perceptibly uniting feature between the white ruling and white working classes that has continued to mask their fundamentally diverse interests, and the similarities between those of the white and black working classes that still run deep today. The Grunwick dispute of 1976 where Asian and white women and men stood together, on equal terms, to fight for justice is an early, perfect illustration of these material similarities and ability to foster togetherness in Britain. For two years they battled, with over 500 arrested in the process as once again the state intervened in full force to shut down these acts of solidarity challenging the capitalist status quo[317].

ESTABLISHMENT-LED POPULISM

'In every age it has been the tyrant, the oppressor and the exploiter who has wrapped himself in the cloak of patriotism, or religion, or both to deceive and overawe the People' (Eugene V. Debs, 1918 speech in Canton, Ohio[318])

Today's populism denotes the remarkable persistence of this very process, with some white working-class people believing that they have more in common, and are at all represented by, the likes of Nigel Farage and Boris Johnson. These men are not anti-establishment; they are the same establishment responsible for continually neglecting the 'left-behinds'. Boris was not driving a no-deal Brexit for so long because he has lots of respect for leave voters in Sunderland, Sheffield, or the East Midlands. Alongside famously writing two columns for *The Telegraph* – one in support of remaining in the EU and one in support of leaving, before opting for the latter – he told Baron Andrew Adonis that he

---

317 On matters of 'race', I am always drawn to Eduardo Galeano's *A Feast on Foot*: 'Adam and Eve were black? The human adventure in the world began in Africa. From there, our ancestors set out to conquer the planet. Many paths led them to many destinies, and the sun took care of handing out colors from the palette. Now the rainbow of the earth is more colorful than the rainbow of the sky. But we are all emigrants from Africa. Even the whitest of whites comes from Africa. Maybe we refuse to acknowledge our common origins because racism causes amnesia, or because we find it unbelievable that in those days long past the entire world was our kingdom, an immense map without borders, and our legs were the only passport required'

318 Incidentally, this speech landed the then-Socialist Party Leader 10 years in prison. He accrued nearly 1 million votes running for President from a prison cell at the Atlanta Federal Penitentiary in 1920

was 'buggered' if he knew which side to take[319]. He was doing it because a) he is completely self-interested and wanted to remain as Prime Minister at any cost, and b) because his wealthy associates benefitted from him doing so. One view – in the vein of disaster capitalism well theorised by Naomi Klein – is that millionaire politicians are actively motivated by the dismal financial effects of Brexit. It is very difficult to attribute an accurate cost thus far, but: GDP was £130 billion lower at the end of 2019 than projected had we not exited the EU which is one measure used, and this figure was estimated to hit £200 billion by the close of play in 2020 – before the pandemic struck[320]. Others have tacked on costs such as the loss of £73.6 million *per day* in exports to our closest European trading partners between July 2020–2021[321], and the £8 billion spent on initial preparations for Brexit (including for a no-deal outcome) meaning that the cost of Brexit has probably outweighed the entire contributions paid by the UK to the EU over the course of its 47-year membership. For clarity, the Office for Budget Responsibility has UK contributions to the EU during its membership (1973–2020) totalling £222 billion in real terms. Pro-remain and neutral observers have been quick to calculate the many millions of nurses, teachers, improvements to transport, and everything else that such money could have gone towards.

Such crises are attractive to certain elites as economic uncertainty makes the public more accepting of financial hardship, particularly in this instance where they voted for it. This enables the continued underfunding of public services and so forth, which is absolutely what is happening. In order to drive capital and investments away from the EU Britain will now compete by slashing taxes further and continuing to de-regulate employment rights and protections. And this is not even a well-kept secret – consultations between the Business Secretary and industry leaders were arranged to discuss what would be retained under EU agreements post-Brexit, with such parties unlikely to lobby for better rights and protections for their employees. Business Secretary Kwasi Kwarteng claims that these consultations are not taking place anymore, so we will have to take the word of a man who co-authored (alongside Liz Truss, Dominic Raab, and Priti Patel) a 2012 book

319 Prospect, 'Boris Johnson: The Prime Etonian', 9 July 2021
320 Bloomberg Economics, '$170 Billion and Counting: The Cost of Brexit for the U.K.', 10 January 2020
321 *Byline Times*, '£515 Million-a-Week Hit in UK Exports to Top European Partners', 2 November 2021

entitled *Britannia Unchained* calling British workers 'among the worst idlers in the world', and for radical free-market economics, including fewer employment regulations.

On the issue of Britain becoming established as a tax haven next to the EU market, we can take a character we will re-visit in the next chapter as one example, Jonathan Harmsworth. Formally known as his Lordship the Viscount Rothermere, Harmsworth is the chairman of the Daily Mail Group. He inherited the company from his father[322] via a Jersey trust and offshore entity registered in Bermuda, enabling him to avoid corporation tax. Far from being content with this – and despite being born in Hammersmith, schooled in Scotland, and owning a mansion in Wiltshire with 240 acres of land – he claims 'non-domicile' status and claims allegiance to France for the purposes of avoiding other taxes, as did his father before him. All told, the owner of the *Daily Mail* – found to be the second biggest media supporter of Brexit[323] who continually told readers to 'believe in Britain' – helps the cause by not paying tax into British coffers on his billionaire fortune. This, despite his newspapers being very vocal about how much tax the rest of us should be paying, and spurious of those who rely on taxpayers' money while in-between jobs. Such tax abusers are being targeted by the EU Anti-Tax Avoidance Directives, which have been strengthened, and thus they are very keen to be outside of EU jurisdiction and in the much safer hands of our governments, which do very little to tackle tax avoidance by their wealthy acquaintances.

Another example of someone who warrants attention in the next chapter is Rupert Murdoch, owner of *The Sun* and *The Times*, both pro-Brexit newspapers. The media baron has a portfolio stretching across the world (America, UK, Asia, Australia) and therefore potentially has designs on expanding into our European neighbours. Despite the many shortcomings of the EU, its might has occasionally proved effective in standing up to monopolies, with the antitrust commissioner quashing the UK merger between mobile-phone network providers 3 and O2 among many high-profile

---

322 His great-grandfather Lord Northcliffe was the Rupert Murdoch of the 20th century. He is credited with popularising sensationalist news for the working classes via his papers the *Daily Mail* and *Daily Mirror* alongside brother Harold Harmsworth, an overt supporter of Oswald Mosley's British fascists and Hitler. Harold's son Esmond was an Eton-educated Tory MP. The family has been disseminating hate and division to the working classes continuously for well over a century

323 Oxford University Reuters Institute for the Study of Journalism, 'UK press coverage of the EU Referendum'

scalps. Having reportedly told Senior Commentator at the *Evening Standard* Anthony Hilton that his reasoning for being anti-EU is because 'When I go into Downing Street they do what I say; when I go to Brussels they take no notice', it all falls into place[324]. Our politicians can be gotten at quite easily if you have money – £50k guarantees you an evening with the PM. So, for the wealthy in our society unadulterated Tory rule with senior politicians more than happy to lend their ears leaving the EU was a no-brainer. One cannot help but see the irony in many Leave voters not wanting to be told what to do or think by unelected elites (in Europe), when this is exactly what they have done, only by media barons instead.

Farage might pose with a pint from time to time in a bid to portray himself as a man of the people, but this is wide of the mark. Another public schoolboy, Nige claimed in a *Daily Mail* interview in 2017 to be 'skint'[325], despite living in a £4 million Chelsea townhouse, earning around £90k per year (plus expenses) as an MEP, and depositing hundreds of thousands of pounds from engagements such as media appearances into Thorn In The Side Limited: a company he is listed as sole director for, as a way to avoid paying 40% income tax (instead expending 20% corporation tax). He has made a fantastic career for himself out of becoming the face of everything anti-EU, and this was no more the case than on 23 June 2016. Farage publicly conceded defeat in the referendum less than a minute after voting closed, despite hedge fund associates of the former financial services worker having paid (and received) information from YouGov and other pollsters indicating a win for the Leave camp. The ability to help create fluctuations in the valuation of the pound led to accusations of 'shorting' the market, from which many of his allies got rich[326].

This is the thing with populism: those who portray themselves as anti-establishment are left in a conundrum if they are elected into power, as they become the very things that they protest against. Particularly politicians who jump on the right-wing populism bandwagons and are thus being pragmatic for votes have the issue when – being the establishment themselves – they actually have no real interest in following through on many of the promises

---

324 *Evening Standard* comment piece, 'Anthony Hilton: Stay or go – the lack of solid facts means it's all a leap of faith', 25 February 2016

325 Mail Online, '"I'm 53, separated and skint"', 15 December 2017

326 Bloomberg, 'The Brexit Short: How Hedge Funds Used Private Polls to Make Millions', 25 June 2018

they made (the classic example being £350 million per week sent to Brussels that would be spent on the NHS instead, plastered on the side of *that* bus). As right-wing populists rarely do anything tangible of value for society and thus have little to garner support *for*, they depend entirely on division and base their arguments on being *against* things. At the next election we can expect a ramping up of the 'culture wars', as Tory MPs and the media band those terms like 'woke', 'lefties', 'Marxists', and whatever else around very frequently and position the opposition as some vague combination of the above. And in power populism must continue to chunter along while the wheels come off for as long as possible, with the blame for their failures placed on anyone but themselves.

If this book has argued anything it is that life has got decidedly worse for much of the population, and the global financial crisis revealed that we are not a rich country who will be able to bounce back from a cyclical economic downturn, but that there are underlying, decades-old issues in many parts of the country. Despite being in power for 28 of the last 41 years, the Tories have done a fantastic job of blaming everyone else for the country's downward fortunes: blame was apportioned to coalition partners the Liberal Democrats when the promises of 2010 were not met at the end of their first term. During this time so-called benefit scroungers were also the reason why the country could not progress. Towards 2016 when there was concern that the right-wing vote would be split with UKIP and David Cameron called the EU referendum, European migrants were next to be blamed. More recently it was EU regulations and bureaucrats in Brussels. Who is going to be next? They are not afraid to chuck anyone under the bus, with Public Health England – whose advice they were selective about following in the first instance, and then dropped when it was too cautious for their own political aims – took blame during the pandemic. The public themselves were then held responsible by Health Minister Matt Hancock despite the government's many failings and the vast majority of people respecting lockdown rules. It is quite a feat that they – supported wholeheartedly by friends in the media – convinced the public to dislike NHS staff during a pandemic: the very people who kept us alive. Teachers were another targeted group, demonstrating that quite literally anybody can be 'got at' except the actual decision-makers themselves.

In some ways white working-class liberation appears unlikely as, in contrast to other disadvantaged groups who receive regular reminders of their social standing via overt discrimination and more unconscious biases, aligning themselves to the Nigels and Borises of this world reduces the likelihood of unity with their oppressed counterparts. Particularly with the aforementioned hollow patriotism propagated by such individuals, and the nostalgic harking back to notions of the British stiff upper lip/spirit of the Blitz via wartime slogans such as 'Keep calm and carry on'. This represents more effective marketing by the Tories rather than an honest assessment which would read something closer to 'yes, your lives are getting worse, but it's unbecoming to not plod on regardless'. Or worse, 'yes, your existence is miserable, but at least there's not a war on' – the class war aside, of course[327].

It is also worth reflecting on what exactly 'we' are taking back control of. We have already outlined who owns much of the land, and most of the public services and infrastructure has passed into private hands. The next sections of this chapter study how undemocratic many of our own governance structures are, not to mention the unelected House of Lords, which raises many questions around what control you or I actually have – and of what. What we actually seem to mean is that our ruling elites have taken back more control than they already had, but large numbers of the population believe that this somehow means they will have a greater say in how the country operates – or at least that is my interpretation. I am yet to hear a clear and convincing statement of what control Joe Public will have post-Brexit, as it appears to be another big win for a small group of elites.

HOW (ACTUALLY) DEMOCRATIC IS OUR DEMOCRACY?

'The democracy of Parliament is, in short, the democracy of Capitalism. Capitalism gives to the worker the right to choose his master, but insists that the fact of mastership shall remain unquestioned' (James Connolly, Parliamentary Democracy, 1900)

---

327 During World War II people really did have to demonstrate 'spirit' in lieu of support from the government. Recognising that effective shelters would need to be deep underground the government opted for less expensive, less effective shelters above ground. During air raids people were thus forced to head for London tube stations, where the government sent police to block their entry – prioritising people moving around the transport links for work over preserving lives. It was a similar story outside of the major cities where people chose to camp out in the countryside, and the government directed local authorities not to provide any sanitation facilities due to their concerns about absenteeism from work, demanding civilians returned. See Richard Overy (2013) *The Bombing War*, Allen Lane

Perhaps the best answer to this question is with another question: how much of your life has been spent governed by people you voted for, or feel represent you and your interests? For swathes of the population, the answer might be very little of it. This should be a pretty good indication that our form of democracy is flawed. We have highlighted some of the questionable, if not downright catastrophic policies and approaches taken by our elected rulers. We know that life for the majority has not got any better over the past certainly decade. It surely cannot be the case that hordes of people are simply foolish enough to vote for things that have an adverse effect on their own lives. Likewise, it cannot simply be a case of a few 'bad apples' who are not practising democracy well enough, as there are too many of them, and it has been happening for too long. We have to ask whether there is something wrong with the system itself.

Take the Iraq War as an example of choices made by politicians that do not reflect the wishes or values of the population they serve to represent. In the US system George Bush received approx. a half million fewer votes than Democrat opponent Al Gore yet became president in 2000 (not least in controversial fashion, with the decision not being made by American citizens but a small number of unelected judges in the Supreme Court). On home soil Blair had been re-elected PM with Labour taking 62.5% of seats in the House of Commons with only 40.7% of the vote. Yet both men were deemed victors in their respective democratic systems and led the countries into a war most people did not agree with; by two men most people did not vote for but were legitimately elected and had every right to do so. This was not an anomaly; consider the fact that Thatcher's Tory government received 700k fewer votes in the 1983 election than they did in 1979 yet gained 50 more seats in the first-past-the-post system. This translates to one seat per 32,777 votes for the Tories; meanwhile, the Social Democrat-Liberal Alliance obtained one seat per 338,302 votes received[328].

Clearly something does not add up when only a tenuous link exists between votes cast and constituencies won, resulting in electoral defeat or success. There are other problems: we may end up with a coalition between two parties that was not even an option on the ballot sheet and therefore a government no-one actually voted for. Choice is constrained by the fact that only really parties or candidates with connections to corporate donors or mass media can seriously contest an election – diminishing the extent to which ordinary

328 Roslyn Fuller (2015) *Beasts and Gods: How Democracy Changed Its Meaning and Lost Its Purpose*, ZED Books

people are likely to have someone in office who can resonate with their lived experience and therefore represent them well. Further, it is highly likely that elected representatives are going to appease the wishes of their major donors rather than those of the everyday voter.

When you step back and consider what democracy means in Britain, people are merely entitled to vote – occasionally – for the people who will actually make all of the decisions. In the four or so years between elections politicians are somewhat free to simply ignore much of the population who often feel limited in their ability to effect change before their next opportunity to vote. As David McNally puts it, 'between elections, these representatives assume virtually total power over the ostensibly sovereign people'[329]. In fact, the system works best (for the governing elites and their sponsors) exactly when the majority are not governing themselves and are thus detached and alienated from politics. Despite 'democracy' evolving from 'Demokratia', which translates to 'people power' in the birthplace of democracy Ancient Athens, there is relatively little public inclusion in actual decision-making beyond the act of voting itself.

We are familiar with how the 'first-past-the-post' system works: our country is divided into constituencies, the candidate with the most votes in each constituency becomes the representative for that area, and the head of the party which has the most candidates becomes the prime minister, usually for four years before the process is repeated. Among the issues are 'gerrymandering', i.e. the drawing (and re-drawing) of constituencies which favour one political party more than another. For example, 'stacking' indicates drawing boundaries in such a way that a party will accrue a large number of surplus votes beyond those needed to win a constituency, which is considered unfavourable as many of these votes are therefore somewhat wasted, as they do not translate into people's desired government and votes counting towards that happening.

Meanwhile, 'cracking' is the drawing of boundaries to help ensure that a political party wins constituencies with smaller majorities, thus spreading around surplus votes into other areas and aiding their attempt to win more seats. In such a situation, the party accrues a lower number of 'wasted' votes than their opposition. This links to the point above (illustrated by the Social Democrat-Liberal Alliance) whereby one party receives a large number of votes but this does not translate into seats, thus depriving people of a meaningful

---

329 *Another World Is Possible: Globalization and Anti-Capitalism* (2006), The Merlin Press

vote. Alternatively, 'cracking' can dilute a party's potential to win by spreading the support across more than one constituency. Perhaps the most abhorrent example of this was the drawing of boundaries in Northern Ireland by the British government in 1920, ensuring that a subsequent vote on whether to remain part of Great Britain was rigged with a maximum number of Unionists and minimum number of Republicans in many areas[330]. The threat of gerrymandering never quite goes away: as boundaries are redrawn following the Parliamentary Constituencies Act passed in December 2020, psephologists agree that extra seats being gained in the (Tory-dominated) south-east and south-west will result in an additional 10 seats for the Conservatives at the next election[331]. Further, the (also Tory-dominated) County Councils Network had been calling for the abolishment of smaller councils to be replaced by bigger local authorities[332], with the potential for 'stacking' Labour support into certain areas and being creative with the new boundaries not unimaginable.

In a meaningful democracy the people should have a range of means to influence political decisions during the time between elections. This is important beyond the obvious, because sustained and direct engagement makes a population more politically aware and better informed to make important decisions. Consider the situation in Switzerland, where by virtue of their system of direct democracy key issues are put to referendums and votes multiple times each year. So informed are the electorate that in 2012 two-thirds voted *against* increasing their annual leave allowance from four to six weeks, on the grounds that their economy largely consists of small- and medium-sized enterprises who feared the effects that this increase in holiday would have. At the same time, people in the city of Zurich voted for the creation of shielded car spaces where sex workers could legally ply their trade. Essentially, a petition on any issue, budget, or law that receives the support of 100,000 Swiss citizens eager to open up a debate earns the right to a referendum.

Contrast that to the situation here in Britain: if 100k people sign a petition a backbench MP *might* decide to bring it for debate before the Backbench Business Committee, which *might* decide to allocate time to discuss it during

---

330 John O'Brien (2010) *Discrimination in Northern Ireland, 1920–1939: Myth or Reality?*, Cambridge Scholars Publishing

331 *Financial Times*, 'UK constituency boundary shake-up expected to boost Tory party', 28 December 2020

332 CNN, 'Evaluating the importance of scale in proposals for local government reorganisation', August 2020

backbench time. Let's face it, how many people have the time to devote themselves fully to activism when petitioning ultimately seems rather futile? We are kept so busy with work and other life commitments that it can seem like too much of an uphill battle. As for alternatives, our most fundamental right as citizens in a supposed democracy – to voice our concerns and protest injustice – was curbed when all of the Tories voted in favour of the Police, Crime, Sentencing and Courts Bill in March 2021, a piece of legislation that would, in the words of DUP MP Gavin Robinson, 'make a dictator blush', although that did not perturb him from voting for it[333]. This Bill makes it virtually impossible to attend a demonstration without committing a criminal offence, where even making noise can lead to hefty fines or a prison sentence, and yet none of this should surprise us. As far back as 1911 James Connolly made the point that forms of direct action are not to the liking of lawyers, politicians, or employers as 'it keeps the two former out of a job, and leaves the latter out of pocket... [it can be] a potent weapon in the armoury of the working class'[334]. When our decision-makers are politicians, many of whom were lawyers, and most funded by employers, one does have cause for alarm.

Many of the threads discussed thus far wed together into a rather disconcerting picture. It feels like we have a fair amount of freedom in our society, to do and be what we want. Yet, it is clearly very difficult to actually affect change politically; mentioned in Chapter 1 is the fact that most people are forced into wage labour for the vast majority of their lives; as Chapter 2 discusses most people are forced to take on debt to buy a home and such things; we do not get any real chance to influence what constitutes unlawful behaviour (as one illustration, there are countless examples of differing responses by law enforcement to protests and demonstrations, as was seen by pro-Trump supporters storming the Capitol building in January 2021). When actually stepping back to consider the bigger picture, we have a degree of autonomy over what we do on a day-to-day basis but really are quite limited in what we can do at a more structural level. Or at least that is what they would have us believe – every major progressive change and civil rights movement began from a position of perceived near-impossibility.

---

333 *Huffington Post*, 'Controversial Anti-Protest Bill Wins Vote As Not A Single Tory Stands Against It', 17 March 2021

334 James Connolly (1911) 'Direct Action in Belfast', in Aindrias Ó Cathasaigh (eds) *James Connolly: The Lost Writings*, Pluto Press

MONEY WINS ELECTIONS

'We may have democracy, or we may have wealth concentrated in the hands of the few, but we cannot have both' (Louis D. Brandeis)

The Electoral Commission provides figures on party donations running up to elections. In the first week of campaigning for the 2019 general election, £6.5 million was received by the political parties, of which £5.6 million went to the Conservatives (over 22 times the amount received by the party with the second highest amount of donations – the Brexit Party). The total donations at the end of those six sweeks look like this:

Party	Donation total
Conservative Party	£19,370,908
Labour Party	£5,121,172[335]
The Brexit Party	£4,150,000[336]
Liberal Democrats	£1,245,998[337]
All other parties receiving donations	£<1,000,000

In effect, the party that received comfortably more money than all of the other political parties combined, also won comfortably more seats than all of the other political parties. There is great precedent here: in the 2014 election victory the Tories received a whopping £29 million, 10 million pounds more than Labour; likewise in 2010 Tory spending running up to the election was double what Labour spent at £16 million. This should not be surprising as the party that is most aligned with the interests of the wealthy are obviously going to have a large number of million- and billionaire donors, with almost one-third of the richest people in the UK having donated money to the party

---

335 Donations came almost exclusively from trade unions, i.e. from members of the working class. The majority (£3 million) came from Unite the Union, £540k from the GMB, £450k from Unison, and £425k from the Communication Workers Union.

336 The bulk of this money (£3.4 million) came from one individual, Thailand-based Mr Christopher Harborne. A Tory donor until 2018, the Offshore Leaks Database links him to five companies named in the Panama Papers

337 Earlier that year Lord David Sainsbury gave £8 million to the Lib Dems, Britain's biggest ever political donation

(comfortably over £50 million, all told)[338]. New Labour made themselves more appealing to such individuals and in the 2005 election that Labour won, spending by both parties was at a similar level (nearly £18 million), reiterating how important money is. In the last section we came across the recently passed Parliamentary Constituencies Act which will increase spending limits from £19.5 million to £33 million, clearly designed for the benefit of the party of the rich and powerful. This long trend of those with the greatest money to spend winning the right to rule over us is disconcerting for a number of reasons. Primarily, parties in a democracy should compete on good ideas and policies, not on who can convince a relatively small group of wealthy, typically white middle-aged men to open their wallets. Such an unrepresentative group would only donate to a party if they benefit from said party being in power, where motivations could range from seeking to avoid tax, gain lucrative public contracts, or continue underpaying workers.

In *The Corruption of Capitalism*, Guy Standing highlights how the 2014 'Black and White Ball', essentially a fundraiser for the Conservatives, was attended by guests worth an estimated £22 billion. By the following year, 27 of the 59 wealthiest hedge-fund managers on the *Sunday Times* rich list had donated over £19 million to the party, including Michael Farmer, whose £6.5 million donation helped his becoming party co-treasurer and receiving a peerage. In 2016 the ball was sponsored by Shore Capital, an investment bank registered in the tax haven of Guernsey, ran by Tory donors. In contrast and as noted in the footnote above, much of Labour's donations come from trade unions, where workers contribute a small amount each month that is then funnelled to the Labour Party unless they opt out of doing so. The average donation made to the Labour party was in fact £26[339]. It is therefore a party funded by a very large number of workers as opposed to a wealthy few.

Money does of course dictate everything in our society. The British intervention in oil-rich Libya had very questionable motives, but despite one-third of the Libyan population having to flee to neighbouring Tunisia, and half of the population who remained requiring aid, some folks did quite well out of it. Ian Taylor, CEO of Vitol Oil, was a visitor to Downing Street

---

338 Evolve Politics, 'One third of ALL the UK's billionaires are bankrolling the Conservative Party', 18 November 2019

339 Labour.org.uk 'Labour's people powered campaign hits £1 million in small donations in 10 days', 7 November 2019

a few weeks after Colonel Gaddafi was murdered. He had not long since donated nearly £500k to the Tories, and then David Cameron's Minister of State for International Development Alan Duncan – a former Vitol Oil trader – had advised the Home Office to sanction the purchase of crude oil from Libyan rebels and supply fuel in return. Vitol Oil were handed a nice £600 million contract to ship supplies in and out of Libya. In the same Downing Street meeting was one Mr Ruddock – who had given the Tories over £500,000 and had a stake in private healthcare firm Circle Health, handed a highly controversial ten-year, £1 billion deal to take control of the NHS Hinchingbrooke Hospital in Cambridgeshire[340].

Donors are often invited or additionally pay money to meet with the PM and cabinet ministers, and it is unlikely that they are lobbying for higher corporation taxes or stricter environmental controls. Take for example the second largest political donor of 2019, Lord Anthony Bamford, who donated £4 million to the Tory party. The chairman of JCB is inextricably linked with the Tories, with former Brexit secretary and MP for Haltemprice and Howden David Davis on their books as an 'external advisor' for £60k per year[341]; David Cameron and Boris Johnson (receiving £10k for the privilege) made separate visits and spoke at the company; Bamford himself is a director of Margaret Thatcher's preferred think-tank, the Centre for Policy Studies. His donations to the Tories amount to millions before the 2019 sum, and he was rewarded with a peerage from David Cameron in 2013, and the construction index shows that JCB 'won' a lucrative stake in the Tories' £950 million regional growth fund grants a year after Cameron's election win (coincidentally the same day younger brother Mark Bamford donated £150k to the party). Lord Bamford, who at the start of 2020 also received a £600 million taxpayer-funded government loan, had complained about EU red tape driving up business costs to his associate Boris. One finds it hard to believe that the *Forbes*-listed billionaire – whose possessions include a

---

340 Circle Health's management of the hospital was a much-criticised failure, and they walked away from the contract early. Circle had Tory MP for Boston and Skegness Mike Simmonds on a handsome (second salary) £50k-per-year contract as a strategic advisor when they were given control of Hinchingbrooke NHS hospital

341 One would expect a full diary serving the interests of his East Riding of Yorkshire constituents, yet the diligent Davis not only earns £50 per minute at JCB but is a board member of German manufacturer Mansfelder Kupfer Und Messing GMBH. Information on parliamentary members' financial interests or received benefits can be accessed via the 'Register of Members' Financial Interests' on the parliament.uk website

$70 million-valued yacht, private jet, rare Ferrari collection, award-winning vineyard in Southern France, and a villa in Barbados[342] – cannot afford to pay his staff a fair wage, but his lordship suggests otherwise.

The ease with which money buys access to the prime minister was laid strikingly bare by *The Sunday Times* undercover video of then-Tory treasurer Peter Cruddas offering favour from his party for donations, principally of £100k or more[343]. Appeal Court judge Lord Justice Jackson said the behaviour of Cruddas was 'unacceptable, inappropriate and wrong', but it does not appear that this corrupt behaviour has ceased in any way. The issue of money is pervasive throughout our political system. Take the House of Lords, which provides a second chamber through which the (potentially compromised) decisions made in the House of Commons by our elected masters can be scrutinised and revised. It is therefore of particular interest to us who sits in this chamber, despite the fact we have no means of electing them ourselves. Nominations for what we might call the expected peers, i.e. former parliamentarians and those who have held major public office, made up nearly 70% of nominees between 2005–2014. All political party donations made by this c70% of nominees amounted to £735k. Of the remaining c30% of nominees, they collectively donated just under £34 million. In other words, for those without the type of CV one would expect to become a peer, it is plausible that others are effectively buying their nominations for peerage. Just 27 of these individuals were responsible for over 95% of the donations[344]. The same issues raised above come into play here: unelected wealthy individuals being able to influence British politics does not typically lead to any increase in 'the lot' of ordinary citizens.

DO WE NEED THE HOUSE OF LORDS?

In principle it makes sense to have a second House, which can ensure that bills passed by the House of Commons receive further scrutiny. The House of

---

342 Super Yacht Fan database: Lord Bamford
343 Video available on *The Times*, 'Sunday Times wins appeal over Tory "cash for access"', 18 March 2015
344 University of Oxford Dpt. of Economics discussion paper, 'Is there a market for peerages? Can donations buy you a British peerage? A study in the link between party political funding and peerage nominations, 2005–14'

Lords has the power to amend bills, and restricted ability to reject them. So is it worth it?

Essentially, most members do not receive a salary but are entitled to claim an attendance allowance if they wish of up to £323 (tax-free) per day, compliments of the taxpayer. This represents a 'pay' increase above the inflation rate and average UK worker pay rises. There are typically 150 sitting days in a year, to which if all peers attended each day the total cost would be comfortably over £37 million. Naturally they do not, but expenses have still soared in recent times: the total cost of peers' expenses and attendance allowance claims hit £23 million between March 2018–March 2019, a huge increase of 29% on the year before. There are some peers doing very well out of their positions: those attending the 150 sitting days can earn nearly £50k that year, which is tax-free and does not require national insurance contributions. It is also difficult to determine who has and has not engaged in 'parliamentary work' because there is no agreed definition, opening up these earnings to possible foul play. Even those who do 'sit' can claim this full amount without actual contribution of note, with public data analysis showing that about one in nine peers did not speak or contribute to any committee, and 46 did not register a single vote (including on crucial issues such as Brexit)[345].

As with MPs in the Commons, there is something that does not sit too well with people earning anything up to £81,932 and beyond who apparently cannot afford food and drink so are able to claim it back, deciding that those unable to find work can live off under £4,000 per year – or £15k annually if on the national 'living'/minimum wage. Occasionally there are 'good eggs' who enter into politics; for example, Labour MP in Nottingham Nadia Whittome pledged to 'take home' what she described to be an average worker's salary of £35k of her £81,932 and is giving the rest to worthy local charities and causes. But these are few and far between, and a truly rare sight in the Lords. There are debates concerning whether the House of Lords should be abolished, which draws mixed reviews.

Is there anything truly democratic about a House full of unelected individuals, profiting from their status, who have a say on our laws without any

---

345 *The Guardian*, 'Peer who never spoke in Lords last year claims £50,000 expenses', 30 May 2019

accountability[346], many of whom do not even actually provide any input, and we pay for the privilege? Let us begin with the more popularly accepted idea, namely that the number of peers be reduced and capped, as suggested by the very own Lord Speaker's committee (to the tune of 600 Lords)[347]. In reality the opposite is happening: while the number of peers was 663 in 2000, the recent 36 nominations from PM Boris Johnson continues an upward trend that puts the number comfortably over 800, so the costs to the taxpayer are only going one way. The absurdity of this is reflected in the fact that this is way beyond the 650 MPs elected to the Commons, and the House of Lords is now the second largest legislative chamber in the world.

This is especially problematic when, on the one hand, we are led to believe that money is tight for public services, yet friends and donors of the PM are an expense we cannot do without. Parliamentary advisor Meg Russell suggests introducing some enforceable constraints on PM nominations, perhaps via devolving some power to the House of Lords Appointments Commission (which currently cannot police the number of nominees, suitability of nominees, etc.)[348] as a sensible reform. Biases in the Lords across party lines were largely eliminated by Blair's decision to introduce the 1999 House of Lords Act, removing the vast majority of hereditary peers. Yet, the fact that PMs nominate whichever and however many peers they see fit means that the chamber is far more political and partisan than proponents suggest. Even the right-wing media lamented the rather astonishing cronyism of David Cameron's resignation honours list in 2016, with cross-bencher Lord Digby Jones suggesting Larry the (No. 10 Downing Street) cat might be next[349]. As an example, Laura Wyld, who was the PM's head of the Lords appointments unit, effectively gave herself a peerage, and more recently Boris gave one to his brother Jo.

At the time of writing, Conservative members make up the largest group within the House of Lords at 246 members, with the other largest party-

346 Such little accountability that in August 2021 a formal complaint was submitted to the Lord's commissioner for standards as 42 peers failed to declare details of private companies they act as a director for – something they are required to do but for years simply had not

347 'Report of the Lord Speaker's committee on the size of the House', 31 October 2017

348 The Constitution Unit, University College London: 'Boris Johnson's 36 new peerages make the need to constrain prime ministerial appointments to the House of Lords clearer than ever', 31 July 2020

349 *Daily Mail*, '"He might as well have given a peerage to Larry!" Anger grows at Cameron's decision to pack the Lords with his senior staff while handing gongs to his spinner and even his HONOURS chief', 5 August 2016

affiliated groups being 173 Labour peers and 88 Liberal-Democrats[350]. While there is a clear incentive for PMs to pack out the Lords with allies in what effectively becomes an arms race, the taxpayer is left to cover their expenses while they continue to decide upon laws that will affect us for the rest of our lives – if they choose to do so, of course. There are the usual representative issues alongside this, including the fact that over half reside in London and the South East/East of England, and the average age is 70. It is hardly surprising that there is demand to reform an unelected, unrepresentative yet expensive institution. Coupled with the flaws in the first-past-the-post system and question marks around how representative the House of Commons is, the current system hardly seems the best we can hope for.

IT DOES NOT MATTER WHO YOU VOTE FOR, THE GOVERNMENT ALWAYS WINS

'Under capitalism, democracy is permitted as long as it doesn't fundamentally threaten the ruling class and their power – once that line is crossed, the democratic façade crumbles rapidly' (Daniel Finn, *Jacobin*)

As we saw when the business world, media barons (including the supposedly liberal outlets) and even his own party had to quash Jeremy Corbyn and his ideas of radically changing society to make it more equal.

2022 began with a perfect illustration of how our system is rigged entirely to protect those in power. While most people faced a cost-of-living crisis, we had a prime minister who genuinely believes that it is one rule for him and his associates, and another for everybody else. Despite his being unfit for office, the country was effectively paralysed while he refused to stand aside, and MPs deliberated on what was best for their party's fortunes and their own careers rather than the good of the country. We had the Met Police refusing to investigate the government's lockdown parties until civil servant Sue Gray found evidence of them – before then insisting that her evidence must be hidden from the public – despite themselves issuing more than 18,000 fines to 'ordinary' Brits for Covid breaches. A broken media well illustrated by the Deputy Editor of *The Sun* James Slack having one such party named

---

350 Peers can be seen on the UK Parliament website, under 'Lords membership'

in his honour. Not only did his own newspaper therefore refuse to break the story, but this episode revealed what has long been suspected – there is much that is withheld from the public, strategically disseminated to us when one faction of the ruling class decides it is in their interests to do so. At the same time, taxpayers were effectively funding Prince Andrew's legal defence against allegations of sexual abuse. Just one of these things warrants a debate about major constitutional reform, never mind every institution in our society simultaneously embroiled in scandal.

Even when governed by a party you did not vote for or are ideologically opposed to, there appeared to be some semblance of integrity to proceedings that no longer exists. The hostile treatment and deportation of black British citizens who had answered the call to come and help rebuild Britain after the war, the so-called Windrush generation, was a level of disregard for humanity not often seen within our own borders. Stripped of dignity, livelihoods, access to healthcare, and the landing cards that guaranteed their rights after they were destroyed by the Home Office in 2010, this is a scandal that should have shocked even the most ardent anti-immigration bod. Instead, the Tories were emboldened to strip a person's citizenship without notice, even retrospectively, via clause 9 of the Nationality and Borders Bill. Other crises, the likes of Grenfell and more, seemingly happened with some expectation that wrongs would be righted, but time elapsed and they simply were not. The Conservative Party renaming their twitter account to 'factcheckUK' in the run-up to the 2019 general election and spreading lies about the opposition would surely have been unthinkable in bygone years, or the leader of a party hiding in a fridge to avoid interview scrutiny mere weeks before an election sounds more like something you would watch on *The Thick of It*. The same leader who just a few weeks before that had unlawfully prorogued Parliament in a bid to – again – avoid scrutiny.

And yet that is 'Boris'[351]: playing up to this caricature of a bumbling comedic man-child who has never overtly cared about anything in his entire life. Indeed, while his shabby appearance might be half deliberate, his statements such as having an '*oven*-ready' deal with the EU, 'to pop into the *microwave*'[352] demonstrates that this is a man who has never had to even take care of himself,

351 Aptly named, to sound like a lovable, non-consequential Labrador rather than his actual (government) name Alexander de Pfeffel Johnson

352 *Daily Express*, 'Boris says his "oven-ready" Brexit deal ready to be "put in microwave" after election', 31 October 2019

let alone anyone else. There is little evidence that Boris has any actual ideology, beliefs or vision beyond himself in No. 10 Downing Street, evident in his effectively handing the reigns to chief advisor Dominic Cummings, another power-mad, unapologetic, and arrogant sociopath. What worse indictment can there be than his own brother Jo resigning from his position in the cabinet as Business Minister and quitting the party as then-MP for Orpington in protest to how unscrupulous antics became – including purging people willing to put personal values before political advantage and replacing them with 'yes' men and women. A cabinet of incompetent and ambitious people is not the kind you want in charge of Brexit negotiations or a pandemic, whatever your views on either. Yet, Boris was painted as an anti-establishment person whose buffoonery was a breath of fresh air from the usual dull politician, or somehow relatable.

There is much that is different about Johnson's Tory party from those that went before, reinforcing the idea that the Tories are pragmatic – they will say or do anything to achieve their aims, namely to sustain power and continue protecting the interests of the elites. On the subject of Brexit, all of the typical entities that the Tories represent – the likes of industry via the Confederation of British Industry and so forth – were not in favour of Brexit, and Brexit itself threatens the union among the UK countries, something else Conservatives have long stood for. As ever, the vast concessions made to ensure that they retain power will be paid for (financially and otherwise) by those outside of the wealthiest top percentiles. Collectively we seem to have forgotten the entire point of taxation and a welfare system: ensuring that everyone can live a decent life. People appear to be more supportive of a reduction in taxes and the size of the state, recognising that life will be made more unbearable for some, than they are to tackle the billions of pounds our governments waste and share among themselves. There is enough to go around: those with power in our society can legislate for a fairer and more equal existence; there just needs to be the appetite to do so. We have become a very accepting society – nothing shocks us, and if it does, it is quickly forgotten about. Perhaps much of this stems from an element of reluctant acquiescence, i.e. 'But what can I do about it?' The answer is quite a lot actually.

FOUR

THE MEDIA

'Nothing appears more surprising to those, who consider human affairs with a philosophical eye, than the easiness with which the many are governed by the few... [A]s FORCE is always on the side of the governed, the governors have nothing to support them but opinion' (David Hume, *Of the First Principles of Government*)

'The most potent weapon in the hands of the oppressor is the mind of the oppressed' (Steve Biko)

The composition of the British media has changed markedly over the last century. While the partisan nature of different media outlets is fairly well established, people historically had a greater range of opinions to choose from. The industrialisation of the press and associated high costs of production ameliorated much of the thriving alternative media, with those backed by wealthy individuals able to rapidly beat out the competition in terms of price and outreach. This led to the transfer of ownership and control of the media away from the working class (who typically faced closure, bowing to advertiser pressure and changing content, or targeting smaller audiences while maintaining manageable losses) to wealthy businessmen[353]. This is concerning because most of our news therefore comes from those with a particular set of interests, i.e. wealthy capitalists, bringing forth a number of consequences. To highlight that this has indeed been the case, it is worth looking at ownership of the most popular media outlets in Britain.

---

353 See Edwards and Cromwell (2006) *Guardians of Power: The Myth of the Liberal Media*, Pluto Press

WHO PROVIDES OUR NEWS?

After 42 years as the UK's 'most-read' paid-for newspaper, *The Sun* was reportedly overtaken by the *Daily Mail* in mid-2020. *The Metro*, a free newspaper, is the most circulated newspaper in the UK. Below are the major news outlets ordered by average daily circulation[354]. Alongside this we consider two important questions: who owns these outlets? And does it matter?

- **The Metro**: 1,326,213 papers (free newspaper): owned by the *Daily Mail* and General Trust PLC. Our friend from the Brexit discussion earlier, Jonathan Harmsworth, known formally as the Viscount Rothermere, is Chairman and controlling shareholder.
- **The Sun**: 1,210,915 papers: News Corp owner Australian media mogul Rupert Murdoch features in two 2018 *Forbes* lists: #68 richest person in the world, and #39 most powerful person in the world. Another tax-shy individual, based in New York, his portfolio boasts *Fox News*, *The Wall Street Journal* and a wealth of media outlets across the world. The Murdoch family were in charge during the *News of the World* phone-hacking scandal – discussion pending.
- **The Daily Mail**: 1,132,908 papers (owned by DMGT, as above).
- **The Sun on Sunday**: 1,013,777 papers (News Corp, as above).
- **The Mail on Sunday**: 952,914 papers (DMGT, as above).
- **(London) Evening Standard**: 700,191 papers (free newspaper): owned by Russian Alexander Lebedev, former KGB officer and ex-oligarch, with his son Evgeny Lebedev (recently handed a peerage by Boris Johnson).
- **The Sunday Times**: 647,622 papers: another pillar of Rupert Murdoch's media stranglehold, focusing on broadsheet readers.
- **Daily Mirror**: 442,610 papers: owned by Reach PLC (formerly Trinity Mirror), themselves embroiled in a decade of phone-hacking allegations and pay-outs to victims.
- **The Times**: 365,880 papers (Murdoch again).
- **Sunday Mirror**: 354,375 papers (Reach PLC).
- **Daily Express**: 289,393 papers (recently acquired by Reach PLC).
- **Daily Star**: 276,453 (also Reach PLC).
- **The Sunday Express**: 252,118 (Reach PLC again).

---

354 Figures of sales for 2 to 22 March 2020, as per Audit Bureau of Circulations, which represents the last month that *The Sun* and *The Times* submitted their figures to the ABC (for use of comparison)

- **i:** 215,640 papers (another of the Daily Mail and General Trust PLC portfolio).
- **Daily Star – Sunday:** 163,695 papers (Reach PLC).

Notable omissions from this list are the *Daily Telegraph*, which stopped submitting circulation figures after December 2019 (with an average circulation that month of 317,817, and the *Sunday Telegraph* 248,288) but enjoys a healthy online subscription from over 600k readers. The Telegraph Media Group presents another interesting ownership situation: billionaire identical twin brothers Sir David and Sir Frederick Barclay enjoy their business not being scrutinised (having sued the BBC[355], *The Times* and *Private Eye* among others). Indeed, their 'modest' abode is a castle on the private Channel Island Brecqhou – but they also boast a home in the tax haven Monaco. Latterly, the *Independent* became digital-only in 2016 and therefore does not record print circulation figures (itself also owned by Russian businessman Alexander Lebedev alongside the *Evening Standard*).

Evident from this is that there is effectively just a few proprietors, typically living offshore, with enormous control over our media: DMGT and News Corp control seven of the nine most circulated newspapers in the UK, with Reach PLC, Alexander Lebedev and Telegraph Media Group making up the rest of the entire top 17. In effect, just five outfits dictate the overwhelming majority of the information we are given, not given, and the way it is presented to us. This is problematic for reasons discussed below, but crucial in creating the illusion that we receive our news from a variety of sources and are thus able to make a balanced, informed opinion on the big issues affecting us. These are incredibly wealthy individuals who care so much about the British public they purport to represent, that they go to great lengths to deprive us of millions of pounds' worth of tax for our beleaguered public services. Questions abound regarding whether we can trust these people to give us honest news, not least as they have a vested political interest in protecting their wealth[356].

Take the *Express* papers, which until recently had been under the ownership of Richard Desmond since 2000 (another individual with a chequered history of tax evasion). This is the Conservative Party donor who personally donated £12k to the Tories two weeks after Housing Secretary Robert Jenrick rushed

---

355 The BBC ran a *Panorama* exposé titled 'The Tax Haven Twins', aired in 2012
356 A YouGov poll in 2015 revealed that 74% of the British public believe that, in order to own a UK newspaper, radio station, or TV channel, companies should be based in the UK and pay full UK tax. There is also high demand for controls on media ownership and influence on editorial output, but none of these things have been regulated by successive governments

through planning permission on his Westferry Printworks redevelopment scheme. Redacted emails show Jenrick's insistence that permission be granted the day before a change to the London Community Infrastructure Levy that would have seen Desmond's Northern and Shell company pay Tower Hamlets council an additional <£50 million, in a move Jenrick accepted was unlawful. This after the pair were seated together at a fundraising dinner event in the previous November, where Desmond played the Housing Secretary a promotional video of his planned development and text messages were exchanged afterwards[357]. According to the government's own borough profiles, Tower Hamlets is the tenth most deprived local authority in England, with the highest rates of both pensioner and child poverty in England[358]. Therefore, one could say that the council, whose Mayor John Biggs indicated has been starved of £190 million per year in funding since 2010 already, needed that money to improve the lives of the public residing there. Indeed, the government's own planning inspector advised against the scheme, citing the need for affordable housing in the area but was overruled by the Housing Secretary. True to form, PM Boris Johnson quickly released a statement proclaiming his unwavering support for the Housing Secretary, and that was the end of the matter. A clear signal if we did not have it already, that corruption – the use of public office for personal gain – is completely acceptable to our government.

Desmond appears to be flexible with his politics depending upon who is likely to be most useful at a given time. He donated £100k to the Labour Party around the time then Trade Secretary Stephen Byers approved his approach to buy the *Daily Express*. This the same Stephen Byers who regularly courted controversy, not least during the expenses scandal brought to light in 2009 and offering to pimp himself out to a fictitious company for money, resulting in a suspension from parliament[359]. Desmond then switched allegiances to the Tories before switching again, donating over £1 million to UKIP in 2015 – despite not being sure at the time whether leaving the EU was a good idea or not[360]. This was due, in large part, to a fall-out with the 'rude' David Cameron.

357 This is one of the rare occasions where media outlets unanimously covered the incident and information on the details of the story are very easy to find from most sources

358 All relevant information available on the Tower Hamlets Authority website: https://www.towerhamlets.gov.uk/lgnl/community_and_living/borough_statistics/Income_poverty_and_welfare.aspx

359 Video footage and information: *The Telegraph*, 'Stephen Byers: I'm like a cab for hire' 22 March 2010

360 *Financial Times*, 'Lunch with the FT: Richard Desmond', 12 June 2015

If there is one thing that can be said for the ex-pornographer, oft foul-mouthed and thrifty billionaire, it is that he too is fed up 'with the floppy-haired Eton club'[361] however, for different reasons than many of us – his rationale seemingly due to the Tories uncharacteristically refusing to grant him a peerage.

Again we are left with an issue of trust: the owners of the press rub shoulders with members of the government, donate to their parties, and receive favours in return. Can we trust the content they provide? You and I do not receive such favours; indeed, we are adversely affected time and time again by such corruption. And thus, the rich media barons ensure that the majority votes in favour of the few.

'IT'S THE SUN WOT WON IT'

Between 2011–2012 it appeared that Murdoch's pervasive influence on British politics might finally be curtailed, particularly when six members of a UK parliamentary committee declared Rupert Murdoch 'not a fit person to exercise the stewardship of a major international company'[362]. However, he was somewhat spared by friends among the Conservatives, with the four Tory representatives on the committee of ten (five Labour, one Lib Dem making up the six who voted contrarily) refusing to find him an unfit media proprietor. This committee met in direct response to the *News of the World*'s (effectively now *The Sun on Sunday*) forced closure, in the face of advertiser boycotts following the public outcry over its phone-hacking scandals. These surfaced in 2011 when it was revealed that *News of the World* (*NOTW*) reporters had hacked the phone of murdered 13-year-old schoolgirl Milly Dowler, victims of the 7 July 2005 London bombings, relatives of deceased British soldiers, and many others. During the ensuing Leveson Inquiry Murdoch admitted that there had been initial attempts to cover the scandal up, with a long list of morally questionable actions in the process. For example, the Commons Home Affairs Committee found the company (News Corporation at the time) had 'deliberately' blocked a Scotland Yard investigation into phone-hacking in 2005-06[363].

---

361 *The Guardian*, '*Daily Express* owner Richard Desmond hands Ukip £1m', 16 April 2015
362 House of Commons: Culture, Media and Sport Committee. 'News International and Phone-hacking' Eleventh Report of Session 2010–12
363 House of Commons Home Affairs Committee, 'Unauthorised tapping into or hacking of mobile communications' Thirteenth Report of Session 2010–12 (among others)

Equally disconcerting are the links between unscrupulous characters in the media and our government(s) and their agencies. As one illustration, Director of Communications for David Cameron's Tories Andy Coulson was a former editor of the *NOTW* (indeed, the phone hacking of Prince Harry and Prince William after Lady Diana's death prompted his resignation), who in the run-up to the election sought advice from Neil Wallis, former *NOTW* deputy editor (who later served just under five months in prison for conspiracy to intercept voicemails). This is the same Neil Wallis who was hired by the Met Police between October 2008 and September 2009. Meanwhile, David Cameron's chief of staff Ed Llewellyn turned down an offer by the Met Police for a briefing on investigations into phone-hacking on 20 September 2010.

This is a link that has precedence, with Larry Lamb who, as editor of *The Sun* for much of the 1970s, introduced the Page 3 feature (dramatically increasing its sales) and was a crucial source of support for Margaret Thatcher during the 1979 election. Indeed, so much so that he was knighted in the Queen's 1980 Birthday Honour's List on her recommendation. As strategies go to radicalise a nation it is quite brilliant: reel in working-class men with pictures of boobs and then bombard them with unflinching right-wing propaganda. When the right-wing think-tank Taxpayers' Alliance (a regular source of information in *The Sun*) denounced higher 'green' taxes for companies detrimentally affecting the environment, topless bombshell Keeley posed the question, 'Why should Britain pay over the odds when our energy usage is lower than other countries?'[364]. And it has worked wonders, with Rupert Murdoch effectively able to pick and choose who he wants elected as Prime Minister in every single general election since 1979:

- **1979 General election:** saw Margaret Thatcher to victory with a front page that stated 'A message to Labour supporters, vote Tory this time'.
- Continued support for Thatcher resulted in victories in both the **1983 and 1987 General elections.**
- **1992 General election:** After a relentless campaign to turn voters away from Labour leader Neil Kinnock, on the day of the election their front page ran with: 'If Kinnock wins today will the last person to leave Britain please turn out the lights'. The Liberal Democrat leader Paddy Ashdown

---

364 As cited in *Democracy for Sale: Dark Money and Dirty Politics* (2020) by Peter Geoghegan. A comprehensive overview of shady practice around the Brexit referendum abounds in this text

sustained a fair amount of flack that year too, including the infamous 'Paddy Pantsdown' headline after a reported affair. The following day, after helping John Major's Conservatives to an unexpected win, the now-immortalised headline: 'It's The Sun Wot Won It' bore the front page.

- **1997 General election:** 'The Sun backs Blair' adorned the papers in the run-up to a landslide 179-seat majority for New Labour.

- **2001 General election:** 'It's in the bag, Tony. You might as well call election now' was their unequivocal support for a second Labour term.

- **2005 General election:** Akin to the smoking chimney one sees when a new Pope is about to be introduced, 'Sun smoke goes RED for Blair' as Labour won for a third consecutive time.

- **2010 General election:** 'Labour's Lost It' was the proclamation, as allegiance switched back to the Tories – as did the nations with David Cameron's Conservatives able to form a coalition government with the Liberal Democrats. An interesting subplot here: former *NOTW* editor Andy Coulson (then-director of comms for David Cameron) and Rebekah Brooks (then-CEO of News International) spent a weekend at chancellor George Osborne's country residence in September 2010[365]. Just over a month later the Murdoch posse informed the European commission that they planned to take over BSkyB – one of the most important bids in broadcasting history with which the buck stopped at Osborne. Ken Clarke, appointed Cameron's Secretary of State for Justice after the election win, believes that a deal was struck between David Cameron and Murdoch (regarding BSkyB) in exchange for the switch in allegiance from Gordon Brown, Blair's successor.

- **2015 General election:** The famous image of Ed Miliband eating a bacon sandwich came with the caption 'This is the pig's ear Ed made of a helpless sarnie. In 48 hours he could be doing the same to Britain SAVE OUR BACON, Don't swallow his porkies and keep him OUT'. Media Standards Trust found that 95% of *The Sun*'s editorials in the run-up to this election were anti-Labour, most of which directly vilified the Labour leader[366]. *The Sun*-backed David Cameron won a second term, before resigning after his failed support of the EU 'remain' campaign.

---

365 *The Guardian*, 'George Osborne's secret meeting with Murdoch clan at country estate', 12 May 2012
366 Media Standards Trust, 'Election Unspun: Political parties, the press, and Twitter during the 2015 UK election campaign'

- It is impossible to pick one anti-Corbyn headline from *The Sun* across **the 2017 and 2019 General elections**, the first of which ushered in a Theresa May-DUP coalition, the latter a Tory majority with Boris Johnson. Just to offer a flavour of the content being put out, this is fairly tell-tale from June 2017: 'THE SUN SAYS: Don't chuck Britain in the Cor-bin – vote Tory unless you want a friend of terrorists who's ready to open our borders and hike up taxes as your next PM'.

Ironically, *The Sun* began life as the *Daily Herald*, an independent left-wing newspaper owned for a decade by the Trades Union Congress (TUC). How they must lament selling their remaining stake in 1964 given how much of a potent weapon it has proved in disadvantaging the labour movement since. *Dial M for Murdoch* offers a more detailed, personal, and sinister account of the steps taken to intimidate politicians by those employed under the Australian tycoon, including having Labour MP and vocal critic of Murdoch's corporation Tom Watson followed by 'surveillance expert' Derek Webb in the run-up to the 2010 general election. The ability of the most circulated newspapers in Britain to influence public opinion is testament of the almighty power of the media in this country. Let us take arguably the two most significant election results, whereby allegiances both by *The Sun* and the British people switched, first from Labour to Conservative (1979) and then back to Labour (1997).

MURDOCH'S 'DEAL' WITH MAGGIE

Both Rupert Murdoch and Margaret Thatcher had a great deal to offer each other in the early 1980s. Thatcher was very mindful of her perception in the public polls and wanted to boost this, not least due to the fact that she was attacking working-class rights and protections at the time. Murdoch's *The Sun* had the eyes of many working-class communities and thus he represented a useful ally. Meanwhile, Rupert wanted to add *The Times* and *The Sunday Times* to his portfolio of British newspapers, which presented a problem. Should he acquire the two broadsheets, he would thus control approx. 40% of the British press, which would not be accepted by the Monopolies and Mergers Commission. On 4 January 1981 the two met at the PM's Chequers retreat[367] and a deal was struck: in return for unwavering support for Thatcher

---

367 A fact denied in *The History of the Times: the Murdoch Years* (published by Murdoch's company HarperCollins), but confirmed in documents revealed by the Margaret Thatcher Archive

in his newspapers, Murdoch's bid for the sister *Times* papers was allowed to circumnavigate the Commission. In securing this pact, Murdoch committed to irreversibly damaging the lives of the very working classes who lined his pockets.

What better illustration of this fact than the 23 May 1984 'Mine Fuhrer' depiction of Arthur Scargill, leader of the National Union of Miners, as Hitler. Sanctioned for print by *The Sun*'s editor Kelvin MacKenzie as an attempt to paint the striking miners in a negative image, given that they were in direct opposition to Margaret Thatcher[368]. The National Union of Journalists (NUJ) members at the printers refused to publish this, partly out of solidarity but also knowing that if the miners lost their 'battle' then they could be next. The front page that then went to print contained the message: 'Members of all *The Sun* production chapels refused to handle the Arthur Scargill picture and major headline on our lead story. *The Sun* has decided, reluctantly, to print the paper without either.'

With the miners eventually defeated, the print workers indeed followed suit soon after, in the 'Wapping dispute'. News International (Murdoch's umbrella company that included the aforementioned four newspapers) decided to move operations to a new plant in Wapping, East London. As part of the negotiation, Murdoch demanded the unions accept flexible working, agree to a no-strike clause, adopt new technology, and abandon their closed shop, which the NUJ rejected. As talks collapsed and a strike was announced in January 1986, the 6,000 newspaper workers were immediately served dismissal notices. This incident is significant for the following reasons: firstly, it represented a united attack by Thatcher's Conservative government and the press against organised labour, with the police utilised against the workers. Amid violent battles police adopted heavy-handed tactics to ensure strike-breaking workers could get into the Wapping plant (and lorries carrying newspapers out) and lawyers were able to ensure the sacking of thousands of workers without legal repercussion. The workers were replaced by members of the Electrical, Electronic, Telecommunications and Plumbing Union (now part of Unite) which again was very controversial in an age of solidarity and sympathy strikes. What all of this meant was that production continued as normal, while the striking workers went a prolonged period of time without jobs and pay – meaning the

368 See Seamus Milne (2004) *The Enemy Within: Thatcher's Secret War Against the Miners*, Verso

collapse of the strike was inevitable. Across the year-long dispute, c400 police officers were injured and over 1,200 arrests made.

It was an enormous defeat for what had been a labour-intensive, unionised industry and meant that any threat to managerial prerogative (and worker security) could be 'got at' – in industries previously untouchable in that regard. The labour lost during a strike in other industries could be recovered in overtime, but one day's newspaper production would be lost forever, which had given the workforce a significant level of power in their employment relationships. With new technology, less labour, and less representation/ protection, Murdoch, with help from the government, had changed everything for journalists. This is a position that has not really changed: 'We beat strike thugs' was the headline at the end of the Wapping dispute (27 January 1986), and among an extensive list of recent examples, 'Sack the docs' during the junior doctors' strike (24 March 2016) offers a fairly representative flavour of *The Sun*'s regard for workers' rights and conditions. The feeling is mutual: Unite, Unison, GMB, PCS, and the BFAWU have all passed national motions to boycott the paper, as well as not allowing *The Sun*'s staff on their premises. *The Sun* has a new powerful friend, however. When campaign group Stop Funding Hate encouraged student unions to stop stocking the paper, Boris Johnson wrote for *The Sun* calling them 'Leftie activists trying to silence newspapers'[369].

We can gain a picture of who Rupert Murdoch is from his associates; for example, Andrew Neil (former presenter of *Politics Live* and *The Andrew Neil Show* on the BBC) worked as editor of *The Sunday Times* under Murdoch in the '80s and '90s and was appointed chairman of Sky TV (part of Murdoch's News Corporation): 'When you work for Rupert Murdoch you do not work for a company chairman or chief executive: you work for a Sun King. You are not a director or a manager or an editor: you are a courtier at the court of the Sun King – rewarded with money and status by a grateful king as long as you serve his purpose, dismissed outright or demoted to a remote corner of the empire when you have ceased to please him or outlived your usefulness'[370].

---

369 Our PM here using 'leftie', i.e. 'left-wing', as a dirty word. It is defined in the Cambridge dictionary as 'relating to the belief that wealth and power should be shared between all parts of society', and the *Encyclopaedia Britannica* as 'the portion of the political spectrum associated in general with egalitarianism'. Understandable why the elite would wish to tarnish those interested in greater equality

370 Andrew Neil (1996) *Full Disclosure*, MacMillan

During the Leveson Inquiry former *The Sun* and *Times* editors (David Yelland and Harold Evans) attested to the pervasive influence of the owner. Evans reported almost coming to 'fisticuffs' with Murdoch after allowing economist James Tobin to publish an article with views that differed to Rupert's. Andrew Neil clarified these views: 'Rupert expects his papers to stand broadly for what he believes: a combination of right-wing Republicanism from America mixed with undiluted Thatcherism from Britain' (*ibid*). It is pretty clear why he would shepherd the British public, most of whom whose interests simply are not served by the Tories, to vote for the party that he wants to see in power. Why then a shift to New Labour between 1997 and 2010?

MURDOCH'S 'INCESTUOUS' RELATIONSHIP WITH BLAIR

At the time Blair replaced Neil Kinnock as Labour Party leader, Murdoch's relations with John Major were becoming increasingly strained. During the Leveson Inquiry, Major revealed that Murdoch directly challenged him to switch his policies on the EU or risk losing the support of his papers[371]. Indeed, his Home Secretary Mr Howard was thought to be one of the infamous three Euro-sceptic 'bastards' TV microphones picked up from John Major off the record, whom *The Sun* backed as a potentially preferred PM. Unlike his predecessor Thatcher's close relationship, a file released in the National Archives reveals that Major instructed his cabinet to avoid a Murdoch soiree in September 1993, following a series of unflattering articles that appeared in *The Sun*. Major himself formally met with Rupert just three times during his seven-year tenure, much less than both Thatcher and the incumbent Labour PM Tony Blair.

Indicating the influence Murdoch had on British politics, relations between the two began when Blair courted Labour controversy by attending and addressing a Murdoch event in Australia 1995, in what he later described as a 'necessary evil' to avoid another Murdoch-fuelled electoral disaster as happened in 1992. In subsequent years the two men became such good friends that in 2010 Blair became godfather to Rupert's eight-year-old daughter Grace. Part of the basis for this relationship was one of mutual gain: indeed, during the 2012 Leveson Inquiry Blair contended that newspapers had become an instrument of political power, and courting the powerful press baron was the

---

371 For video, see 'Leveson Inquiry: John Major reveals Murdoch's EU demand', BBC 12 June 2012

difference between savage media attacks that would have made it difficult for him to govern. The relationship went further, with Blair conceding that former News International chief executive Rebekah Brooks had access to him whenever she wanted it, and such was their friendship that he even sent her a message of support during the phone-hacking scandal in 2011.

It is difficult to know exactly how much influence Murdoch was able to exert over government policy between 1997–2007. During the Leveson inquiry Blair pointed to examples where Labour did not bow to News International pressure, including boosting the role of Ofcom (the UK regulatory and competition authority for broadcasting), increasing the BBC licence fee, and their role in blocking BSkyB (of which Murdoch held a substantial share) from taking over Manchester United Football Club. Yet, a lot is left open to interpretation: in his written statement during the inquiry, Blair claims that his Labour Party 'more often than not' rejected the views expressed by the Murdoch media. His spoken address stated that he had decided to 'manage' rather than 'confront' the press. Various editors under Murdoch during Blair's reign as PM suggest that this managing of the media included lots of concessions on the part of the PM in exchange for unwavering support, creating unprecedented media influence on British politics[372]. What we can be sure of, is that New Labour saw the route to electoral success as being partly achieved by constructing policies that would be deemed acceptable to such wealthy news proprietors (and donors), in effect abandoning Labour's founding principles and ultimately losing in order to 'win'.

More recently, the Hacked Off Campaign[373] found that phone-hacking scandals, unnerving political influence, and being 89 years of age was no impediment to his continued influence in, and on, British politics. There were a whopping 206 meetings between Murdoch company staff and the government over the course of 2018–2019; including three personal meetings between Murdoch and Boris themselves during that period.

ANTI-CORBYNISM IN THE MEDIA

Building on the work of others, in *The New Working Class* Claire Ainsley argues that policies themselves will always be viewed within the frame of reference people view the party presenting said policy, i.e. the story and identity a party

---

372 *The Murdoch Dynasty*, BBC (aired July 2020)

373 Founded in 2011 to support victims of press abuse after the phone-hacking scandals emerged, and also to campaign for a free and accountable press. Report: https://hackinginquiry.org/unelected-insidious-influence-murdoch/

creates for itself is of great importance. It is plausible that this explains some aspects of Jeremy Corbyn's Labour Party, where in their own right each policy (free broadband for homes, abolishing university tuition fees, etc.) should have been, and probably in fact were, very popular. But because the Tories again wilfully aided by the media, have managed to position Labour as fiscally irresponsible and socialism in general the same, swathes of the population did not seem to buy into them as a collective set of policies through a notion that it was not financially possible to do so (without major borrowing and tax hikes)[374].

Despite a constant stream of deliberate lies, conjecture and bluster Boris got an incredibly easy time of it from his former employers and allies in the media – who were happy to point out that the 2019 election was characterised by a frenzy of disinformation but did not hold his party to account over it at all[375]. Meanwhile, it is very difficult to find any close comparison to the character assassination delivered on his opponent Jeremy Corbyn during his tenure as Labour Party leader. Research conducted at Loughborough University found that more than 70% of news items covering Labour were framed negatively, and that the Conservatives were the only party to receive more positive than negative stories across both the print and TV press[376]. As early as 2016, former chair of the BBC Trust (the body tasked with ensuring independent, quality output for licence-fee payers) Sir Michael Lyons commented on the 'quite extraordinary attacks on the elected leader… I can understand why people are worried about whether some of the most senior editorial voices in the BBC have lost their impartiality on this'[377]. Even the perceived liberal (albeit more closely aligned to 'New Labour') *Guardian* pulled no punches. For example, former Columnist of the Year Polly Toynbee began an article on 19 April 2017 with 'Was ever there a more crassly inept politician than Jeremy Corbyn?'.

The media were not taking any chances after the close-run 2017 general election where Corbyn came within 2,227 votes of being able to form a coalition

---

374 This problem is particularly acute given people's reliance on these outlets to base opinion on. For example, a poll conducted in January 2020 by the Irish online publication *The Journal* found that more people (27.8%) read news articles about political party policies than actually read the parties manifestos (24.6%). Similar research, e.g. in 2017 BMG Research, found that 67% of voters do not actually read party manifestos

375 See Peter Oborne (2021) *The Assault on Truth*, Simon & Schuster

376 Centre for Research in Communication and Culture, Loughborough University, 'General Election 2019 Report 1'

377 *The Guardian*, 'BBC may have shown bias against Corbyn, says former trust chair', 12 May 2016

government (e.g. key marginals such as Southampton Itchen saw their Tory MP win by just 31 votes). Indeed, writer and political activist George Monbiot tweeted 'The biggest losers today are the billionaires who own the *Mail, Sun, Times* and *Telegraph*. And thought they owned the nation'. As the Corbyn smears ramped up, newspaper headlines on 12 December 2019, the day of the general election, looked something like this:

> *'If Boris wins today, a bright future begins tomorrow… but if Red Jez gets in, the lights will go out for good'* (*The Sun*, invoking its 1992 Kinnock headline)[378]

> *'Your vote has never been more vital. Today, you MUST brave the deluge to go to your local polling station and back… BORIS'* (*Daily Mail*)[379]

Indeed, Britain's most-read newspaper offered its readers a tactical voting guide to keep the Tories in No. 10[380]. What of the other widely read news outlets?

> *'Vote Conservative Today: Brexit and Britain in your hands'* (*Daily Express*)

> *'The Tories are the only rational choice'* (*Daily Telegraph*)

> *'Tories face last-minute threat from Brexit Party'* (*The Times* with a more measured headline, but a story centred on Johnson's warnings of the 'terrifying prospect' of letting Jeremy Corbyn into No. 10 and the risk that votes for the Liberal Democrats could 'hinder the Tories')

The *Independent* was not drawn into decisively backing any candidate, *The Guardian* erred towards Jeremy Corbyn (after a sustained attack on him throughout the pre-election period), with just the *Daily Mirror* actively instructing its readers to vote for Labour. This offers a partial picture of what

---

378 Former MP and Ed Miliband adviser John Prescott tweeted that Rupert Murdoch stormed out of *The Times'* election party after seeing the 2017 exit polls, in which the Tories lost their majority

379 I have focused enough here on Murdoch, and consequently *The Sun*. For a change of pace, Britain's highest selling newspaper was not taking any chances with those who do not buy the paper, providing a scathing attack on the Labour leader online: https://www.dailymail.co.uk/debate/article-7782995/DAILY-MAIL-COMMENT-Boris-Johnson-choice-Briton-bit.html

380 'Revealed: The 100 seats where tactical votes could win it for Boris and Brexit', *Daily Mail*, 7 December 2019

was a very clear steer by the media with regards to who voters should opt for in the election. But this was simply the cherry on top of what had been an annihilation of one man's character and reputation for a number of years.

This is very deliberate. YouGov polls demonstrate that many voters will not even give a party or their policies a 'fair' hearing if they do not take the leader as a serious potential PM[381]. For those who are hard-pressed for time (as many of us are) and thus do not have scope to forensically examine the voting history of those around a party's leadership, manifestos, and so on, party leaders offer a barometer, i.e. are thought of as embodying many of the ideals of said party. In other words, it is convenient and relatively logical to form a view of who is preferable between two (or more) party leaders and use this as the basis for a decision regarding who to vote for. If much of your information comes from the news then it is pretty clear why so many people did not envisage Jeremy Corbyn as an appropriate leader. Among the highlights included this from *The Sun*: 'Is THIS the most dangerous chicken in Britain?', complete with Corbyn's head imposed on a chicken's body. On exactly the same day, reporting on exactly the same story, where the Labour Party were delaying the opportunity to hold a general election in 2019, the *Scottish Sun* (*The Sun*'s sister paper north of the border, run by exactly the same Murdoch corporation) went with the first page 'Floppy Johnson can't get an election'. This is commonplace with very little attempt to hide the prejudices of its owner; backing the SNP as Labour's main rival party in Scotland, as part of a multi-faceted attempt to keep the Tories in No. 10 Downing Street.

One has to wonder what reasons there could be for such an unprecedented smear campaign across all media outlets and genuine plea for the public not to vote for an individual. One particular headline that sticks with me is 'Corbyn's plan to kill British soldiers' ran by *The Sun*. This is a man who not only voted against the Iraq war but also has stated his belief that Blair should stand trial for war crimes and was lambasted for refusing to commit to nuclear genocide in the run-up to the 2019 election. The fact that a lifelong anti-war pacifist can be painted out as devising strategies to have British soldiers killed shows how deeply the media wishes to interject in politics. The most widely circulated newspaper, the *Daily Mail*, typifies the spin that we are given on news stories. In the March 2020 *Private Eye* they point to an editorial published the day after Labour's 2019 general election manifesto which led with the headline 'Corbyn's

---

Blueprint to Bankrupt Britain' with such eye-catching quotes as 'Jeremy Corbyn would spray your money around like a drunk at the races'. A year later in the same paper, one day after Rishi Sunak announced the Conservative budget would increase public spending by £175 billion and take the national debt above £2 trillion for the first time ever, their headline reads 'Dr Feelgood to the Rescue: Biggest Budget splurge in 30 years to boost Britain'.

In terms of rationale, there has already been mention of the tax evasion rife among those controlling our media. So it is a fairly safe conclusion to assume that they would not like a politician breaking the mould of bowing to their wishes in return for favourable press coverage and threatening action on tax evasion. Only one has been brave (/daft?) enough to try, and the evidence presented above serves to demonstrate that this was not well received. Jeremy Corbyn released a video via his personal Twitter account publicly calling out said tax-evading media barons and issued a warning that 'change is coming'[382]. Naturally the crushing defeat in the 2019 general election means that he will not be leading said change from the front, nor will the Tories. They benefit enormously from the tirade of pro-Conservative, anti-Labour content that passes for 'news' and will not be looking to change this scenario, thus the situation will remain the same – with hugely negative consequences for the public.

This is not a futile, after-the-fact plea for anyone who disliked Corbyn to concede that he had unfair treatment in the media. This is merely an illustration of how far removed we are from neutral, objective, quality journalism, that the main opposition leader and party can be obliterated and the public directly instructed to vote another way by self-interested billionaires. We should be terrified that as soon as we get a politician who wants to challenge the establishment and promised real change, the establishment media colludes into a group of hysterical liars, thwarting any possible ascendency to power. It is a complete undermining of democracy that this happens, and is allowed to happen, as a government who benefits from not regulating the press properly sustains this arrangement.

ANTI-WORKING CLASS?

In posing the above questions we are simultaneously asking ourselves what possible reason the billionaires who own our media have for deliberately targeting working-class readers, and doing their utmost to sway them towards

---

382 https://twitter.com/jeremycorbyn/status/966013570273234944?lang=en

the Conservative Party when this is a party that does not objectively serve most people's interests. The motivation is actually very simple. The Tory track record is lower taxes for the rich, and little to no regulation on the media or workers' rights. As a result, our multi-billionaire news corporations save a hell of a lot of money by keeping political parties out who are likely to tax them more and improve their workers' terms and conditions (subsequently increasing their costs and obligations). Because voting for the Conservative Party is completely against the interests of the working class, the elites have to find ways of encouraging them to do so. The barrage of headlines offered to illustrate that this actually goes way beyond encouragement to complete defamation of the Labour Party and its top brass, with literal instructions on who to vote for, should dispel any myth of neutrality.

A cursory search of *The Sun* articles that cite the terms 'working class' and 'labour' reveals an incessant tirade of claims, such as 'Why the Tories are now the party of the working class' (10 December 2019) written by Sascha O'Sullivan. According to her LinkedIn profile and other discernible internet sources, Sascha appears to have arrived from Australia a few years ago. She was recruited from Murdoch's conservative broadsheet newspaper *The Australian*, has settled in London, and is therefore clearly well placed to speak on behalf of the British working-class. Phillip Blond offered this catchy headline 'Corbyn turned the working classes blue by being an anti-military, terrorist-sympathising, Islington snob' in *The Sun* on the eve of the 2019 general election[383]. Phillip, former university lecturer in theology whose admiration for David Cameron was reciprocated with input into the former Tory prime minister's speeches, is a self-proclaimed 'Red Tory' who created what is described as a progressive conservative think-tank. Just as one final example of these questionable sources used by *The Sun* to speak for the working class, Tom Newton Dunn led his 11 May 2017 article about Jeremy Corbyn with 'WORKING CLASS ZERO'. An interesting fact about political editor Tom Newton Dunn is that in December 2019 he posted an article titled 'HIJACKED LABOUR' claiming that a 'hard-left extremist network' was operating at the centre of the Labour Party. Among the sources he used to inform

---

383 Lest we forget, the 1996 Scott Report revealed that Thatcher's government supplied arms to Saddam Hussein, provided training and weapons to Afghan terrorists associated with both the Taliban and al-Qaeda, sent the SAS to train troops fighting alongside the Khmer Rouge, was responsible for up to 2 million deaths in Cambodia, and Thatcher referred to brutal dictator General Pinochet – a man who oversaw the torture, internment, and execution of tens of thousands of Chileans – as a 'true friend'

this assertion were various fascist, anti-Semitic websites such as 'Aryan Unity'[384], and the article was deleted that same day. The irony of accusing others of extremist views based on extremist views evidently not lost on *The Sun* bigwigs.

The Sun also regularly runs negative news stories about trade unions, which remain the most representative, democratic workers structure in our country. There is a bottomless pit of examples, but this from December 2018 is about as anti-union and anti-worker as can be: 'THE CORBYN UK Labour plot to tear up trade union laws and plunge Britain back into a 1970s-style strike chaos'. The UK has the most stringent and thus repressive anti-strike laws in Western Europe thanks to the 2016 Trade Union Act, despite being a relatively de-regulated labour market. How could anyone purporting to represent the working-class attempt to drum up criticism and apathy towards the most effective vehicle workers have for improving their terms and conditions? Former *Daily Express* journalist James O'Brien reflected live on his LBC radio show that his old colleagues had to publish anti-union stories at the will of their billionaire boss, from whom only their trade union membership offers them a veil of protection[385]. Earlier that year *Express* staff, then working for Richard Desmond, wrote to their local MPs appealing for their eighth year without a pay rise to be raised in parliament, amid his refusal to co-operate over collective bargaining. This changed little, as *Express* staff (who, according to the National Union of Journalists, dubbed Desmond 'Britain's greediest billionaire' in 2014) continued to run anti-Corbyn and anti-trade union stories. A month before the 2019 election was announced we were treated to such headlines as 'Corbyn plot to hold Britain to ransom in vice-like grip of union baron friends – exposed' (14 September 2019) and 'Jeremy Corbyn would turn Britain into a basket case like Zimbabwe' (18 September 2019). There are similar attacks on the most vulnerable, notably welfare recipients as part of the divide-and-conquer approach colluded by politicians on 'the right' and the media barons. In fact, given that a substantial proportion of journalists are privately educated university graduates who must be very competent purveyors of the English language, it must take a fair degree of skill to write such tosh. The language and framing of said articles tend to be

---

384 For worrying signs of increased reliance on right-wing conspiracy theories/questionable sources see Daniel Trilling's opinion piece, 'Why did the Sun publish a far-right conspiracy theory?' *The Guardian*, 9 December 2019

385 See video: https://www.lbc.co.uk/radio/presenters/james-obrien/james-obrien-link-southern-strike-daily-express/

delivered in a way that can only be described as a patronising depiction of what they consider to be working-class 'speak'.

Government commissioned research in November 2016 found that just 11% of journalists are from working-class backgrounds[386]. More recent evidence suggests that 44% of our most influential newspaper columnists attended Oxbridge universities (as opposed to <1% of the general population), and exactly the same proportion attended fee-paying schools (in contrast to 7% of the general population)[387]. There is thus a significant lack of representation between those who provide us with our information, and those they are professing to represent. It is difficult to see how this situation will change without proactive intervention: only those from 'well-off' families can afford expensive journalism master's degrees and then survive during unpaid internships, and are more likely to have the all-important industry contacts to land any meaningful job. If these highly educated individuals were using said advantages to offer the public quality, objective journalism then there would be no issue at all. But given the nature of the headlines presented in this chapter, we are seeing an agenda being pushed, and not from, or for, the people at large. Indeed, if almost half of our journalists are from similar backgrounds, it is highly likely that the perspectives and insights of swathes of society will be missed completely. This is unlikely to improve as the media sector, much like all others, has seen a trend towards increasing casualisation and precarious contracts. These ideas are picked up below.

THE PRETENCE OF OBJECTIVE NEWS

There are other reasons why our media is not providing the kind of service we need to be able to understand the world we live in and be in a position to make informed decisions, political or otherwise, that go beyond the motives of the billionaire owners who oversee the type of content our media produces. Here are but two:

---

386 Social Mobility Commission (2016) 'State of the Nation 2016: Social Mobility in Great Britain' report
387 The Sutton Trust (2019) 'Elitist Britain 2019' report. Similarly, around 94% of journalists are white (NCTJ, 2017 'Diversity in Journalism') with such statistics possibly a contributing factor to a lack of reporting over issues like cladding pre the Grenfell Tower tragedy, and stereotyped portrayals of minority ethnic groups in the press

ATTRACTING AND APPEASING ADVERTISERS

Media companies are businesses and are thus driven by profit. They exist to make money and resultantly creating revenue streams is their priority, which comes before acting as watchdogs for the public, unearthing scandals and defending ordinary people from abuses of power, including holding governments to account. Much of their revenue derives from advertising, and for those who have not introduced a pay-wall to view their articles online or via an app – for example, *The Guardian* and the *Independent* – advertisements account for as much as 75–80% of their intake. Naturally, attracting and appeasing advertisers is therefore one, if not the, main driver of their activity. This obviously creates conflicts of interest, as papers are not going to print stories that bring their main source of income into disrepute, or espouse values that go against those of their funding partners. This was highlighted in 2015 when Peter Oborne resigned from his position as chief political commentator of *The Daily Telegraph* as the newspaper suppressed negative stories about its chief advertisers, notably HSBC[388]. One can only imagine what is omitted in the press given the possible effects of challenging corporate capitalism, notably its destruction of the planet.

NOTIONS OF PROFESSIONAL JOURNALISM

'Professional' journalism is a relatively new concept and gained much traction around the time big corporations took control of the media. The logic is simple: portray your journalists as neutral and unbiased, and as having received formal journalistic education and training. The next step is to claim that these trained professionals operate with autonomy and artistic licence to 'tell it like it is' and you are well on your way to presenting a neutral service to the public. Furthermore, by positioning their sources as legitimate, i.e. 'official' members of the political and business community, this air of objectivity is reinforced. The are many problems with this, not least the fact that politicians and business leaders are concerned about positive PR, thus inclined to misrepresent, misinform, and mythologise. This problem is further exacerbated by the fact that around 60% of the content produced by such outlets as *The Times*, *Guardian*, *Independent*, *Telegraph*, and *Daily Mail* were word-for-word reprints of press releases or came from wire copy providers

---

388 Peter Oborne wrote an open letter about advertising affecting which stories were published, and how, on OpenDemocracy: https://www.opendemocracy.net/en/opendemocracyuk/why-i-have-resigned-from-telegraph/

(such as Reuters and Associated Press), further reducing the actual sources we acquire news from[389]. Equally disconcerting, the same study found that the accuracy of stories was only checked 30% of the time.

This is a situation that is only worsening in an age of digital media, where the desire to be the first to break a story is not conducive to fact-checking or the type of rigour and ethics one would hope of journalists. Dominic Cummings is the master of this dark art: take for example the BBC article proclaiming that new PM Boris Johnson was boosting school coffers with £7.1 billion. The Tories paid substantial sums for Facebook ads targeting millions of British users, one of which promoted the BBC headline but with a doctored figure of £14 billion – that was removed two weeks later amid criticism but the 'damage' of misinformation had already been done[390]. His VoteLeave campaign similarly spread lies about immigration and the financial benefits of leaving the EU to millions of Facebook users, unlawfully breaking campaign expense limits in the process.

During the 2019 general election campaign the Tories continued their shockingly brazen dishonest campaigning. As noted earlier, this included changing their official Twitter account to 'factcheckUK' and tweeting out yet more lies during a live television debate. Less than 24 hours later they had paid Google to put a website – labourmanifesto.co.uk – complete with Jeremy Corbyn's picture and the heading 'Labour's 2019 manifesto', at the top of its search engine results for unsuspecting voters attempting to educate themselves on the opposition's pledges. Naturally having no plan for Brexit was part of the website's purported manifesto. This was not long in the wake of their doctored video of then-Shadow Brexit Secretary Keir Starmer, to make it look like he had stuttered on the key leave/remain question when in fact he had not.

In an age of 'quick' news we see think-tanks and the like presented as expert opinion without critical engagement with who these organisations are. There are too many examples to mention, but consider the think-tank Policy Exchange which influences much of Boris Johnson's undertakings. Describing itself as a neutral education charity, it was set up by two actual and one future Conservative MP (Francis Maude, Archie Norman, and Nick Boles), with Michael Gove as its first chairman. Not only has Policy Exchange been instrumental in attempting to undermine and ultimately reduce the power of potential 'challengers' to the government (the judiciary, civil service,

389 Prof. Justin Lewis and Cardiff University colleagues (2008) 'The Quality and Independence of British Journalism: Tracking the changes over 20 years'
390 BBC News, 'Facebook removes altered Conservative advertisement', 14 September 2019

broadcasters, civil service, local government) but it lobbies in the way you would expect[391]. For example, in 2019 it labelled Extinction Rebellion personnel as dangerous extremists – widely covered by the media in typical fashion – but *Vice* identified big energy among its funders (E.ON, Cadent, Energy UK, and Drax), although a lack of transparency hides this fact pretty well. We also have organisations in the world like American Majority whose purpose is to skew public opinion via likes/dislikes and ratings which helps to elevate certain issues and create conservative 'impressions' of them.

Given the distinct lack of diversity among journos and the oft-precarious nature of their employment, there is conformity to these notions of professionalism desired by employers. The BBC's Mark Mardell describes journalists considered more liberal to 'crave the ideologically soft centre' given their own life situations, i.e. not being on minimum wage or relying on tax credits, yet equally unlikely to own big corporations or homes in the Cayman Islands, which amounts to 'group-think in the muddled middle, a fear of thinking outside a comfortable box'[392]. This is why, despite democratic socialism attracting more than 40% and 30% of the 'popular' vote in the 2017 and 2019 general elections respectively, it has never had a fair hearing. This comfortable box becomes an echo chamber, as broadcasters often 'round up' and discuss what the biased printed press says, with a narrow group of favoured commentators repeatedly invited for discussion.

And yet the more liberal journalists know this but are incentivised to pick their battles. For example, you are more likely to see attention drawn to the lack of recruitment of ethnic minority individuals and/or people from poorer backgrounds (albeit not nearly enough) than you are questions of the elite ownership, for obvious reasons. Journalists are unlikely to commit career suicide by criticising actual or potential employers, so even those who begin a career in journalism to 'expose the truth', are likely to dilute their aspirations and become co-opted into the system. One only has to look at New Labour's campaign against the BBC – who opposed the Iraq War on the basis that there was no evidence Saddam Hussein had weapons of mass destruction[393] – with

---

391 *The Guardian*, 'No 10 and the secretly funded lobby groups intent on undermining democracy', 1 September 2020
392 BBC News, 'Labour leadership: Beware the muddled middle', 30 July 2015
393 Saddam Hussein had actually destroyed and halted his WMD programme previously, at the instruction of UN weapons inspectors. There was also no evidence, then or now, that Iraq played any part in the 9/11 terrorist attack. But air strikes that kill the innocent indiscriminately are easier to justify with misinformation from the media

chairman Gavyn Davies, director general Grey Dyke and reporter Andrew Gilligan all forced out. The rest of the media were largely supportive of the war effort, as they were when Cameron backed an intervention in Libya nearly a decade later, again despite there being no evidence that Colonel Gaddafi was poised to commit genocide on his own people. Coincidentally, both countries possessed some of the biggest oil reserves outside of Saudi Arabia. What state were Libya left in? According to the United Nation's measure of country advancement, the index of human development, Libya fell from 53rd in 2010 to 94th by the end of the intervention in 2015. Where were the dissenting voices when British troops and innocent civilians were dying?

Indeed, we might have the illusion of some semblance of dissidence from the likes of *The Guardian* and *Independent*, but they do not – in large part – fundamentally challenge the elite. The recent peerage given to the owner of the *Independent* by Boris suggests one of two things: appreciation that any criticism of his government is kept relatively light, or a gesture of goodwill between future allies. If the coverage of Corbyn's campaign taught us anything, it is that these people subscribe to some vague, centrist notion of civility. In the end, they do nothing more than to uphold the liberal wing of the establishment, unwilling to see real societal change as they have it relatively comfortably as things are. As such, the media does not perform the basic tasks we would expect as a society. In *The Assault on Truth* Peter Oborne, who has kept track of political lies told, writes, 'I have never encountered a senior British politician who lies and fabricates so regularly, so shamelessly, and so systematically as Boris Johnson'.

THE BBC

Our national treasure the BBC has long been lauded as independent and a source of non-biased news upholding a semblance of real journalism in an age of corporate media. Interestingly, suggestions that there is a left-wing or liberal bias has taken on new life recently, cumulating in a letter sent to Tim Davie, Director-General of the BBC, in August 2020, by West Dorset MP Chris Loder and 13 of his fellow Conservative MPs calling for changes[394]. This followed the attempted coercion of party leader Boris Johnson, who has dangled the threat

---

394 'Changes needed at the BBC', https://www.chrisloder.co.uk/bbcletter

of the licence fee – the chief source of income for the BBC – being scrapped once its guaranteed period (up to 2027) has been reached. Even if this does not happen, it is a clear ploy to begin constraining the Beeb's funding with negotiations over how much the BBC can charge for the licence fee due in 2022. One is still left with the question, how likely then are BBC reporters to provide appropriately uninfluenced news offerings about the people who can effectively dissolve them as an institution?

It would seem that holding the government to account is no longer acceptable, even where criticism is very much in the national interest. No more did this become apparent than when friends in the media (e.g. *The Telegraph*) were given the honour of announcing pandemic lockdowns before the government itself, and others – e.g. *Channel 4 News*, *The Daily Mirror* and more – banned from press briefings and from speaking to government ministers as they were considered 'too critical'[395]. Indeed, in September 2020 the Council of Europe – set up in 1949 under the Treaty of London to monitor human rights, democracy, and the rule of law – issued the government with a formal warning relating to media freedom after it blacklisted *Declassified UK*, the investigative journalism website on UK foreign policy.

By and large there are many examples that illustrate the BBC's criticism does not really go far enough. There are clear reasons for this, going beyond its chief source of funding, the licence fee, being determined by government. The BBCs constitution, the Royal Charter, is subject to review by the Secretary of the State – Priti Patel at time of writing. Those in senior positions are technically appointed by the crown but very much on the advice of the Prime Minister and government advisors. The most recent (February 2021) was Richard Sharp to the position of BBC Chair. A cursory search of the electoral commission shows that Richard has donated nearly half a million pounds to the Tory party, presided on the board of the Thatcherite think-tank Centre for Policy Studies (alongside the likes of JCB Chairman Lord Bamford and Viscountess Rothermere) and was a City banker (largely at Goldman Sachs, some of which was spent as Chancellor Rishi Sunak's boss) with no experience of journalism.

Non-executive director Sir Robbie Gibb, formerly an advisor to Theresa May's Conservative government, attempted to block *HuffPost UK* editor

---

395 Unsurprisingly, the government is attempting to privatise Channel 4, by as soon as 2024 according to Culture Secretary Oliver Dowden. This in a bid to install a favourable new ownership following the commitment of Director of Programmes Ian Katz to 'asking the most difficult questions' and 'making space for the arguments and issues that others won't'

Jess Brammar's appointment as BBC executive news editor – citing that it would damage the government's already fragile trust in the BBC[396]. In other words, appoint someone who will act as a cheerleader for those in power. As is often the case, Jess was targeted by a huge smear campaign by the rest of the mainstream media, prompting the Policy Editor of BBC *Newsnight* Lewis Goodall to condemn what he described as 'misogynist attacks' in the *Daily Mail* via his Twitter account. Lewis later removed the tweet at the behest of BBC management, who apparently do not support journalism that is not in keeping with their particular ideology. For context, the aforementioned Director-General Tim Davie was previously the deputy chairman of the Hammersmith and Fulham Conservative party and stood as a councillor for the Conservative Party in Hammersmith in 1993 and 1994. Additionally, integral bodies to impartiality and integrity such as the BBC Trust (now defunct) were populated by what were essentially political appointees despite their masquerading as independent and non-partisan. Such individuals, also overwhelmingly from the privileged, 'establishment' classes, determined the management and output (for example, were bestowed with the power to allocate resources to certain programmes and not others), and thus, what did not make it onto our screens very often.

Mentioned above was the fallout between New Labour and BBC Chairman Gavyn Davies and Director-General Grey Dyke over the Iraq invasion. Both men had been donors to the Labour Party, with Davies not only a member of the party until 2001 but his children were bridesmaid and page boy at Gordon Brown's wedding. With such levels of cronyism it is unsurprising that feuds between governments and those they select for top broadcasting jobs are few and far between. The revolving door between politicians, press barons and our taxpayer-funded broadcaster is an active one, perhaps well illustrated by Michael Gove, whose trajectory took him from BBC news reporter, to a journalist at Rupert Murdoch's *Times*, to a potential Conservative Party leader. Allegra Stratton – forced to resign after rehearsing how to lie to the public about government parties during lockdown – moved from the BBC to ITV News as National Editor, and then to Director of Strategic Communications for Chancellor Rishi Sunak before becoming the Tory press secretary in 2020. Sunak was best man at her wedding to the political editor of *The Spectator*,

396 *Independent*, 'BBC urged to sack director with links to No 10 who 'tried to block editorial appointment on political grounds', 10 July 2021

James Forsyth, demonstrating the closed shop operated by influential media and government. James Slack switched from the *Daily Mail* to the Tories' official spokesperson and latterly Boris Johnson's Director of Communications, before returning to the right-wing press as deputy editor of *The Sun*.

This extends to the top jobs at the Beeb, including recent head of BBC News (2013–18) James Harding, who had also worked under Murdoch at *The Times*. That personnel will move from the media to the BBC does make sense in some respects, if they are clearly good at what they do and their news output is award-winning. But given the state of the British press, are these the people we want managing the service we should most expect good journalism from? Are we going to get significantly different output than what they are accustomed to providing for their former bosses? Should we not be worried about the close links between government and what is meant to be the sole non-partisan news outlet?

BBC top brass also have links to corporations in other sectors. Consider the Health and Social Care Act 2012, outlined in the previous chapter, with very little debate or critical coverage of this pre- or post-introduction from the Beeb. One only needs to take a closer look at the main figures at the time: Dr Mike Lynch OBE, then of the BBC's executive board, was a non-executive director of Isabel Healthcare Ltd.; on the advisory board of Apax Partners, investors in healthcare; and Director of Autonomy PLC, whose customers include healthcare and pharma companies. His colleague, former Tory MP and then-chairman of the BBC Trust, Lord Patten of Barnes[397], was (and still is) advisor to Bridgepoint, a private equity firm that had been involved in 17 healthcare deals, including the procurement of Care UK[398]. These are hardly the types of resumes we would hope our guardians of impartial reporting possess during a time of controversial NHS reforms. Perhaps indifference also played a part given that senior BBC staff themselves do not depend upon the NHS like most of the public do. A freedom of information request by campaign group Taxpayers' Alliance[399] revealed that

---

397 Incidentally, Thatcher's Secretary of State for the Environment, responsible for the poll tax, which the BBC described as her 'biggest political misjudgement', bringing her career 'to an ignominious end' two years after he departed

398 You may recall, Tory donor and education minister John Nash had been chairman of this company

399 Despite its claims to be a non-partisan think-tank and lobbying group, it was set up by Matthew Elliot (CEO of Vote Leave) which has been embroiled in a number of Brexit-related scandals, but also packed with right-wing individuals seeking tax cuts and reduced public spending, including a privatised health service

the BBC spent over £2 million of public money on private healthcare for senior Beeb staff between 2008–2010[400]. Not something you will hear much about as the media instead targets their favourite scapegoats, immigrants, with so-called 'health tourism' actually estimated at a mere 0.3% of NHS spending[401].

Ultimately, the BBC is not independent as is often propagated: and the political influence on it has been apparent since its inception. As with other national institutions, Thatcher made clear moves to shape the Beeb in ways that were fitting of her government and ideology. Rifts between the Board of Management and Board of Governors emerged as the latter, politically appointed and powerful body took issue with some of the programmes, as did the home secretary Leon Brittan. In particular, Maggie was unhappy with BBC coverage of the Falklands War, the miners' strike and a *Panorama* broadcast in 1984 titled 'Maggie's Militant Tendency', which asserted that members of the far-right had infiltrated the Tory party. What followed was the forced resignation of Director-General Alasdair Milne, considered too left-wing by Thatcher, who was replaced by an accountant Michael Checkland and latterly John Birt – men trusted by the right-wing governors to ensure coverage befitting a drive towards neoliberalism. Those in defence of Birt suggest that he saved the BBC from being privatised, but the price paid was to implement private-sector managerial practices and the dumbing-down of content such that any form of critique, and holding of those with power to account, became impotent and infrequent.

It certainly does produce shows that offer critical commentary (the likes of *Panorama*) and will criticise the government across its various programmes, but it is given enough independence as is seen 'strategically expedient from the perspective of the government'[402]. In other words, there is a degree of self-policing to maintain its status as quasi-independent, as those in charge at the BBC know that should they push the boundaries too far they may become at risk to greater commandeering from the government, or have its chief supply of funding pulled. Notions of a supposed left-wing bias typically relate to liberal attitudes towards sexuality and race relations, but fundamentally there is a subscription to neo-liberalism and the status quo

---

400 Taxpayers' Alliance, 'BBC and S4C spend millions on private healthcare', 27 May 2011
401 Full Fact, 'Health tourism: what's the cost?', 21 December 2016
402 For a comprehensive overview of the BBC's history, including its transition away from a more radical source of journalism in the '60s and '70s, see *The BBC: Myth of a Public Service* by Tom Mills

with the economic system, capitalism, and so forth not critically engaged with at all. For example, decades-long research found that the BBC fell well short of its legal commitment to impartiality, truth, and accuracy when reporting on Hugo Chavez's presidency in Venezuela[403]. Little to no mention of the successes of renationalisation, the enormous reduction in poverty, or the greatest literacy programme ever seen on this planet (from which over 1 million illiterate Venezuelans learnt to read and write within one year of its commencement).

To be clear, this is not an automatic call for arms to dismantle the BBC completely, as any replacement would be subject to the same agendas of billionaire ownership and advertisers as a source of finance. But we should expect a much better service from the BBC – after all, our taxes do fund it, meaning that we are effectively shareholders whose interests it should serve. According to statistics, BBC News also dwarfes all other media outlets as an online source of information (45% of news accessed, with *The Guardian* second at 18%, the *Daily Mail* 15%, and Sky News 10%)[404]. Our old friend Peter Oborne reports that senior BBC executives think that it is wrong to expose lies told by a British prime minister because it undermines trust in British politics. This hardly seems like a sufficient reason for giving Johnson free rein to make any false claim he wants, and this memo clearly did not get through when it came to Jeremy Corbyn. As testament to this, former political editor of the BBC (and president of the Oxford University Conservative Association during his time as a student) Nick Robinson reported being 'shocked' by the BBC's treatment of Corbyn, writing to several BBC colleagues concerning bias in their political coverage in 2015[405]. This seemingly fell on deaf ears as the negative coverage continued. Other people will perhaps take the view that all politicians lie and just shrug their shoulders, but it is not true that all politicians lie. Treating all politicians as liars gives a licence for the total collapse of integrity of British politics, a collapse that habitual liars such as Johnson are delighted to exploit.

---

403 Lee Salter and David Weltman (2011) 'Class, nationalism and news: The BBC's reporting of Hugo Chavez and the Bolivarian revolution'. *International Journal of Media and Cultural Politics*, Vol. 7, Issue 3, pgs. 253–273

404 Statista, 'Leading online news brands accessed in the United Kingdom (UK) as of February 2020'

405 *The Spectator*, 'Nick Robinson tackles anti-Corbyn bias at the BBC', 16 November 2015

AN OPEN AND FREE DEMOCRACY

'The further a society drifts from the truth, the more it will hate those who speak it' (George Orwell)

The media have an enormous part to play in constructing our reality. It is true that words are attached to things in arbitrary fashion: for instance, the word 'tree' only represents what we know 'tree' to denote because enough people within a given society have accepted the meaning of this word (whereas to a dendrologist the tree is likely to have a different label). Thus, words can be rendered meaningless and subject to change – consider how identity politics reclaims certain terms and highlights the unacceptability of others over time. Yet, language shapes our understanding of the world around us enormously and can create very 'real' social conditions. It is therefore important that we have a media that is fit for purpose, and if those with the power to legislate in order to make this so do not, we are again left with questions regarding their reliance on the current weight of misinformation and partisanship.

Governments tend to de-regulate markets rather than protect our interests, with the media being no exception. The Leveson Inquiry report in 2012 recommended that all newspapers sign up to an independent press regulator but this has not happened[406]. What we have instead is the Independent Press Standards Organisation (IPSO), a self-regulatory body that is funded through the regulatory funding company (RFC). Those who signed up to IPSO, i.e. the major media moguls themselves, nominated directors for the RFC, and as such the eventual list included Paul Ashford (editorial director of Richard's Desmond's media company, Northern & Shell), Christopher Longcroft (chief financial officer of Rupert Murdoch's News UK), and Paul Vickers (Trinity Mirror's secretary and legal director). That the same media that needs to be regulated is effectively funding and regulating itself falls somewhat short of the standards the public should expect, and explains why many newspapers continue to publish fabrication and lies. And then there is Ofcom, the government-approved regulatory and competition authority. As with the BBC the government has made a huge attempt to appoint friendly faces at the helm, in this case spending well over a year attempting to make Paul Dacre (former

---

406 In 2018 the Conservatives also decided to axe the second phase of the Leveson Inquiry, intended to examine the relationship between journalists and the police

editor at the *Daily Mail* and vocal BBC critic) its chair. Even a government-appointed advisory committee could not find him fit to lead Ofcom, yet instead of appointing another candidate the government scrapped the process and restarted it in a bid to get him the job. The problem? No-one with any credibility would agree to this rubber-stamp charade[407].

To be clear, this is not an attempt to censor or impinge on free speech – the press are entitled to be partisan, but they *should* also have a responsibility that the public be accurately informed and not subject to a bombardment of fabrication, misinformation, and misrepresentation of facts. As stated by Newton Lee in *Counterterrorism and Cybersecurity*, journalists should be watchdogs, not lapdogs. If a political party is fulfilling its role of looking after the interests of the people, then there would be no need for the press to do any of those things. This is entirely the situation we should be in: and those news outlets that support either the Conservatives, Labour, or another party can do so, and the public be in a position to make an informed choice. However, this is exactly why appropriate regulation is not introduced. The media selectively reporting some stories and not others, or putting a spin on the information disseminated, means that our governments can, to an extent, do as they please[408].

A more open and free democracy is more readily achievable than what we may think it can be. If enough people make a stand against the press that fails to do the duty we, collectively, attest it needs to be doing, such as holding powerful actors in our society to account, then we can boycott it. *The Sun's* circulation in Liverpool is notoriously low after blame was attributed to its fans for the Hillsborough disaster of 1989 and suggestions that fans were pick-pocketing victims, ironically with the article headed 'The Truth'. These are profit-driven businesses: if we refuse to give them our money in principle, advertisers will very quickly follow suit and change would be very rapid. Likewise, we can choose to give our money to forms of press that do operate with integrity, the types of press that do not rely on advertisers and have the freedom and

---

407 *The Guardian*, 'Ministers struggle to find people to interview Paul Dacre for Ofcom job', 31 August 2021

408 As one illustration, George Monbiot co-produced an independent report for the Labour Party, which both the right-wing press and the Tories used to falsify claims about Jeremy Corbyn. While IPSO conceded that this had occurred, the process was long, arduous, and with little outcome – often a minor note of correction on an obscure page, or gestural fine to be paid by appreciative billionaire associates. See his account in *The Guardian*, 'Why do I have to break an embargo in order to expose press lies about Labour?', 10 December 2019

licence to tell the truth without agenda. Again, all this takes is people paying subscriptions (to sustain said outlets in lieu of advertisers and billionaire owners) and getting a much better service in return[409]. The more people who subscribe, the smaller the subscription charges. At a time when right-wing media increases in forms and size, with GB News a perfect illustration of this, it is not too late to reclaim a fair and just democracy.

*

The irony is not lost on me that a fair amount of the criticism levelled at various individuals and entities in this book are sourced from the exact media that is being criticised, which serves to illustrate the problem that we need more independent, transparent journalism sooner rather than later. Every attempt has been made to source information from the different news outlets with wide readership as opposed to relying on any one or two, to minimise accusations of bias.

---

409 It is worth checking some out, the likes of: *Tribune*, OpenDemocracy, Novara, *Morning Star*, New Socialist, *Byline Times*, Double Down News, *Red Pepper*, *Socialist Worker* – even just for a different perspective than is offered by the mainstream outlets. There are also fantastic organisations holding the mainstream media to account, including the likes of Media Lens and the Bureau of Investigative Journalism

FIVE

AN ALTERNATIVE, 'GREAT' BRITAIN IS POSSIBLE

'The sad, horrible, heart-breaking way the vast majority of my fellow countrymen and women, as well as their counterparts in most of the rest of the world, are obliged to spend their working lives is seared into my consciousness in an excruciating and unforgettable way. And when I think of all the talent and energy which daily go into devising ways and means of making their torment worse, all in the name of efficiency and productivity but really for the greater glory of the great god Capital, my wonder at humanity's ability to create such a monstrous system is surpassed only by amazement at its willingness to tolerate the continuance of an arrangement so obviously destructive of the well-being and happiness of human beings. If the same effort, or only half of it, were devoted to making work the joyous and creative activity it can be, what a wonderful world this could be' (Paul M. Sweezy, foreword to *Labor and Monopoly Capital: The Degradation of Work in the Twentieth Century* by Harry Braverman)

In ode to Erich Fromm and what would constitute a 'sane society', when you sit back and truly reflect on how we have decided to organise our lives, acknowledging that we are a very capable, innovative, pioneering species, you have to wonder is this the best we can do? Long working hours, a lack of quality housing, education and health for all as a basic right, gross inequality, allowing just a few to control naturally provided resources and extort others for its use, consumption for consumption's sake, and much more. We *are* society and can shape it how we wish, provided enough people want to. Naturally opinions will differ, but we can point to certain things that do have popular consensus, or could, when articulated in palatable fashion. Fromm's suggestions about what a 'sane' society might look like overlap with some of the ideas identified here, with the first being worker co-operatives. Via this organisational structure people are less likely to be 'alienated' from their work: taking meaning, satisfaction, and ultimately having some autonomy in what they do, reaping the benefits also. As another example, localised forms of democracy where people are actually informed, not lied to by self-serving politicians with the media onside. Ultimately a society conforming to the needs of its citizens.

The premise of outlining ways in which our society is grossly unequal, unfair, and unsustainable is to lay the foundations for an alternative. It is important to make the case for a different way of life before conceiving of the possibilities. I would hope that the case for change is pretty clear, given that the lives of most people are not improving as they were previously (if at all), and this to the ever-increasing benefit of a minority. People deserve better and it should be our goal to make life as fulfilling and happy as it possibly can be, not least for future generations. Equally, outlining alternative futures is important, as without conceiving of what is possible it is difficult to make a fair and accurate appraisal of our current state of affairs. It is not necessarily a finished utopia that we ought to desire, but a world where imagination and hope are alive and active[410]. Even reflecting on failed attempts at progressive change in the past is helpful in establishing parameters for what could work; mindful that as the technological, social, and economic environments change things that may not have worked before might lead to different outcomes today or in the future.

The following measures should not be viewed as a chronological and neatly integrated action plan, rather a range of measures that warrant consideration as we plan for a better future. To illustrate this point, advocating that people join trade unions and yet pushing for increasing automation and a reduction in work may seem contradictory to the role and functions of unions as we conceptualise them today. While unions clearly have a part to play in measures

---

410 Borrowing from Bertrand Russell (1917) *Political Ideals*, The Century Co.

such as tackling wage inequality, traditionally unions have resisted technology as they have looked to protect jobs. Their role in the medium term proposed here would be to advocate what 'good' work looks like in a much-changing employment sphere, including to help ensure full employment on reduced working hours. If we advocate a transition to worker co-operatives and a reduction in the role and influence of capitalists, we are effectively asking trade unions to sign their own death warrant. Yet, as technology is not discovered and implemented as soon as it becomes of apparent benefit to humanity, employers will continue to introduce it in ways that suit them – often ways that scupper the potential to unionise[411] (as we see in the platform economy). The proposition here is therefore not a bad role for unions moving forward given the alternative ways they may cease to exist, and the fact that the ultimate goal of the working class should be to eradicate both work and class as much as possible.

Naturally, some of the measures here *will* reinforce others in ways that are part of a more coherent, holistic change in how society is organised. For example, reducing our time spent working should lend itself to a reduction in consumption for a number of reasons. As one, a huge amount of 'compensatory' consumption[412] has built around our long working hours that will not be needed to the same extent, not least the convenience foods, coffee shops, transportation services, and so forth that ensure people turn up to work on time and with a degree of energy. Secondly, a reduction in meaningless jobs that produce unnecessary goods and services, and less marketing that currently interrupts almost every activity we attempt to engage in will be factors here. Combining this with the fact that we are overworked and left without time and energy, thus more susceptible to capitalism dictating what we should find pleasure in, we can envisage conceptions of 'the good life' and fulfilment in other non-material, spiritual, communal, and many other ways. Not to mention that basic needs being met and wages being brought into kilter means that people will be able to access what they need, thus incentives to accumulate wealth for pointless consumption will be entirely unnecessary.

The suggestions that follow encompass changes that we as individuals should lead on but would be greatly enhanced with a more progressive 'state' to both aid and implement what is necessary to achieve the transformations

---

411 See Aaron Benanav (2020) *Automation and the Future of Work*, Verso
412 See Kate Soper (2020) *Post-Growth Living: For an Alternative Hedonism*, Verso

below. A continuation of free-market capitalism is to guarantee further financial crashes, spiralling inequality and planetary catastrophe. Further, free-market capitalism brings out the worst in people – we are cynical, in competition, individualised, and this simply need not be the case. Taking inspiration from Thomas Sankara, it took 'the madmen of yesterday' for us to be able to think and act with the clarity we have today. Let us all be madmen and women; we must dare to invent the future.

RENATIONALISING KEY SERVICES

Privatisation has been a disaster. Chapter 2 offered just some of what is an extremely long list of catastrophic failures. Various polls evidence the public's appetite for bringing key services like rail and water back into public ownership[413], and with good reason. Those sectors with a private monopoly continue to rip consumers off and public control of transport is the only legitimate way for a speedy transition to a green and quality service, itself ensuring a reduction in traffic and pollution. Benefits tend to proliferate: with fewer car parks needed there is scope for more green areas, housing, or space for worker co-operatives in 'prime' locations of business. The economic case for renationalisation is resounding: WeOwnIt report that we waste approx. £13 billion per year on privatisation, money that lines the pockets of shareholders instead of being reinvested for better infrastructure and services, which remains unlikely when profit rules supreme.

In terms of specific examples, research from the University of Greenwich calculates that we could save over £3.7 billion from bringing energy back into public ownership and over £2.5 billion from renationalising water *annually*[414]. There have been some localised attempts to do so, notably Robin Hood Energy set up in 2015 as a non-profit by Nottingham City Council, but recently acquired by British Gas[415]; Bristol Energy established by Bristol City Council a year later but also acquired – this time by Yü Energy in 2020; and the People's

---

413 E.g. YouGov, 'Nationalisation vs privatisation: the public view', 19 May 2017

414 David Hall (2019) 'Benefits and costs of bringing water, energy grid and Royal Mail into public ownership'

415 Thousands of British Gas workers staged around 44 days of strike action over the course of 2021 after the company adopted a 'fire and rehire' approach to cut wages by 10%, despite operating profits of over £900 million. BT engineers also went on strike after attacks on pay, conditions, and freedom of association

Energy company in Scotland. People guffawed at the Labour Party's intent to roll out free broadband before the 2019 election, which would have been achieved via public ownership of Openreach. The cost of doing so, according to an independent report conducted on behalf of the Department for Digital, Culture, Media and Sport, would be £20 billion; whereas the cost of waiting for private companies to achieve this via big subsidies (to undeserving companies like our old friends Virgin) would be more than £32 billion[416].

We could take heed from Hamburg, where the city's residents voted in favour of renationalising the energy grid during a referendum in 2013 following a 'Our Hamburg – our grid' campaign. Testament to the ability to move beyond profits when utilities are publicly owned, at the time of writing plans are afoot to develop a hydrogen electrolysis plant, powered by wind and solar (thus renewable) energy, extracting 'green' hydrogen from water in a carbon-free process. This is what a real 'taking back control' would look like. Rather than empty gestures like waving Union Jack flags at every opportunity, true nationalism would be the British public as chief stakeholders in the services they require – getting a genuine say in how they operate and their satisfaction with the service being the primary goal in how they are run. Renationalisation will also facilitate many of the measures outlined in this chapter, such as a move to full employment but with everyone working fewer hours, particularly valuable as the public sector should operate with a duty to act as the benchmark for good employment practices. Historically the sector offered high levels of unionism, and relatively good terms and conditions, thus delivering money to local economies via public-sector workers who enjoy secure employment and incremental pay rises. Most supplies and costs come from the external, commercial sector, ensuring activity here continues to be a source of wealth alongside better public-service provision.

A key question here would regard whether to nationalise the banking sector. This, again, is not a new idea: in the aftermath of the 2008 financial crisis the UK government took on majority shares of Northern Rock, RBS and Lloyds-HBOS. Instead of the typical approach, which is to rescue banks and return them to private ownership, these could be placed under full public ownership. As mentioned previously, the bank bail-outs revealed how the central banks can create new money at will, but the current system

---

416 Frontier Economics, 'Future Telecoms Infrastructure Review: Annex A. A report for DCMS', 13 July 2018

directs this towards the private-banking sector and creates notions of state expenditure being constrained, much like a household. In co-operation with the central bank, operating as a government body, the state can create money debt-free. Further, by granting a monopoly of banking activities to the public sector this can be both regulated (e.g. taxing 'speculation' to phase it out[417]) and democratic (e.g. the people decide how much money to allocate to, say, provisioning agents such as an environmental funding body). Private banks could be allowed but on a number of provisos, such as they operate as worker co-operatives, expropriating current shareholders who have enjoyed enough compensation up until now as it is[418]. Or that they retain a utility function, i.e. still provide services such as payments, transfers, and so forth, but their ability to create new money through bank loans is restricted to certain agreed priorities – those for the common good. A consequence of this would be to shrink the banking sector and thus drive financial activity towards activities linked to people's actual needs.

Progressive local authorities can of course be the catalyst to municipal renationalisation of sorts. There is a proud tradition here – in 1870 Birmingham mayor Joseph Chamberlain bought the local gas and waterworks, running them for public profit in an early instance of municipal socialism. In the modern day, local authorities in cities such as Leeds, Bristol, and Nottingham have established municipal energy companies that deliver affordable power for their communities[419]. Where privatisation is failing some authorities have also brought back service provision in-house; for example, Metro schemes in London, Birmingham and Newcastle, and recently the bus services in Greater Manchester by Mayor Andy Burnham. There is evidence of local communities organising in ways that actually or potentially can amalgamate worker co-operatives and service provision where privatisation has failed. The irony that austerity has ravaged bus services was not lost in one of its chief architect's

---

417 Regulation has been used before, when speculation was somewhat curtailed by the Bubble Act in 1720 after the first documented stock market crash – caused by the collapse of the South Sea Company – wherein the British government had promised investors monopoly trade in South America (notably of slaves) but whose assets were seized as war renewed with Spain. This was repealed in 1825 and unhindered buying/selling of shares resumed thereafter

418 The British Co-operative Bank rode the initial crisis well, until it took over Britannia Building Society. Likewise, the only state-owned bank in the US, North Dakota State Bank, survived the crisis well

419 Hall and Hobbs 'Public ownership is back on the agenda in the UK', Chapter 9 in *Reclaiming Public Services* by Petitjean and Kishimoto. Transnational Institute 2017 Report

David Cameron's constituency of Witney, where locals banded together to create West Oxfordshire Community Transport. It is a non-profit co-operative, where paying just £1 ensures a number of things, including the ability to participate in big decisions such as how to reinvest profits, notably a real living wage for drivers[420].

REVOLUTIONISE WORK

'Man is born free, and everywhere he is in chains' (Jean-Jacques Rousseau, *The Social Contract*)

Naturally, there are many ways in which we could reshape how work is undertaken in Britain and some of these ideas are picked up below. Here, we will focus primarily on worker collectivism and solidarity, worker co-operatives, and tackling endemic wage inequality.

WORKER SOLIDARITY: UNIONISE

Nowhere near enough recognition is given in mainstream media, education curriculums, and so forth to the role that trade unions have played in our society. Workers collectivising together in the past is the only reason why work is remotely bearable for many people in the present day, given their role in acquiring the basic rights and protections many of us are lucky enough to still take for granted. Instead of this, you are much more likely to hear the usual negative tropes about unions being greedy or causing trouble during potential bouts of industrial action, or vague references to their being the cause of England becoming unproductive, and even anarchic, in the late 1970s. The value and importance of worker solidarity is evident globally; for example, in his address to the Illinois State Convention of the AFL-CIO Martin Luther King Jr described the labour movement as 'the principal force that transformed misery and despair into hope and progress'.

In the first of any real progressive move towards a radically different, better life for the majority, people would be well served by joining a trade union. This is already happening, with four consecutive years of trade union membership growth between 2016–20 bringing total membership to approx. 6.56 million

---

420 *The Guardian*, 'The town that refused to let austerity kill its buses', 6 June 2018

workers[421]. The caveat to these positive figures is that those aged 16–24 make up just 4.4% of members, suggesting a membership 'time bomb' of sorts. Yet there is great incentive for people to unionise; for example, the Labour Force Survey reveals a 17.7% wage premium for trade union members over non-members in the public sector, and 3.6% in the private sector. This is partly due to the fact that there is might in the collective that an individual does not possess on their own, with a recognised union legally entitled to collectively bargain terms and conditions, possessing the ability to go on strike (and thus better positioned to obtain concessions from an employer) and consultation rights in the event of significant changes to working conditions.

This would represent a positive change without unsettling the fabric of current life too much, for those who are uneasy about taking a leap into the utopian unknown. Unions function to improve workers' standing in the capitalist system rather than over-throwing it. Consider the fact that one of their primary functions is to *protect jobs*, this is the antithesis of markedly changing the system. Indeed, when a union 'wins' in either the collective bargaining or dispute processes the outcome is to return to work – albeit on slightly better terms and conditions. There also lies a contradiction at the heart of their nature, in that while they express working-class resistance to capitalism their role requires that they contain this too. For example, the job of a full-time union official (employed by the trade union) is to negotiate the terms of compromises between labour and capital: their interest is therefore vested in the continuation of the wage labour and capitalist economic system from which unions derive their function and to which their livelihoods depend. The best way to think about this is that if a more militant and broader struggle emerged among workers that threatened the capitalist system, this would also pose a threat to full-time union officials' precise raison d'être[422].

Union struggles that are workplace- or industry-based tend also to be isolated from broader political and social movements, thus they often end with a fairly localised agreement or disillusionment if the desired outcome is not obtained. Therefore more work is needed via a stronger union base to address this latter point. For example, the workplace issues that trade unions engage in with capital are also likely to affect the wider community (whether it be work

421 Department for Business, Energy & Industrial Strategy, 'Trade Union Membership, UK 1995–2020: Statistical Bulletin', 27 May 2021
422 General secretaries of the larger unions also earn the type of salary one would be a tad reluctant to give up

intensification and pay freezes, through to things like tenancy rights) and thus multi-union committees building class-wide rank-and-file networks are one possibility[423]. Particularly as most people are without a formal political education the experience of struggle, at work or otherwise, is often the shortest road to political awareness. Activists could focus more of their efforts on lobbying working people, with the trade union-backed False Economy project a prime example. This provided a public-facing, grassroots online platform to host and discuss alternatives to austerity and information contrary to the mainstream media[424]. In Croxteth residents and volunteers set up Communiversity to help adults upskill[425]. Activists and union structures are key to drawing attention to workplace issues that workers can share experience of, humour, survival tips, and ultimately transformative change via direct, member-led democracy.

This would help circumnavigate the Trade Union Act 2016 which should be repealed to counter-balance the unequal power dynamic between employer and employee. This was one of Keir Starmer's pledges and it will be very interesting to see if he gets the chance to do so, and whether he is true to his word, although current signs suggest that this is unlikely. It will also help to restate the working class at the heart of the 'left's' attempts to improve Labour's position in society: there is too much of a disconnect at the moment with middle-class sects who are happy to shout about revolution while living comfortably, and a vast array of social movements and identity politics that are not being bridged well enough by either side to foster cohesiveness. Solidarity among workers breeds a greater awareness of others' working conditions and thus we are more likely to behave in similar ways as consumers, i.e. by boycotting products or services from organisations we know to exploit its workforce or those within its supply chain. This would force the Amazons of this world to change their practices overnight; we are that powerful. Social media also increases the ability for greater awareness of potential issues, providing a platform for people to engage in sympathy protests, and so forth.

The proportion of UK workers covered by collective bargaining agreements has naturally fallen significantly, and we see the stark effects. The

---

423 A fuller discussion of how this could work can be found in Cohen (2006) *Ramparts of Resistance: Why Workers Lost Their Power, and How to Get It Back*, Pluto Press
424 To illustrate this point, such initiatives as the False Economy were practically ignored by said media
425 Mary O'Hara (2014) *Austerity Bites: A Journey to the Sharp End of Cuts in the UK*, Policy Press

goal of workers joining unions has to be a *real* living wage (as per the Living Wage Foundation), side-stepping the government's cynical rebranding of the National Minimum Wage to the National Living Wage. Presently around 20% of the British workforce are paid less than the real living wage (£9.90 per hour). The pandemic has re-emphasised this need with a recent report from the Living Wage Foundation finding that those already paid an amount below that required to 'get by' have seen their pay decreased further, with consequences that include one-quarter skipping meals for financial reasons, one in five unable to heat their homes, and a range of unfavourable effects on their health and happiness[426]. As advocates of 'good' work unions will play a pivotal role as we address other issues facing society. For example, high-carbon industries face a very uncertain future as there clearly needs to be a 'green' revolution. The longer-term strategy needs to be one akin to degrowth (see below) but the initial drive towards greening our current industries could potentially result in a repeat of the deindustrialisation experienced in the 1980s – devastating whole communities[427]. Knowing that they are contributing to a sustainable planet and thus performing what clearly constitutes meaningful work will provide intrinsic reward to such workers, and unionising will help to ensure other staples of 'good' work such as job security and apt working hours too. As a further illustration, at the time of writing this the Communication Workers Union secured a four-day working week for postal workers in Northampton, beginning in April 2021, with plans to expand to other sites pending review[428].

WORKER SOLIDARITY: CO-OPERATIVES

'And really in the end he [the landowner or magnate] is more dependent upon them than they on him. Were they to die out, he also would die with them, he being but a parasite whose life is dependent upon their continued existence; whereas, his disappearance as a class would free the other classes from a great weight with which they are now burdened' (Keir Hardie, *From Serfdom to Socialism*)

---

426 Living Wage Foundation, 'Life on Low Pay in the Pandemic'

427 A fate that already awaits industrial regions due to government inactivity as other countries steal a march on green innovations. For example, while British steel continues to burn coal, Swedish firm Hybrit produces 'green steel' using hydrogen extracted from water, via taxpayer-funded government grants and public shares

428 CWU, 'South Midlands Mail Centre's four-day week is a win for all', 28 April 2021

What does have more transformative potential to put wealth into the hands of those who create it yet can, and does, fit within our current system are worker co-operatives. According to the International Co-operative Alliance, a co-operative is an autonomous association of persons united voluntarily to meet their common economic, social, and cultural needs and aspirations through a jointly owned and democratically controlled enterprise. Well-known variances of worker co-operatives are John Lewis Partners, the Co-operative Group (banks, supermarkets, etc.), and, to an extent, Richer Sounds since 2019 after founder Julian Richer transferred 60% of his shares into an employee-owned trust. If you are equally interested in sustainability and cutting down on a meat-based diet then the likes of Suma offer a succinct summary of how co-operatives are run and the many benefits on their website. There are other instances where owners have transferred control of their businesses to employees, such as Novograf in Scotland (responsible for signage and surfaces across the likes of Tesco, Greggs, Pizza Hut, and many more), which experienced a real upturn in financial performance and a recruitment drive in the year that followed.

In the typical employment relationship it is the capitalist who benefits from the surplus value produced by the workforce whereas worker co-operatives enable those involved to distribute the value evenly among themselves and thus better provide for their families, or simply produce just what they require and then cease work for the day to enjoy more time engaged in other activities. Value is created by the co-operation between workers who can produce more together than separately, thus the capitalist is dispensable in this arrangement. If the main offering of the capitalist is the means of production, then we could follow the example set by Cuba where workers are offered these means via favourable rental terms on public property/assets (e.g. one year free on a ten-year lease), lower tax rates, preferential credit options, and raw materials at wholesale rather than retail prices[429]. Corporations are already offered a huge amount of 'welfare' by way of huge grants, subsidies, and various other incentives or 'handouts', so preferential terms for worker co-operatives does not require a new source of funding. Likewise, the argument already put forward for renationalising public services compliments an approach where, in situations that it makes sense for governments to subcontract out work,

---

429 See Peter Ranis (2016) *Cooperatives Confront Capitalism: Challenging the Neoliberal Economy*, Zed Books

organisations – whether worker co-operative or not – should be selected based on their ability to demonstrate that they provide 'good' work to the local community and are demonstrating a desire to deal with local suppliers themselves (as is currently the case in the city of Preston, Lancashire). Serco and the like have had it far too good for too long, and simply donating to the ruling party should not be the deciding factor irrespective of the fact that the public are failed time and time again.

Worker co-operatives are a source of British pride, with many scholars attributing the archetypal co-operative society to that achieved by Robert Owen in New Lanark from 1800. Not only were Owen's cotton mills profitable, but workers enjoyed unprecedented conditions including receipt of four months of full wages during the American embargo in 1806, and profits reinvested into the community to boost local education, supplies, and so forth[430]. This model of society was hugely influential to the writings of Marx and Engels yet remains little taught or known among Brits. Work would still be central in such a society, with worker co-operatives a way to avoid unemployment (and thus poverty) and also to develop the capacity for autonomy, problem-solving, and other useful skills required for long-term work organised in this way. Rather than the undemocratic, oppressive state of affairs many workers are subject to in contemporary society, people could have a say regarding what they produce, how that work is organised, and so on[431].

There are many examples of effective worker co-operatives. The Basque Mondragon Corporacion Cooperativa, founded in 1956 is the world's largest co-operative encompassing approx. 75k members and a turnover of around £13.5 billion. Their key principles are that all members are fundamentally equal; the management body is democratically elected by all; members vote on substantive issues (for example in favour of or against a pay cut during financial difficulty); a portion of profits are paid out to employees while the rest is either reinvested into the co-op or flows into the Central Fund for Cooperation (which implements new projects, creates new jobs, goes to the local community for

---

430 A good account of these achievements can be found from numerous sources, including A.L. Morton (1978) *The Life and Ideas of Robert Owen*, Monthly Review Press. See also the Rochdale Society of Equitable Pioneers

431 The International Co-operative Alliance is a good place to start for underlying principles, of which they propose seven for members: 1) Voluntary and Open Membership, 2) Democratic Member Control, 3) Member Economic Participation, 4) Autonomy and Independence, 5) Education, Training, and Information, 6) Cooperation among Cooperatives, and 7) Concern for Community (see ica.coop website)

purposes such as educational initiatives). Wider solidarity comes in the form of co-ops working together during demand fluctuations, the co-op bank offers favourable loan terms to struggling co-operatives, and a solidarity fund to help floundering operations within the group. Ultimately, the guiding principle is not profit given that there are no shareholders in the traditional sense and so all earned revenue can be used for the common good[432]. The Emilia-Romagna region of Northern Italy has a burgeoning co-operative economy accounting for around 40% of the area's economic activity, and Quebec boasts an extensive 'social' or 'solidarity' economy in Canada (see *Fonds de solidarité* FTQ as one illustration of this). In fact, there are examples of successful co-operatives in a variety of sectors internationally, e.g. in banking (the likes of GLS Bank and Sparda-Bank are billion-pound organisations) right through to agricultural co-operatives in the Egyptian desert like Seliem. Organisations like CECOP (the European confederation of industrial and service co-operatives) offer a means for international solidarity between national federations of co-operatives across Europe.

In today's digital age, and demonstrating the potential overlap between worker co-operatives and social enterprises, i.e. trading with a social purpose or using profits to benefit the community, we have *Interessengruppe Premium* (also known as Premium Cola). This is an internet collective that has been trading since 2001 with no office, fixed salaries, or formal boss – just a moderator for their discussion board. Founded in Hamburg, the c1.7k partners are paid a uniform wage, freely select their working hours, and only sell to outlets with a similar ethos to their own, i.e. localised, environmentally sustainable, fully democratised, and not profit-driven. Practices include the offer of an 'anti-volume' discount to small distributors who cannot compete with larger outlets, who then pay slightly more for Premium Cola and the three other beverages they have diversified into, including an organic Pilsner. All decisions are taken by the collective as a whole with the elected moderator there to ensure full and fair participation in decision-making. Similarly, as precarious and unfair as the platform economy has become, the likes of Uber do demonstrate – given that Uber drivers essentially need to provide all of the tools to work themselves

---

432 Naturally there are some limitations as Mondragon aims to compete in the global marketplace, e.g. it was forced to lay off some workers after the 2008 financial crisis, but such things are viewed as deficiencies in practice to be rectified, rather than the capitalistic view of advantages to exploit (e.g. most of the aforementioned workers were rehired by other parts of the co-op in the wider network)

(vehicle, valid licence, smartphone), including repairs, insurance and so forth – how easy it could be to establish platform worker cooperatives to provide such services. Uber does not really do too much beyond market itself as *the* app to use for transport, admittedly with very effective technological innovations and algorithms[433].

REDUCING PAY INEQUALITY

'I mean, your society's broken, so who should we blame? Should we blame the rich, powerful people who caused it? No, let's blame the people with no power and no money and these immigrants who don't even have the vote, yeah, it must be their fucking fault' (Iain Banks, the final interview)

In the kind of democracy we purport to live in, there would at least be some semblance of a conversation facilitated by mainstream journalism regarding the rapid increase in salaries of those 'at the top' and the real wage decline for everybody else. If the wage ratio continues on its current trajectory CEO pay at the large companies in the UK will be on average £112 million per year by mid this century. At some point we must say enough is enough and begin to think about what constitutes a fair ratio between highest paid and lowest paid in society. It is not for me to decide what would constitute fair in this regard, or what the maximum wage rate should be; this is a matter for real democratic deliberation.

Just to illustrate how this could work in practice, we might decide that the maximum salary someone would require for a comfortable life is £120k per year. If we also decided that the most anyone should be paid in relation to anyone else is five times their salary, i.e. a ratio of 5:1 (highest paid:lowest paid) then the minimum wage people would receive in this society is £24k per year. These amounts could all be phased in incrementally over time; for example, wages adjusted from their current ratio of 119:1 to 100:1 after one year, to 20:1 after three years and reach the agreed target after five years. If people did not want to work for that amount of money? No problem, they are not cut out for a modern, progressive, and egalitarian society and are free to continue chasing unabated levels of wealth elsewhere. In other words, we are better off without

---

433 And of course they do take on additional 'employer' responsibilities such as performance management, which companies like Deliveroo have been much more effective at concealing in courts of law

them. It works for Mondragon Group previously mentioned, where the wage differential stands at around 9:1, which is a far cry from the ratio for those companies that are not worker co-operatives.

There is already appetite for this: 78% of the public say that the gap between those on high and low incomes is 'too large', a figure that has never been below 72% and did reach 85% while records have been kept[434]. Such a move would necessitate that we dispense with the present bonus culture too, as clearly any shortfall in salary would be manoeuvred into a benefits package. Incentives and additional rewards could instead be offered to those contributing to the common good rather than success for a small group of elitist shareholders. The reason why this is so important is not only to reduce inequality – which is a good enough reason itself – but reducing the incentive to accumulate individual wealth, at all costs, is imperative to shifting focus onto broader social needs. We can hardly contain environmental destruction or offer peace and love to thy neighbour when putting profits over people and planet. That our survival is subordinated to shareholder dividends was laid strikingly bare in Goldman Sachs' 'The Genome Revolution' report, advising biotech companies that curing patients was bad for business. The evidence has also been presented that the ultra-rich are very rarely justifying their colossal sums of money. The salaries and bonuses being banded around are as undeserved as they are seemingly arbitrary in many cases. What is unquestionable, is that such amounts are unnecessary in relative terms to basic needs. If salaries are so disconnected from effort and relative value (as showcased during the pandemic and by various types of work, notably the feminised sectors, for a long period of time), it would benefit significantly more people to use this as the basis for more progressive salary-setting.

Undoubtedly there would be great hostility to this idea, including somewhat bizarrely from those in the bottom and middle parts of the income spectrum. There is almost a sentiment among some that to be accepted as a competent social actor one needs to subscribe whole-heartedly to meritocracy even to a point of self-deprecation when they are not in a top job themselves. A perfect illustration of this came in November 2019 when McDonald's workers went on strike asking for £15 per hour and were met with disdain from much of the public across various social media platforms. Swathes of people comparing their own educational backgrounds, occupations, and salaries

---

434 British Social Attitudes survey 36 (2019 edition) p. 152

to what McDonald's staff were requesting and remarking how all manner of people, from nurses to time-served welders and lab technicians with chemistry degrees, would be changing careers. The point these people appeared to be making, often unwittingly, is that they too are underpaid and participating in a 'race to the bottom'. McDonald's revenues were over $21 billion that year, and then CEO Steve Easterbrook was paid approx. $16 million per year. Why do the workers who contribute to this success not deserve a living wage? Why are corporations like McDonald's allowed to make so much money, pay senior management so handsomely, and rely on the taxpayer to subsidise their employees' wages via in-work tax credits?

Another criticism that might be levelled is that it would be unfair for those performing highly skilled work, such as brain surgeons or rocket scientists, receiving pay not too dissimilar from those engaging in 'unskilled' work. If we can use perhaps the closest real-life example to the kind of things being put forward here, it is actually such professionals employed in the public sector that have most bought into the Cuban revolution[435]. In the Cuban case, because those who are now operating Airbnbs or taking tourists for drives in their classic American cars can make more in one day than a doctor can in one month (anything up to circa $30), university professors and such ilk genuinely moonlight as taxi drivers to supplement their incomes. This would not be the case here – those essential, highly skilled occupations would be towards the upper parameter of £120k, with jobs that are less essential or skilled (again, to be decided democratically, such as by referendum) towards the bottom end of said spectrum.

RE-THINKING WHAT IS IMPORTANT TO US

'Normal is getting dressed in clothes that you buy for work, driving through traffic in a car that you are still paying for, in order to get to a job that you need so you can pay for the clothes, car and house you leave empty all day in order to afford to live in it' (Ellen Goodman)

In the preface to *Affluenza*, Clive Hamilton and Richard Denniss note how the public have unintentionally answered the question many philosophers have pondered – namely, what is the meaning of life? This answer appears to

---

435 Peter Ranis, *ibid*

be acquire a bigger house, a nice car, and experience an epidemic of stress, overwork, waste, and indebtedness in the dogged pursuit of such goals. Capitalist society depends upon workers engaged in relentless production and consumers in relentless consumption. As such, it creates the notion that our aspirations should be hard work and productivity on the one hand, and economic success via high-status consumption (owning nice, expensive things) on the other. This keeps the machine ticking over. The result?

Permanent dissatisfaction as forever seeking – but crucially never finding – satisfaction through consumption is a key reason for societal unhappiness and insecurity. The idea is constantly sold to us that if you only looked/dressed/lived/married/drove/shopped/holidayed like *this* you would be happy. Fuelled by social media, where complex algorithms and morally questionable data mining ensures that we receive ads and information tailored specifically to our whims and desires, the next purchase is never far away. Yet with no end to consumption and new innovations being created all of the time, this would be an endless, futile pursuit. Corporate interests require us to pursue a version of happiness that serves profits before people. It is no coincidence that every new [insert product here – for the sake of example, a mobile phone] adds just one or two new features and a slightly longer battery life. If the Apples of this world gave us the product they are capable of we would not need to upgrade every couple of years – which is exactly what their business models are premised on: permanent dissatisfaction, longing for more, and ultimately waste[436].

When we move beyond largely consumerist goals, we will not feel the need to work so much in order to acquire these things we are told we desperately need for some opaque notion of self-fulfilment. This sense that 'we're all middle class' and the aspiration that this encourages brings with it more work and the requirement for more money – both of which are ills for a better society. Those participating in societies that are seeing unprecedented levels of wealth and comfort are continuously found to be less happy while economies have thrived. Part of the reason we feel unhappy is the very real, objective fall in the value of our earnings as wage growth for most has not kept pace with the increasing costs of living. As outlined by Tim Kasser in *The High Price of*

---

436 In June 2021 ITV revealed that just one Amazon 'fulfilment centre' in Dunfermline, Scotland, had a target of destroying 130k largely new/unused items per week (incidentally with fewer than 28k marked for donation). The company had previously illegally fired two employees, Emily Cunningham and Maren Costa, simply for speaking out about the firm's environmental practices

Materialism materialism and consumerism actually undermine our quality of life as we spend less time working on our relationships, interests, and activities that actually carry meaning and purpose – all of which will improve our lives tenfold. Not least, we rid the superficial, individualistic, and selfish aspects of society when we shift the focus to *something else.*

Anthropologist Marshall Sahlins calls into question the typically dim view of the hunter-gatherer of old, suggesting that our ancient ancestors' needs were satisfied because they did not conceive of, or demand, as much as we do now. Contrasting what he calls the original affluent society with the situation today, in this world of plenty, where we have a dazzling array of products and services 'within a man's reach – but never all within his grasp [sic]' and thus are truly deprived and unhappy[437]. Now I am not advocating that we return to a primitive way of life; having seen such riches we would of course struggle to live with being 'poor'. But there is something to be said for finding a better balance between being materially rich and thinking about other routes to happiness and freedom from materialistic ambitions. As Sahlins puts it: want not, lack not.

In another interesting text, *Change Everything: Creating an Economy for the Common Good*, Felber and Pettifor (2015) point out the peculiarity with which the values we hold for the economy (systematic pursuit of profit, egoism, individualism, greed, and envy) stand completely at odds with those we apply to our daily interpersonal relationships (building trust, empathy, respect, and co-operation). And yet the outcome of betraying our more personal convictions and values is ecological destruction, inequality, and lots of time spent working with varying degrees of unhappiness. We largely have economists to thank for this like the pioneer of political economy Adam Smith, who position the rational 'dollar-hunting animal'[438] as the centre-piece of our economic systems, someone who behaves in simplistic fashion far removed from the complex, flawed, agential, and relational beings we know humans to be. Trickle-down economics and the apparent belief in the free market to take care of everyone better than any other system has been rebuked by the evidence, not least of growing inequality, and rather serves as useful rhetoric for elites interested in sustaining their advantages[439].

---

437 *Stone Age Economics* (1972) Aldine Atherton Inc.

438 To quote CS Devas (1883) *The Groundwork of Economics*

439 Those not fooled by trickle-down economics included Pope Francis who, in the first apostolic exhortation of his papacy in 2013, stated, 'This opinion, which has never been confirmed by the facts, expresses a crude and naïve trust in the goodness of those wielding economic power… Meanwhile the excluded are still waiting'

In capitalist society our goals tend towards 'varied and interesting work', perhaps achieve success in the narrowly defined terms of promotion and status, with a higher standard of living. But this is largely a means to the end of material acquisition rather than of genuine intrinsic value, and is it even that lofty as far as ambitions go? Why persist in sustaining a system that does not make us the happiest we can be, while also inflicting so much suffering on others? Realistically how many people would prefer to conserve the privileges of the rich more so than they wish to conserve the planet? We allow ourselves to be wooed and guided by notions of Gross Domestic Product as a performance metric for how society is doing, despite the fact that GDP probably means very little to your average person. Paraphrasing Robert F Kennedy, he suggested that 'gross national product measures everything except what makes life worthwhile'[440].

Yet GDP as a primary measure of progress has been used to justify woeful and growing inequality and the destruction of our planet. It was prominent in Rishi Sunak's March 2021 budget as we were told how much GDP had reduced during the pandemic, how much it would grow in future years, how far behind it would be pre-Covid levels, etc. As well documented by Kate Raworth in *Doughnut Economics*, we have moved away from the principle economic goals highlighted by its founders in Ancient Greece, the first proponent of a political economy in James Steuart and others since. The economy is a human-made concept and system, created to be of benefit to people themselves, i.e. to secure a living in a mutually thriving community. We are so far removed from this now that countries willingly sacrifice lives to uphold the economy, as was well-illustrated during the Covid pandemic. In effect, the economy and notions of GDP that are meaningless to many are now something we serve irrespective of the cost. Are there particularly good reasons why we do not replace it with something akin to our more spiritual counterparts in Bhutan, who measure 'Gross National Happiness' based upon bi-annual household surveys that use 33 indicators of life quality? New Zealand PM Jacinda Ardern has toppled GDP in favour of this Happiness Index (herself a proponent of a four-day working week); Icelandic PM Katrin Jakobsdóttir has similarly put such a 'well-being' economy before GDP, with Scottish PM Nicola Sturgeon following suit; indicating that the world needs

---

440 To oversimplify, Gross National Product measures a country's economic activity including endeavours abroad, whereas Gross Domestic Product adds up such activity within a country's borders (including foreign investment)

more female leaders. The London think-tank New Economics Foundation suggest the 'Happy Planet Index', the OECD formulated the 'Better Life Index', and there are many others since Herman Daly's 'Index of Sustainable Human Welfare' in the 1970s.

We come back to the question of what and how to measure, whether it is happiness, a happy planet, or a better life, of which the masses *should* decide democratically. The fact that this does not happen already in a democracy is quite startling – deciding on policies within the parameters devised by elites who then either ignore the public's wishes or undertake them in harmful ways is not the same as all members of a society being able to define what is in their interest and what would make them happy. There are a variety of options through which this could be actioned. Firstly, we could think about incentivising and rewarding those who wish to contribute to such a society, e.g. by lower tax rates, preferential status for public contracts, bank loans with better conditions, all of which are being implemented in modern-day Cuba with some success. We can build towards a new economy and thus society in this way, producing goods and services that people actually need, and for the common good. The market would have no alternative but to respond accordingly when favourable conditions are offered to those that do. Felber and Pettifor (*ibid*) suggest including some common good metrics into organisation audits that organisations are then judged upon, with state backing.

It might be difficult to imagine how this could work, but we are moving away from the current profit-obsessed market so organisations do not need to be judged on profitability when organisations begin benefitting from their contribution to society's needs, the 'green' agenda, and so forth, and our old capitalistic system is phased out. Presently, deforesting the Amazon, destroying the homes of indigenous tribes, polluting water supplies, and so forth are all part of everyday business, but a 1p drop in share price is considered a real crisis. In an age where trade unions have reduced power and governments tend to be pro-business, it is down to the consumer via negative publicity, boycotting, and demonstrations to make corporations listen[441]. Further, we do not need profits and thus rich business owners

---

441 History will remember tobacco companies denying cancerous links, manufacturers suppressing figures on asbestos, more recently Volkswagen deliberately understating NOx emissions from their cars. Today's corporations do not heed the social justice case for change, only the business case

when everyone is engaging in work that is meaningful to them; there is a limit to how much they can earn; and we are trying to work less and enjoy our time on this planet (whilst doing it less harm), and these will be the metrics of success. Once you imagine a world unshackled by this dog-eat-dog, workaholic way of life, its feasibility becomes clearer. We even have societies which exist currently to prove that this can be possible too, as will be demonstrated below. It would also help to recalibrate what we think of when defining 'prosperity' as this immediately conjures up images of doing well economically. Prosperity can mean the flourishing of persons in other, non-material ways. Could we not think of someone who lives in a just society, shares common access to all basic needs, and an ecologically rejuvenated and vibrant environment as prosperous?

It can seem like a tall order to switch from a high-consumption society to something that undoubtedly a proportion of the population would think is simply restraining their choices. But we are capable – consider the changes cosmetic companies have made in response to growing awareness of cruelty-free measures and changing purchasing patterns. The growing scepticism people have to single-use plastic products. The huge increase in people switching to a plant-based diet, with meat consumption one of the world's biggest contributors to deforestation and greenhouse gas emissions. The boycotting of products from certain corporations and countries when people feel aggrieved by their internal or international endeavours. Voluntary schemes such as the Ethical Trading Initiative and the Fair Wear Foundation exist, and perhaps it is up to us to lobby governments to ensure that standards – both employment and environmental – become compulsory to how companies function. Everything is a commodity: human organs can be bought and sold, and wealthy people can pay those less fortunate to wait in queues for them. There is seemingly no moral compass on what should be above having a valuation and price attached to it, ultimately making it purchasable or sellable. It is therefore unsurprising that people find it hard to connect with other people, to have real, authentic experiences, since everything has now been reduced to an economic transaction, or a monetised, market-based solution. When everything is reduced to money or buying something to fill a void, much of what makes us human and the needs and desires that accompany our humanity are relegated.

DARLING, I HAVE NO DREAM JOB.
I DO NOT DREAM OF LABOUR

'*You waste your life to earn your living*' (Andre Gorz, *Farewell to the Working Class*)

The argument has been made for a reduction in our time spent working throughout. We have a plethora of 'bullsh*t jobs'; we have people who feel that they are overworked (as many as three in five people work longer than they would like[442]); and conversely many other people who are either unemployed, temporarily employed, or working part-time who would like to be working longer. Not bringing these things into line seems bizarre, especially as there is even a business case for having people who want to work doing so, and there is little point paying people for additional, disengaged, exhaustive, and ultimately unproductive hours. And having fewer, more intrinsically rewarding jobs where people do not feel overworked is surely the basis for a happy society.

With fewer unnecessary jobs, and subsequently less production and provision of things that we do not actually need, there would be more people available for work. This does not need to equate to a reserve army of labour keeping those in employment precarious and easily replaceable, or an exorbitant welfare bill paying out Jobseeker's Allowance. More people could be trained to do these essential jobs, and with lots of people able to do said jobs, everyone's hours could be reduced. In other words, we could have full employment but with working weeks averaging anything up to 20 hours per person. Hand in hand with degrowth (see below), as we look to reduce consumerism and thus production, we will shed quite a lot of jobs. This should not cause alarm – quite the opposite. Jobs that are no longer required for society's well-being, cohesiveness, and progress can go, and those who worked in such roles can share out the hours required by those jobs society does need. Dispense with some of the highly paid marketing executives, accountants, and consultants who are not pushing a greener or more humanist approach to business and train people instead as doctors, nurses, and teachers. This would create a surplus of these professionals who can then move away from 8–12 hour shifts to 4–5 hours of work per day. Is this not better?! Everyone can feel valued, take a sense of meaning and purpose in what they do, and have more time outside of work to do whatever they wish (if they wish to do more work, so be it).

---

442 CIPD 'UK Working Lives Survey, 2019'

This is all further made possible due to technological advancements, where we could and should be using technology to do the work for us – what is often termed 'full automation'. For too long technology has fragmented work into mundane tasks, thus de-skilling it and reducing discretion, pay, and ultimately the satisfaction one can take in their work – but not the hours worked themselves. Instead of viewing the encroachment of technology as a threat to jobs, let us welcome how liberating this could be. Let us not fight against automation but embrace it and have it take on the productive capacity of as many goods and services as we can. In fact, why not demand its acceleration? This is one of the fastest routes to something resembling a 'post-work' future where we can begin to enjoy an abundance of leisure time. We may not actually have much of a choice one day as technology expands from the more routine, oft-manual positions and work that can be managed by algorithms to those sectors not previously thought to be 'at threat', such as caring roles. There will of course be roles that are always done, or best done, by humans, but this should not prevent us from dispensing with cheap, unhappy labour and making big capital investments where automation is favourable.

This is perhaps an opportunity for something good to come out of the Covid pandemic; instead of spending trillions of pounds in a clamour to get back to what we call normality, we could dispense with those occupations and organisations that simply are not required for the future – or are too harmful to the planet – and use the money to build 'better'. In *Ecocide* David Whyte points out that BAE Systems, involved in a number of ultimately unnecessary (military defence) and environmentally detrimental (air travel) endeavours, quickly switched to manufacturing essential medical supplies during the pandemic such as ventilation units: demonstrating that immense switches in production are feasible to transform our economy[443]. Whyte asks, 'why save corporations that are killing us?'. One does wonder whether this monumental global event that began at a Chinese food market is going to change people's eating habits or lead any real calls for changes in how 'factory' meat farms operate. Corporations will not stop themselves as they continue in the quest for greater profits, with continued land grabs, control of water supplies, and

---

443 As with much else discussed here there is precedent, including the famed 'Lucas Plan' in the 1970s where Lucas Aerospace employees, facing layoffs, devised plans for 150 socially useful products such as wind turbines for renewable energy as globalisation and technological change brought about restructures. Management did not accept the plan, but the efforts and potential demonstrated by the workers inspired similar endeavours internationally

pollutive intensive farming methods depriving local populations of a means of subsistence (often acquired by much more sustainable means), with great power wielded over local authorities.

Whyte also encourages us to question why we continue to support corporations that have harmed people as well as the planet. The roll call of shame includes the likes of (Chevron) Texaco, whose endeavours in the Amazon have been implicated in the cultural genocide of both Tetetes and Sansahuari tribes, and who smuggled oil into Franco's fascist Spain during the US embargo. IBM, ExxonMobile (under its former name), ITT Inc., and General Motors are alleged to have provided vehicles, weapons, and more to the Nazi regime. ITT Inc. were also behind a deliberate plan to adversely affect Chile's economy to preclude a military coup that subsequently overthrew anti-colonial, socialist president Salvador Allende, resulting in tens of thousands of deaths and 'disappearances', for which they were rewarded with approx. $235 million. Other extensive lists include those who have continued to exploit the natural resources in former colonies with many of the usual suspects present – Shell, BP, and more.

A GREEN REVOLUTION AND 'POST-GROWTH' THINKING

'We are sorry for the inconvenience, but this is a revolution' (Subcomandante Marcos, Zapatista Army of National Liberation)

It is becoming increasingly difficult to ignore the effects our global rising temperature is having, with pictures of wildfires, deforestation, and a growing number of environmental refugees becoming very much the norm. Most people understand that the situation is bad, but every now and then we get a reminder of just how bad. My most recent jolt came when reading Jason Hickel's *Less Is More: How Degrowth Will Save the World*. On land, 40% of the planet's soils are seriously degraded according to the UN, with scientists suggesting that the Earth can only support another sixty years of harvests on current trajectory[444]. In the sea, approximately 85% of fish stocks have been depleted, and the situation does not make great reading for species in the air either.

---

444 Chris Arsenault, 'Only 60 years of farming left if soil degradation continues,' *Scientific American*, 2014

All told, since 1970 the number of birds, mammals, reptiles, and amphibians has dropped by more than half[445]. Our planet has seen this before, with four of the five previous mass extinctions involving climate change produced by greenhouse gases. Approximately 250 million years ago 96% of species were wiped out as carbon dioxide warmed the planet by 5 degrees Celsius: currently we are adding carbon to the atmosphere at a rate one hundred times faster than at any point in human history pre-industrialisation[446]. We do not always make the connection between ourselves and the rest of nature but we are fundamentally dependent on other species – insects necessary for pollination, birds controlling crop pests, grubs and worms essential to soil fertility, and so on. We are somewhat sleepwalking into our planet's sixth mass extinction event in its long history, the first to be caused by humans[447].

There are a number of reasons for our seeming cognitive dissonance, not least the fact that those who have contributed the least to climate change are currently bearing the brunt of it[448]. The first documented environmental refugees were relocated from the Carteret Islands (Papua New Guinea) in 2009, with a number of the Solomon Islands (to the east of Papua New Guinea) disappearing due to rising sea levels pre-2016[449]. Among those set to follow are the Maldives over the next 80 years, which may cause more alarm due to its popularity among honeymooners and social media influencers. In 2021 Madagascar suffered the first climate change-induced famine due to severe droughts leaving over 1 million people unable to feed themselves. Yet, even here in the UK we are given reminders that more extreme weather patterns are not just someone else's problem. Over the course of December 2013–January 2014 we had the wettest period for nearly 150 years submerging thousands of

---

445 IPBES, Global Assessment Report on Biodiversity and Ecosystem Services, 2019

446 David Wallace-Wells (2019) *The Uninhabitable Earth: A Story of the Future*, Penguin

447 The term 'Anthropocene' denotes the latest epoch in the Earth's geological history in which humans have, for the first time, become the planet's primary agents of change. The implicit suggestion is that we are all equally accountable, but the reality is that capitalism – particularly in the global north – is the primary culprit. The elites have a different view: take Thatcher's aide Sir Crispin Tickell who, ironically, blamed the poor for climate change, citing that there were too many of them and that they were exploiting 'the commons'

448 A perfect illustration of this being Nauru, formerly (and now ironically) named Pleasant Island. Made of phosphate rock, foreign corporations completely mined the island such that the locals were left clinging to a tiny piece of land, forced to rely on expensive imports. Nauru subsequently became a tax haven and is now essentially a client state of Australia, until recently hosting a highly controversial immigration detention centre

449 Albert et al. (2016) 'Interactions between sea-level rise and wave exposure on reef island dynamics in the Solomon Islands'. *Environmental Research Letters*, Volume 11 Number 5

homes, interrupting power and transport links for a prolonged period as the Environment Agency, gutted of thousands of jobs by the Tory-Lib Dem cuts, struggled to support citizens as money was again put before people's safety. In the same year, nine-year-old Londoner Ella Adoo-Kissi-Debrah became the first person in the UK to have air pollution listed as a cause of death[450].

Our apparent relative indifference to this great existential threat may be due to an 'out of sight, out of mind' approach that may itself be interspersed with hope that a clever scientist will find some miraculous cure to ecocide[451]. Undoubtedly, we feel better about it at some level of consciousness because our leaders – elected to serve our interests, of which survival is surely number one – do not make a song and dance about it. Yet, the reason for this is pretty clear: any attempt to deal with climate change will fundamentally transform the fortunes of many elites, from banning polluting activities and renationalising industries (as part of a general shift away from being so profit-focused to one centred more around a green, effective service), to ending our fetish with GDP. As recently as September 2021 the British government were in court attempting to defend their decision to grant BP a permit to drill in the North Sea oil field without taking into consideration the climate impacts – this just two months before the UN Climate Change Conference in Glasgow. Mere days before world leaders descended upon Glasgow Rishi Sunak announced the 2021 budget, which included a slash on Air Passenger Duty for domestic flights, encouraging more internal air travel at a time the country was supposed to be acting as a benchmark for reducing emissions. Even if countries stick to their emission cut pledges in the Paris agreement global temperatures may still rise by more than 3 degrees Celsius by just the year 2100 – the issues we are already witnessing are at a current level of 1 degree Celsius higher than pre-industrial levels. Hickel notes that at such a level large parts of Spain, Italy, and Greece will have sub-Saharan temperatures and effectively become deserts. We are not even on to rising sea levels, glaciers melting, deforestation, harvest yields failing, and people displacement on a scale unimaginable.

The common denominator underlying the main causes of our impending ecological disaster – emissions into the air, ocean acidification, intensive

---

450 Airly, the data analyst firm monitoring air quality found unacceptably high levels of air pollution (as per the World Health Organization's standards) in around 41% of schools in mid-2021

451 In *After Geoengineering: Climate Tragedy, Repair, and Restoration* Holly Jean Buck (2019) points to a number of such innovative ideas, from injecting sun-dimming aerosols into the stratosphere to reduce global warming, to capturing streams of carbon at industrial sites and storing it in underground wells

farming and fishing practices on an industrial scale, and so forth – are all direct by-products of capitalism's drive for expansion of both production and consumption[452]. What could typify capitalism more than capitalists polluting the air people breathe so badly that people then need, if they can afford to, buy purified cannisters of oxygen, from capitalists! This is common in the 'workshop of the world' China, where clean air is shipped in, complete with all of the usual environmentally damaging productive and transportation practices, from places such as Canada's Rocky Mountains literally by the can. Here the supposedly free market is positioned as the solution as opposed to the problem.

Nature has been perfecting balance for millions of years and we are managing to destroy the whole thing in what equates to just a tiny speck on that timeline. In effect, the entire economic and social system we uphold will need to radically change, and yet an end to our planet and potentially existence as we know it has become more feasible than the end of neoliberalist capitalism. Indeed, the ruling class will only listen to the extent that market solutions are favoured (be it subsidies to change technologies being adopted and so forth) and thus further profit can be gained. So-called 'green' consumption would likely replace current consumption practices, thus would not negate the problems we are facing at all, merely slow them down. Actually consuming less is going to be a tough pill to swallow for those who rely on this very thing to maintain their social standing. Firstly, in their role as capitalists (thus relying on people's over-consumption to derive their profits) but also themselves as consumers, with a study by Oxfam and the Stockholm Environment Institute finding that the wealthiest 10% of Brits are responsible for a carbon footprint the same size as the poorest 50%[453].

In the remarkable text *This Changes Everything* Naomi Klein offers many examples of how our elites will not solve the climate crisis for us. One illustration, is how countries have repeatedly challenged each other's attempts to expand renewable energy with charges of protectionism (the US against Chinese wind power subsidies in 2010, then later India's Jawaharlal Nehru

---

452 Expansion that has fuelled a 'new colonialism' (see *Land Grabbing* by Stefano Liberti) with vast hectares of developing countries bought up by those looking to turn a profit, or concerned about the effects of climate change on their own country's ability to provide subsistence to its population

453 Oxfam, 'Wealthiest Brits have a carbon footprint 11 times that of someone in the poorest half of society', 8 December 2020. On a global scale, the world's wealthiest 1% account for more than double the poorest 50% (!) according to the United Nations (UN) Environment Programme

National Solar Mission; China's complaint in 2012 against renewable energy programmes in places like Italy and Greece). Another is how green activist organisations have often end up being co-opted by the big polluters and their chequebooks in exchange for tokenistic and largely ineffectual gestures at becoming greener – usually after said activists have presented the economic case to them for doing so. Others take to surveillance of activist groups, as was the case in 2011 when EDF Energy were convicted of unlawful spying on Greenpeace. Or as was the case with Lone Pine Resources you could sue a country (in this instance Canada) for banning fracking as unfair under trade agreement terms. Klein describes the collusion between corporations and the state as 'boorishly defiant', with local communities opposed to having their homes, sources of subsistence, and livelihoods destroyed, viewed essentially as a burden to big capital. This would explain why the fossil fuel industry benefitted from subsidies of $11 million *every minute* in 2020[454], while world leaders simultaneously indicated that they would 'get tough' on climate change.

Perhaps the most convincing argument of the lot for radical change, and there are many, is that the choice is not between a new greener world and the status quo – the status quo simply cannot be sustained. As the constantly increasing amount of greenhouse gases (carbon dioxide, methane, etc.) trap more and more heat in the atmosphere, we are seeing ice caps and glaciers melt, which are imperative to reflecting back heat from the sun (dark surfaces absorb heat); permafrost in places like Siberia melt releasing vast quantities of methane from these once permanently frozen marshland[455]; and this is to say nothing of rising water levels or the exorbitant amounts of plastic in the ocean. We have to question whether even the status quo itself is worth saving given that we all continue to be worse off at the expense of a wealthy few. Surely we should be welcoming any reason to change the way things are, let alone having this reason – the threatening of our very own existence as we know it – forced upon us. It is not as if we haven't been given enough warning: Svante Arrhenius broke the news about global warming in 1895. We need to fundamentally change how we live, and things like recycling or not running the tap while brushing our teeth will not suffice. Part of such a transition requires what we might call a 'green revolution'.

---

454 International Monetary Fund, 'Still Not Getting Energy Prices Right: A Global and Country Update of Fossil Fuel Subsidies', working paper, 24 September 2021

455 A process being further accelerated by Mammoth tusk hunters searching for the valuable ivory that has been preserved in these frozen tombs for thousands of years, desired by the wealthy in bordering China

Many of the issues discussed in this book relate to scarcity, e.g. land scarcity creating inequality in wealth, housing scarcity distorting the housing market, finance, and so on. The scarcity over land and natural resources is going to get much worse as people struggle over space and resources as more parts of the world become uninhabitable. Undoubtedly, those who can afford to live in gated communities above sea level near valuable resources will include those who continue to exploit the Earth now and exacerbate this problem[456]. And why stop there – lest we forget, the 1979 Moon Treaty forbidding ownership of any part of the moon's surface was never actually ratified by the spacefaring nations[457]. As with many of today's challenges, we are faced with a government whose members often have financial interests in environmentally destructive corporations or rely on their funding and thus do the bare minimum to curtail this activity. Yet, if we collectively defined it as our most important societal issue we could quite easily force them to set radical measures or risk electoral failure.

Aaron Bastani's *Fully Automated Luxury Communism* makes a clear case that 'going green' does not automatically lead to minimalism. All too often we see messages of cutting down on things (be it time spent in the shower, eating the things we would like, and so on) or that we need to build tree-houses in the forest and sing Kum-bah-yah. In most instances this is not the case at all, one obvious example being that a well-insulated home can keep one sheltered and warm without recourse to round-the-clock heating via non-renewable energy and would be cheaper too[458]. The truth is that there are plenty of resources to go around; it is just that too much of it is hoarded by too few. The fact

---

456 There are examples of this already happening, the privately owned, sea-wall protected, self-sufficient Eko Atlantic off the coast of Nigeria being one currently underway. As our government continued to enjoy wine and cheese parties while simultaneously banning everyone else from seeing loved ones during the Covid pandemic, the rich spent £1 billion on superyachts between January–May 2021 to escape lockdown restrictions in international waters, demonstrating their contempt for rules and for doing the 'right' thing

457 See Rachel Riederer 'Who's Moon is it Anyway?' Dissent 61:4, which reports on Bigelow Aerospace, an entity that has requested government approval for a zone of non-interference around future lunar operations

458 Given that we desperately need affordable homes these threads wed together. We have a large section of society stuck with exorbitant rent costs which make house deposits and good credit for favourable mortgage terms somewhat less plausible. As wages stagnate and much of people's accrued wealth comes from the value of assets, those at the lower levels of society are often forced to work the hardest with little tangibly to show for it. A home should be a safe haven, not a constant source of anxiety. Tackling the housing crisis in the 'right' way presents a great opportunity for a more sustainable society too – if we refrain from handing over cash to the same developers only interested in profit at any cost

that we live on a planet with finite resources is a huge problem for our elite friends. But to be clear, the argument is not that all material desires are bad, or that there is no such thing as a material need; of course there is. But we have other needs too that have been subordinated by the material, and the big corporations, marketing executives, and social media that ram it down our throats. We are directed to occupy ourselves with meaningless social media trends, mediocre TV shows, or gadgets that serve little purpose, and are prone to judging experiences based on whether they offer 'value for money'.

There is another point to make about this perception that scaling things back will lead to our land of plenty becoming a world in which we have very limited choice. Scarcity is at the very heart of the present system – land and resource scarcity are why people are forced into long working hours. The desire to consume more, i.e. artificially created scarcity, is a reason why many people opt to work even longer hours. Financial scarcity is endemic in a world where people rely on long-term debt for basic necessities such as housing and education, and the wealthiest in said societies hoard more and more of the total income. In effect, we are merely granted the illusion of abundance. A world in which all of our basic needs are met is not one characterised by scarcity, and in such a world we are actually unshackled from the *time scarcity* that long working hours burdens us with, such that we can enjoy caring for others, leisure, hobbies, relationships, and interactions. Our employers will not spare us a second's thought once we pass away, but the family we forgo time with to benefit said employer will grieve indefinitely.

What constitutes prosperity should include participation, community, meeting relational needs, ultimately one's fulfilment that is not tied to how much one can afford to buy after subjecting themselves to working misery all week. Going green and becoming more conscious of our finite resources does not mean that the ration book needs to make a re-appearance – although, this is possibly what awaits us if we do not act now and continue to chip away at nature's resistance. Community-enterprise projects based around energy, food markets, horticulture, health and fitness centres, library and writing spaces, sports clubs, martial arts, outdoor pursuits, mindfulness events, music and drama, and much, much more are just some of the things already available in most locales as a viable alternative to our consumption patterns now.

As Tim Jackson articulates in *Prosperity Without Growth: Foundations for the Economy of Tomorrow*, 'It's possible to eat better (or less) and exercise better (or more). It's possible to walk rather than ride. It's possible to own less stuff. It's possible to invest money more ethically. People do these things. For a variety of reasons. And sometimes they feel better for it. It's possible to breathe more deeply. To spend more time with our family and friends. To volunteer in the community. It's possible to be more creative. To be more charitable. To be kinder to each other. It's possible to engage in totally random acts of unwarranted kindness. People do all of these things. And strangely, all of them have been shown to have beneficial impacts on wellbeing. They cost nothing. They contribute nothing to the GDP. They have nothing to do with output or efficiency. They have everything to do with prosperity' (217). If we do not start fostering our sense of community, when climate catastrophe does strike and society begins to collapse it will become every person for themself. We are not equipped to compete with those who have the means and money to better protect themselves with fortified, walled communities on stilts, or whatever dystopian future awaits us.

There is a wider point to be made here too, namely that wanting to see changes in our current system does not mean denying that capitalism has offered us some positives: it took five centuries to double the standard of living between 1300 and 1800 in the US, but just 28 years between 1929 and 1957[459]. Be it the increasingly competitively priced opportunity to see the world and broaden horizons, or to connect with other people. Even the advancements in technology that have enormously helped in the polling of information and writing of this book for one. However, indicative of the situation we now find ourselves in, an improved standard of living is expected to slow back down to a century for the next doubling – although one would have to question this given the degradation trends we are seeing and impending climate catastrophe. Being an 'anti-capitalist' in this moment does not mean rolling back the clock; it means taking the fruits that steamrolling expansion have created and now using them for a more sustainable, fairer world. As was described by Erik Olin Wright, 'capitalism is poverty in the midst of plenty', and that children – who bear no responsibility for their plight – can live in such conditions within rich societies is morally reprehensible[460]. It does not need to be this way; we can have what capitalism has to offer (a choice of foods, entertainment, clothing, whatever) with everybody flourishing rather than a minority[461].

---

459 National Bureau of Economic Research, 'Is U.S. growth over? Faltering innovation confronts the six headwinds', August 2012
460 Erik Olin Wright (2019) *How to Be an Anti-Capitalist in the 21st Century*, Verso
461 There are also many good organisations that provide fantastic ideas, research and forums for debate on what an alternative economy can look like – greener and better for everyone – such as the New Economics Foundation

In effect we could continue to expand our lives, particularly with non-material conceptions of the 'good life' centre stage, but with less guilt and anxiety as is usefully demonstrated via renewable energy advancements. We should take great encouragement from the fact that in just 90 minutes, enough sun hits the earth to provide a year's supply of (solar) energy for every human[462]. Wind power is now Britain's second largest source of electricity (as of the year end 2019) with coal down to under 2%[463]. This is not surprising given both our helpful island location and the fact that wind energy costs are down by 50% over the last decade, with a further 50% reduction in costs on current prices estimated in the next four years[464]. Using the United Nation's estimated cost for a switch to renewable energy, Bastani (*ibid*) calculates that this would cost less than current projections for fossil fuel expenditure over the next twenty years.

Ultimately, governments need to do far more than they have been doing: paltry fines for serious climate offenders are pointless without taking into consideration the corporate revenues of offenders[465]. Handing out what are effectively carbon tax credits to high-polluting corporations who make token, inadequate gestures at turning small parts of their operations 'greener' also will not suffice[466]. There could be a levy on those using natural resources for profit, which depletes our collective resources. Governments should also ramp up initiatives such as ensuring that our homes are as thermal-efficient as possible. Almost two-thirds of UK homes are found to fall short of the government's energy-efficiency standards based on Energy Performance Certificates data[467], meaning that we are using more energy than is necessary and pumping more carbon dioxide into the atmosphere. These types of changes are likely to be labour-intensive, encompassing both skilled and relatively unskilled work, from which meaning can be derived to both sets of workers as it is important.

Part of the challenge, as we know, is that many of the offenders donate tidy sums of money to ruling political parties, members of their senior management are often involved in advising government policy, and huge sums of money are thrown at lobbying and misinformation via various 'think-tanks' and research centres. Undoubtedly some elites are going to lose out in any transition, but

---

462 International Energy Agency, 'Solar Energy Perspectives', 1 December 2011
463 The Independent, '2019 saw the rise of wind power and the collapse of coal', 9 January 2020
464 Ofgem, 'State of the energy market', 2017 report
465 E.g. BP were fined $25 million in 2011 after an oil spill in Alaska, which amounted to 0.007% of their revenue
466 See Naomi Klein (2014) *This Changes Everything: Capitalism vs. the Climate*, Penguin,
467 BBC News, 'Two-thirds of UK homes "fail on energy efficiency targets"', 2 March 2020

they have managed to generate too vast a wealth to the detriment of the rest of us for any guilty feeling; indeed, they should be thankful if people (particularly those in the developing world long exploited) do not demand reparations for the destroying of communities, land, water supplies, thousands of wildlife species, and so forth. For those that do not comply, international criminal prosecutions should not be overlooked; it is time the book is thrown at individuals who hide behind corporations with administered licences to wreak environmental catastrophe. Since 2015, courts in England and Wales have had the power to impose unlimited fines for environmental (and health and safety) offences, technically enabling them to immediately divest an offending corporation of its assets – it is high time regulators sent a clear message to those that repeat their digressions that whatever amount of money is required to re-address damage caused (however subjective) will be collected. Naturally, more stringent monitoring and reviewing of green incentives is required: not doled out as another form of corporate welfare for the chief polluters.

Progressive tax credits and subsidies for those developing green industry do have a place in any green revolution provided they are administered in a transparent and effective manner. As climate change is a global issue and thus requires a cross-national effort, there is a strong argument for allocating some of the taxes acquired from high-polluting organisations and offer them to countries taking positive steps to protect the Earth's lungs. For example, via democratic means the people of Ecuador voted overwhelmingly for a change in the country's constitution in 2008 that assigns legally enforceable rights to *Pachamama* (Mother Earth), ensuring that its forests and other natural resources continue to exist, flourish, and evolve – the first country to do so. To ensure that such an approach is maintained and to help prevent the selling-off of such land in developing countries to private corporations who will deforest and pollute, such a financial incentive is needed and warranted. We should also be sharing innovations and support with developing countries who are embarking on industrialisation, improving energy coverage, and so forth, as it would be unfair of us after heavy pollution has helped fuel our development to then say it is unacceptable for others to do the same.

Other potentially fruitful avenues include Fleming's tradable energy quotas (TEQs) at the national level, whereby carbon-rated energy 'amounts' are allocated to individuals evenly, at no cost. This would make energy-consumption targets more publicly accountable as they are directed by governments, and ensure that they are not exceeded as there is a ceiling placed on how much aggregate energy users can access. This also sits well with wider nationalisation initiatives to better co-ordinate energy consumption with greener public services and so forth. Those who are not heavy users can sell parts of their allocation to those who are, incentivising a reduction in consumption in order to both reduce costs and, for the thrifty, to create a potential revenue stream. Other benefits centre on the fair distribution of resources that are somewhat monopolised by private interest, and greater freedom of choice over individual energy use. As argued by Shaun Chamberlain, TEQs also shift our focus away from money-focused, market-based approaches to problems that are not actually about money – as is the case with carbon tax credits and the like[468].

Mainstreaming ideas related to 'post-growth' and 'degrowth' thinking are necessary in order to meet the climate change targets set by the likes of the UN's Intergovernmental Panel on Climate Change. These concepts signify a number of things: notably to question the reigning logic that growth is good, and to acknowledge that 'more is better' is simply unsustainable with the Earth's finite resources. Capitalism is incapable of knowing when to stop pursuing growth nor what to do when we reach that point, as indeed we have. We are asked to envisage a post-capitalist future and to transition society away from over-production and over-consumption to centre our values on things that are human- and Earth-orientated (enjoyment of life, working less, equality, taking pleasure in and conserving nature, etc.) as a positive thing. We are talking about working part-time, in meaningful, freely chosen jobs; locally produced food and services; pursuing ethical endeavours – nothing scary or implausible.

It is not a return to some kind of primitive past; it is very forward-looking: a way out of inequality, weak democracy, the unrelenting, unhappy pursuit of more material possessions, climate catastrophe. Think about how much energy, traffic, infrastructure, and so on is built around people doing meaningless jobs, and how meaningless consumption is also to our detriment[469]. Even products that are useful are subject to a proliferation of choice – how many combinations of scents do we really need when it comes to shower gel? Why are there so many bad movies made (and why does Netflix offer so many of them up to us)?

---

468 See his chapter in *What We Are Fighting For*, edited by Federico Campagna and Emanuele Campiglio

469 Though dated, Harvard's Clayton Christensen's figure of 30k new consumer products launched each year is still used as an estimate: Harvard Business School 'Clay Christensen's Milkshake Marketing', 14 February 2011

Does the world really need a Donald Trump shower curtain, or a toastie maker that imprints a picture of Jesus Christ into your bread? Or chopsticks that have been made to look like lightsabers from Star Wars? Corporations create demand for things that isn't there – things that we do not desire nor need, at least until we are subjected to multi-million-pound marketing campaigns. As Liegey and Nelson set out in *Exploring Degrowth*, this need not be scary – we already have abundance. A fairer distribution of what we already have would provide more than enough for everyone to live in comfort, without the need for any more growth (as it is currently pursued) at all.

Transcending this fixation on short-term measures such as shareholder value and GDP[470] is key. When Nobel prize-winning economist Simon Kuznets introduced GDP to the US Congress he issued a stark warning alongside it: GDP alone is not a good measure. Today we have such things as the Genuine Progress Indicator as one attempt to measure environmental and social factors alongside the economic (and thus can supplement GDP) to offer a fuller account of a nation's well-being, adopted by a host of US states and in Canada and Finland. Mirroring experiences elsewhere, studies in Finland have revealed that GDP growth was matched by GPI growth as economic prosperity improved general welfare, but while GDP continued to grow in the 1990s, GPI did not as both the environment and Joe Public have not been the principal beneficiaries of recent economic growth[471].

Turning once again to Hickel, degrowth does not have to be quite as challenging as one imagines. Ending planned obsolescence is one example: legislating so that manufacturers cannot churn out products that will only last a few years or ensuring long-term warranties in order to incentivise them not to do so. Sharing goods among our communities; for example, rather than everyone having a garage full of things like lawnmowers, for small patches of grass that are only used perhaps monthly, we become more accustomed to share. Damage and the other associated costs of climate change already cost us billions of pounds; it is not like there isn't a business case to complement the more obvious reasons to tackle the impending apocalypse. The costs of recovery following natural disasters are astronomical: clean-up of the earthquake and tsunami in 2011 that ravaged Tōhoku, Japan, cost over $300

---

470 Gross Domestic Product growth indicates a total monetary amount of production and services traded; environmental implications (nor social) are not factored into this calculation. It is essentially a measure of capitalism's welfare

471 See Jukka Hoffren 'The national GPI calculations for Finland, 1945–2016', April 2017

billion – comfortably more than the entire GDP of many countries. Those more directly attributed to man-made issues are too, not least BP's Deepwater Horizon oil spill in the Gulf of Mexico a year prior. Financially, the costs are estimated at over $60 billion with an unquantifiable amount of damage done non-financially. Climate change will bring about more disasters, and given the non-trivial sums we are talking about here, this is clearly money that can be better spent on proactive preventative measures. Even beyond the obvious things such as a switch to renewable energy, revamping public transport and planting trees, to possibly initiatives like a Universal Basic Income (UBI) or Universal Basic Services (UBS).

A UNIVERSAL BASIC INCOME?

There has been a growing interest in a universal basic income for some time, which is effectively the distribution of a liveable amount of money to all citizens without means-testing them for eligibility. What may have appeared fantasy at one stage is now fully supported by business leaders, such as Facebook creators Mark Zuckerberg and Chris Hughes, to politicians from all parties: Mark Drakeford, socialist First Minister of Wales, backing a UBI trial in Labour-held Alyn and Deeside, and with acting Lib Dem leader Ed Davey particularly leading the charge. Indeed, it is not that radical a departure from what many countries and territories already do. Take Alaska, where since 1982 each citizen has received anything between $1k and $2k annually, derived from the Alaska Permanent Fund, a state-owned investment fund financed by oil revenues, with no strings attached. Often there are; for example the Bolsa Familia programme in Brazil where millions of low-income families have received cash transfers for keeping their children in school and visiting health clinics when advised.

Particularly if we are to advocate technology taking on more of the productive work and people to have more free time, there are some who argue this requires extra support to make ends meet. This is not necessarily true in two ways: 1) having more free time does not necessitate that people will be out shopping or engaging in entertainment activities more than they do presently – the things that we are forced to cram into evenings and weekends in order to feel like we make the most of time outside of work that can simply be spaced out more. We are also advocating for a world where we are happier without having to consume as much as possible, or feel pressured to, which of course costs much less. 2) If we are tackling wage inequality then the cost of living is likely to reflect this new median salary, as things cannot be given an astronomical price when the wealthiest are earning just five times (or whatever is democratically decided) more than the lowest earners. I am inclined to agree with Aaron Bastani (*ibid*) that universal basic services – i.e. the provision of universal, free and quality healthcare, education, housing, and anything else that should be a basic human right – is more convincing than UBI. There are questions regarding whether UBI could be used as a wage subsidy by employers; as a form of substitute for part of the welfare state; and in the current political climate be set at a poverty rate in all likelihood. However, it is worth exploring some of the arguments for UBI[472]:

Although it is typically subordinated to the economic case, there is of course the social justice case that a society's wealth is collective in character, and a healthy, happy, cohesive society is one where people are allowed to be 'well off', but not to levels of excess that leave others miserable. A UBI completely undermines the wage-labour dependency that characterises capitalist societies, with people able to opt out of long working hours if they wish. In isolation this would in turn reduce the reserve army of labour that constrains the terms and conditions of work for those who wish to continue working. This would represent a culture shift towards seeing access to money as a right, rather than linked to an obligation to earn. This means that waged labour is unlikely to be the basis for subsistence in the future as paid work is gradually phased out: partly due to automation which capitalists will be increasingly incentivised to do as humans are no longer forced into unpleasant, low-paid work, or because precarious, boring, or hazardous work would have to be paid a more befitting premium as people are not forced into such roles. With people's physiological needs met, a reduced amount of work could be more enjoyable for those who take intrinsic reward from doing something that they find meaningful, particularly if the roles that remain are those important to society's continued development.

As people are freed up to engage in endeavours they want to devote more time to outside of work, perhaps helping to preserve the environment, building up localised infrastructure for the new communal modes of living identified in this chapter, and ultimately fully functioning members of an informed

---

472 For a fuller, more impassioned case see Guy Standing (2017) *Basic Income: And How We Can Make It Happen*, Pelican Books

democracy. The long-term trajectory of UBI is to move into a society where money becomes less central, as people re-acquaint themselves with the needs and wants we have forgotten amidst capitalist over-consumption. As Peter Frase argues in *Four Futures* if UBI was linked to GDP, people's income would decline with the inevitable reduction in GDP as technology replaces waged labour, with the lower UBI reflecting the simultaneous decrease in the costs of living as GDP itself falls.

UBI could help to overcome pay gaps that are the result of gendered and racialised occupational segregation and so forth. In *Inventing the Future* Nick Srnicek and Alex Williams suggest that the evidence points to political and cultural barriers being more constraining than economic ones, as a variety of progressive taxes, clamping down on tax avoidance, reducing corporate welfare, and doing away with (now-unnecessary) programmes of welfare, tax credits, etc., would ensure its feasibility. The argument is also made that as labour-intensive industries are not those spearheading any semblance of economic recovery in rentier Britain and the continued automation of those and other industries, UBI might become a necessity as more people are unemployed, precariously employed, or relying on top-ups from the welfare state anyway.

UBI trials have been conducted across all continents, albeit typically on a relatively small scale, but with favourable humanistic results. Consider the largest UBI project to date: a $30 million, twelve-year project (which began in 2017) encompassing 20,000 individuals in rural Kenya. Initial indications point to a modest yet positive association with increased well-being across a range of criteria, e.g. hunger, sickness, and depression, despite the Covid pandemic as context. Other interesting findings include social benefits such as reduced hospital visits, and rather than a deterrent from work many respondents were actually taking more 'income risk' such as entrepreneurial endeavours given UBI mitigated potential adverse effects[473]. Researchers at the University of Manchester found that across UBI projects households generally put the money to very good use, via a range of means including boosting educational attainment or increasing their employability – contrary to concerns about the money being used to avoid work. As well as the aforementioned benefits relating to less strain on hospitals and other public services, such people are

---

473 'Effects of a Universal Basic Income during the pandemic' working paper by Abhijit Banerjee, Michael Faye, Alan Krueger, Paul Niehaus and Tavneet Suri. Available on the GiveDirectly website

more likely to boost tax revenues[474].

It is not entirely clear yet what the best implementation of UBI would be. Guy Standing suggests that building a fund from which UBI is drawn, with the level of income increasing gradually as the fund grows would be a sensible idea. As with many things, we become naturalised to a state of affairs and it becomes the status quo. We accept entering into 30-year+ debt with banks just to put a roof over our heads as normal, just and fitting. Is a UBI worse than credit cards and everything else we currently put to great and frequent use?

MORE STRINGENT REGULATION TO PROTECT PUBLIC INTEREST

'If you ain't angry, you ain't paying attention' (Mumia Abu-Jamal)

This ascertains to many aspects of our lives, encompassing areas discussed previously such as more effective regulation of a media that drives a right-wing populist narrative, often misguided, with almost zero attempt or requirement to fact-check what it puts into the public domain. To further illustrate the point that we would be well served by more stringent regulation, we have also considered tax and the seeming lack of appetite by our overlords to recuperate that which is owed. This section will also consider regulation that is much more effective at protecting us from our politicians' conflicted interests.

ACTUALLY RECUPERATE OWED TAX

There is widespread agreement that everyone should pay their fair share of taxes. This extends to a need to move away from the present situation where those with the greatest ability to pay their share are able to purchase expensive legal advice to find loopholes, or worse, have friends in government who do not make the prerequisite efforts to amend and enforce appropriate legislation. There are quite a few options available to us here. Firstly, there needs to be greater diversity on the various panels and committees who input into tax policy development, beyond their domination by corporate interests and the (profit-driven) tax industry. A host of experts, knowledgeable civil society

---

474 Joseph Hanlon, Armando Barrientos and David Hulme (2010) *Just Give Money to the Poor: The Development Revolution from the Global South*, Kumarian Press

groups, and other stakeholders should form part of publicly debated policy drives.

As another example, allowing millionaires and billionaires to claim asylum elsewhere and not pay taxes here is a huge facilitator of tax evasion, and we could follow US tax law which makes US citizens liable to taxes on their worldwide incomes whether they live in the States or not. Transparency is another step to deterring likely culprits, with the British government more than capable – should it want to – of forcing British companies to publish information on what tax is paid and where each year, for the public then to decide whether serial offenders deserve boycotting. Those corporations concerned about their reputations may find that any damage outweighs the already (relative to international standards) low tax burdens imposed on them here. All too often offenders are offered 'sweetheart deals' as settlement by HMRC top brass whom they have close relations with, rather than (again, preferably public) court hearings[475].

Furthermore, a progressive tax particularly on unearned income for those who have colossally greater amounts than they need even for a lavish lifestyle is evidently agreeable to most. There is not much that 'the 99%' does agree on, being a disparate group with different interests, values, and ideas. Yet opinion polls consistently show that there is appetite to tax the wealthiest in our society more (even among Tory voters[476]) – and comparative tax rates demonstrate that there is plenty of scope to do so. Even some of the uber-rich themselves: Disney heir Abigail Disney, co-founder of Ben & Jerry's ice cream Jerry Greenfield, and many more have called for higher taxation on people like themselves[477]. Naturally there needs to be some nuance in what this actually looks like but again there appears to be a degree of agreement on what could be targeted here. For example, our politicians claim that Britain is a meritocratic society; surely higher taxes on inheritance dovetail nicely into this, as allowing

---

475 Perhaps the most publicised was David Cameron's deal with Google to backpay £130 million in owed tax – effectively just 3% of their £7 billion profits, after numerous meetings with ministers (something common folk simply are not able to do). This had followed his Chancellor George Osborne introducing the diverted profits tax, or 'Google tax', an attempt to recoup money from multinational companies shifting profits overseas to avoid paying UK corporation tax. It is forecast not to generate one single pound sterling between 2021–2026

476 A poll by Tax Justice UK found 64% of Tory voters backed a tax rise for wealthy individuals and organisations; the same study revealed 87% want tax loopholes closed by the government

477 Their open letter and signatures at Millionairesforhumanity.com

people to inherit copious amounts of wealth and assets through no effort of their own goes against this mantra. Likewise, those who do pay a fair amount of tax on their huge incomes tend to not pay much on their wealth – with clear incentives then to buy land (à la Mr Dyson) or properties, which are left empty for capital gains purposes or expanding the rentier economy.

Alternatives could be to lift the cap on council tax or even replace it with a land value tax. Council tax was effectively rushed through in the wake of the Tories' poll tax debacle, and the eight equally weighted bands, which were based upon 1991 valuations, have never changed. As such, council tax is only very loosely linked to the value of property and has failed to account for changes in house prices since its inception. This leaves the greatest burden on those with less disposable income as someone with a property worth, say, £150k pays the same council tax as someone with a multi-million-pound mansion in the same area. According to the Resolution Foundation, the average net council tax rate is only 2.7 times higher for the top 10% valued properties from the lowest 10% – despite the average incomes between top and bottom income groups being much more widely apart (45 times higher according to this study)[478]. Such a progressive land tax needn't be overly complicated; for example, there could be a standard per square metre charge on land with regular re-evaluations.

Again, we could follow the lead of the Americans and impose a 'minimum tax', i.e. a set amount on taxable income and gains for people earning over a certain amount, e.g. economics and law professors at Warwick University and LSE found that implementing a 35% rate for those with over £100k per year could raise £11 billion each annum, and not punish high earners who already pay a higher share than those who do not[479]. Alternatively, the same personnel are involved with the Wealth Tax Commission who call for a 'wealth tax' on the value of a person's total assets, which other countries have in place, such as Spain, Switzerland, and Norway. They estimate that extra 1% tax on two-person households worth above £1 million, for five years, capped at £4 million per household, could raise £260 billion over that period of time[480]. At present, this could be a fairer way to raise money in the wake of Covid than what happened in the wake of the '08 financial crash.

Both for this and to truly tackle tax evasion, there needs to be international

---

478 Resolution Foundation, 'Home Affairs: Options for reforming property taxation', March 2018
479 *The Times*, 'The rich pay more tax than ever – but some hand over more than others', 2 July 2020
480 Wealth Tax Commission, 'A wealth tax for the UK' Final Report

agreements – where our global regulatory bodies need to agree that information on who is setting up companies in their hospitable offshore climates should be held and made available. This should be accompanied by favourable trading conditions and other incentives for those countries who, to a degree, rely on providing shady (but perfectly legal) financial services to the elites. In many instances they are former colonies or countries whom we have taken more from than we have given back, economically or otherwise, so this is the least we can do. The decision not to liaise with other governments is a deliberate one, and we could learn quite a lot from our counterparts. In Norway and Finland, for example, everybody has to declare their income, net worth and taxes, with this information made publicly available. There are reasons why *who* owns *what* (particularly when it comes to land) is shrouded in so much secrecy, and why this is allowed to continue. They are the same reasons why those who take a tiny proportion of the tax coffers, such as the disabled and those with impairments that are less visible, are targeted rather than the real scroungers hoarding billions of pounds each year.

MAKE POLITICIANS ACCOUNTABLE TO THE PUBLIC

Quite incredible that this should form part of a 'utopian future' rather than act as a presently available starting point when one lives in a country that considers itself to be one of the chief proponents of civilised democracy, but here we are. That the public are unable to decide what happens with their own money is ludicrous. Who would have opted for Liz Truss to blow £500k of taxpayers' money on a private plane to Australia instead of, say, a year's worth of salaries for 20 new NHS nurses? And yet ministers can squander our money at will. Deciding what role 'the state' should play in an alternative future is highly contentious. Undoubtedly in the first instance a progressive government would be incredibly useful, one that is actually fit for purpose – concerned with those who it is elected to represent rather than accepting money from fellow wealthy individuals to maintain the status quo as much as possible. We the many are a nuisance to them; they have to spend time and money disseminating misinformation, lying, and chucking us the odd bone to stop an all-out revolution. Discussed already are the many issues with our governments and the lack of opportunities for a diverse pool of individuals to become MPs, problems with the first-past-the-post electoral system, and so forth which all illustrate how daunting a task this could be.

Trust in politicians is already low and there are many critics of the main political figures on all sides, and governments have been forced into U-turns when the tide of public feeling is against them. So, with a number of steps it is not beyond the realms of possibility that we can shape up British politics for the better. One obvious measure would be to increase the transparency with which our politicians operate; and instead of toothless watchdogs 'asking questions' we need a *genuinely* independent body that *genuinely* monitors, investigates, and actually places sanctions on MPs for foul play. Consider the earlier example of Robert Jenrick pushing through planning permission for pal Richard Desmond at a cost to the taxpayer of anywhere between £40–50 million. Understandably there was a public outcry, but when an equally unscrupulous prime minister lends their support to a minister with no punishment (as this would be punishing what is normal practice in such circles) what did the public have left at their disposal[481]? We are barely even 'allowed' to protest these days. 'Allowed' being the operative word, as we seem to drift away from having elected representatives masquerading as though they work for us to creeping totalitarianism, recognising that only via protest has any progressive change ever come about in the past.

Similarly obvious yet challenging in practice, we could put a cap on party donations. The difficulties here are highlighted by Peter Geoghegan (*ibid*), who notes that recently millions of pounds have been poured into 'third-party' groups, campaigns, and websites such as the Conservative-aligned Capitalist Worker and the Campaign Against Corbynism, often with little transparency about the source of this money. However, it is much easier to modify the outdated electoral laws currently in place. For example, each prospective MP has a spending ceiling of around £15k, yet it has already been discussed how expensive it is to stand for a seat, and one has to revisit the 1920s for the last time a candidate was convicted of breaking spending limits. Part of the issue is that limits relate to the 25 days before an election, which ignores the campaign trail as a much longer process. It is also easy for rules to be circumnavigated, e.g. targeting specific advertising and other campaign measures to specific areas but allocating it from the national (party-level) budget. Most significantly, the

---

481 Among Boris's cabinet ministers is an exhaustive list of behaviour that was found to be unlawful and/or broke the ministerial code. As just two examples, Michael Gove was found to have broken the law when awarding £560k of taxpayers' money to long-time associates at Public First and for 'blacklisting' Freedom of Information requests; and Priti Patel for bullying civil servants in the Home Office. Boris's backing of Priti led to the resignation of his ethics advisor on the ministerial code, Sir Alex Allan

Speaker's Committee on the Electoral Commission contains five Tory MPs with just two Labour and one SNP MP. Majority not enough, those selected have bugs to bear with the Commission – for example, MP for South Thanet Craig Mackinlay was cleared of knowingly falsifying election expenses in 2019 but his campaign manager received a nine-month suspended sentence for preparing election returns dishonestly. MP for Lincoln Karl McCartney is also part of the committee, who claims he was victim of an Electoral Commission 'witch hunt' in 2017 after being cleared of electoral impropriety[482]. Recent threats include co-chair of the Conservatives Amanda Milling calling for the commission to either be abolished or subject to wholesale changes – because even the remotest sharing of power is too much for them.

IS LAND 'OCCUPATION' ETHICAL?

'Was the earth made to preserve a few covetous, proud men to live at ease, and for them to bag and barn up the treasures of the Earth from others, that these may beg or starve in a fruitful land; or was it made to preserve all her children?'
(Gerrard Winstanley, 'The New Law of Righteousness', 1649)

Land is nature's gift, and not seeing it this way demonstrates just how indoctrinated we have all become to the ills of our adopted economic, social, and political surroundings. In medieval times a large proportion of land was considered to be a commonly held resource that locals could freely use for various things, such as cattle grazing We must remember how many of the privileged classes came to be privileged: appropriating and enclosing land that people relied upon for their survival, thus denying them basic subsistence, imposing private property, and simultaneously creating classes of land and asset owning capitalists (themselves) and classes who previously accessed the commons but now had to sell their labour power to survive (virtually everyone else). In effect, land was fought for, seized, and monopolised, often from their own ranks a priesthood appointed who controlled the education and thus created a system of values that have since guided social behaviour, and laws created (aided by a legal system, police force, and penal system) to stop others

---

482 Karlmccartney.co.uk, 'Karl calls for "heads to roll" at "politically motivated, biased and unfit-for-purpose" Electoral Commission', 10 May 2017

from doing the same[483]. As land belongs to all of us, we should not feel guilty about occupying that which is owned by people who have more than they know what to do with, who effectively took it in the first place themselves.

That there would be so much unease about this reflects the fact that we are more in touch with human nature: we know that for as much as we are individuals, we are social beings who see the recognition and affection of fellow human beings as important to our physical, intellectual, and emotional existence. Those of the privileged class, and via effective social conditioning of others in the wider population (not least through the capitalist system), recognise their dependence upon society but do not experience this as a positive asset, but rather a threat to their economic existence. Thus, while reorganising democracy requires the present arrangement in which dominating classes are upheld to disappear, this is restitution rather than confiscation. As with the slaveowners, no-one should have the right to call for compensation just because their right to steal from others in the future, as they have in the past, is taken from them. Given that people are usually made to pay for both their crimes and their debts (for decades of land theft, earnings theft, etc.) our elites should consider themselves fortunate that we do not seek revenge, merely a fairer, better future for ourselves and our children[484].

There are a range of measures that could be taken here. The obvious starting point is to follow the lead of other countries (such as France, Denmark, and New Zealand) who make it transparent exactly *who* owns *what* land, rather than the secrecy that characterises who owns our country. Progressive taxes targeting the large, luxurious empty properties being used to 'hide' wealth should follow: with Boris Johnson himself suggesting a tax hike of 1,000% on homes left vacant for more than two years during his tenure as Major of London[485]. This could be one way to disincentivise the purchase of properties much bigger than people need too, which would help to redistribute more land. Other 'quick wins' would be to stop the huge handouts of public money via various forms of subsidy to those who inherit land, and to clamp down on inheritance tax loopholes (e.g. our friend James Dyson has been procuring swathes of farmland precisely because it

---

483 See Albert Einstein 'Why Socialism?' (article written in *Monthly Review*, 1949) for his account of how the privileged class established themselves, simultaneously subordinating everyone else in the process

484 Indeed some debts would be unpayable, not least those to former colonies, ancestors of slaves, and the ecological debts owed by major corporations to the world

485 *The Guardian*, 'Boris Johnson calls for massive council tax rise for owners of empty homes', 4 June 2014

is exempt from inheritance tax). Further, owning vast acres of land should come with obligations of stewardship rather than simply rights – notably to protect the ecosystem. Too much land goes unused not to be afforested or repurposed for new woodlands to serve as natural carbon sinks. This is beneficial for the environment but also again will act as a disincentive for those who claim to be the stewards of England when the land tells us a different story.

Such is the conservative nature of our country at present that the following would probably be considered quite radical, despite having precedence in other countries. Numerous authors mentioned in this book have called for the introduction of Community Right to Buy Land reforms, similar to what is present in Scotland. This legislation enables communities to contest the use of land and a right to buy if ownership can be seen as of greater benefit to the local population. According to the Scottish government's own figures, as of December 2018, 593 'assets' (almost exclusively land and buildings) were owned by 429 community groups, covering an area of 209,810 hectares[486]. This has disproportionately included private estates in the North and West Highlands and islands[487].

We could take our lead from the Movimento dos Trabalhadores Rurais Sem Terra (the Landless Workers Movement, informally known as the MST) in Brazil, who demand, and often occupy, large swathes of unused private land until it is partially or wholly transferred into common ownership. This is so that more people can benefit from it, while simultaneously making land less scarce and reducing the monopoly the privileged classes enjoy from it. Despite a violent response from the privileged landowners – it is estimated that 1% of Brazil's landowners own half of the vast country – and the state through which thousands of rural workers have been murdered, the MST has expropriated over 50,000km^2 of land and settled hundreds of thousands of families on it. Once settled, schools are built, agricultural production co-operatives established, real democracy instated (with gender quotas in leadership positions), and social transformation continually sought. When we consider the constraints imposed on such peoples we really do owe it to ourselves to fight for change here in Britain. In November 2020 the leader of the MST in Paraná, Ênio Pasqualin, was shot and killed in a politically

---

486 Rural & Environmental Science and Analytical Services, 'Community Ownership in Scotland 2018', published 11 December 2019
487 The Mar Lodge Estate in Aberdeenshire represents an example from Scotland of how conservation efforts can return land (and depleted species) to their former glory when the right people are in stewardship of it – see *Regeneration* by Andrew Painting (2021) Birlinn Ltd.

motivated attack. In nearby Columbia, simply being a member of a trade union has been enough to get oneself assassinated. According to government statistics 470 trade unionists were killed between 2000 and May 2009[488].

Marinaleda in Andalucía, Southern Spain, offers another alternative to our broken capitalist system. It appears just like any other pueblo in this part of the world; however, the Che Guevara mural adorning the side of the sports centre tells visitors that things operate very differently here[489]. Although age and ill health are not on his side, Mayor Juan Manuel Sanchez Gordillo has been in power since 1979 and has achieved notoriety on numerous occasions, notably in 2012 when leading trade union members on a raid of a nearby large supermarket chain to redistribute produce to food banks. In the same way he is opposed to supermarket shareholders being paid dividends while huge amounts of food are wasted and local townspeople go hungry, the story of Marinaleda began by occupying a parcel of land on the Duke of Infantado's 17,000-hectare estate, possessed for no other reason than to receive farm subsidies. With unemployment in the late 1970s hitting 60% and the locals, mainly land farmers, suffering abject poverty with no land for subsistence, Gordillo led hundreds of villagers to this parcel of land that had been enclosed by the Duke's ancestors, the El Humoso farm. They engaged in peaceful direct action, occupying and leaving the land when evicted by the police each evening. All told, they occupied El Humoso farm around 100 times, organised hunger strikes, picket lines, were arrested and beaten until eventually the Duke agreed to give up the 1,200 hectares around El Humoso in 1991 (albeit with compensation from the Andalucía government).

Most of the townsfolk work in the agricultural co-operative where they democratically voted to harvest labour-intensive crops such as olives and artichokes to ensure near-full employment – working six and a half hours each working day and everyone is paid the same wage (nearly double the Spanish minimum wage). The locals donate time to help build houses themselves, receiving construction materials from the regional government, and everyone then pays just €15 per month for their abode. The co-operative owns the houses so that people do not look to speculate on the property and accumulate capital on it, but each person is essentially free to do as they wish in terms of

488 Daniel Blackburn and Miguel Puerto (2013) 'Columbia: The Most Dangerous Place to be a Union Member' in *Global Anti-Unionism* (Gall and Dundon, eds)

489 The best account of Marinaleda is provided by Dan Hancox (2014) in *The Village Against The World*, Verso

modifying the home for themselves. Internet is free to all, public services are affordable (e.g. pre-school nurseries are charged at €12 per month including three meals per day), and everyone has their chance to pass comment, motions, and directly participate in decision-making via the frequent general assemblies at the town hall. With low inequality there is little crime and no police, and this community built on mutual aid and collectivism fared much better than the neighbouring capitalist cities and towns; for example, unemployment reached 5% during the economic crisis that ravaged Spain following the global financial crash as nearby rates reached between 40–50%.

Perhaps more palatable for people in Britain would be a progressive state bringing land back into public ownership and thus the hands of the people. Ryan-Collins and colleagues (*ibid*) point to Singapore, where around 90% of the land is owned by the state. As such, the land is used for socially desirable means (be them relating to infrastructure or whatever else is required by the population) and other areas offered to private enterprises on long-term leases, providing a handsome source of public revenue. In South Korea, the government-owned Korea Land and Housing Corporation has effectively managed land and home-building such that the ratio of house prices to income reduced by nearly half over the course of 1995–2013. Our local governments have compulsory purchase powers which serve as a pretty useful bargaining tool when looking to (re-)acquire land at a reasonable cost. The fact that many people can benefit from this, and those in possession have often enjoyed enormous benefits from it, I think we can argue that this would be an acceptable step from a moral standpoint.

In theory, there is nothing to stop the government acquiring land without planning permission, granting said permission, and then offering long-term leases on that land at a much higher value than what they paid, if we wanted to illustrate what is possible when a government has the people's best interests at heart, and not those of a wealthy few. Given how many people argue for reduced government intervention as it is seen as clunky, bureaucratic, and inefficient, why not offer them the chance to see a government operating like a business? Instead of a small number of shareholders benefitting, as is the case with private corporations, we all would instead. The New Towns Act 1946 was developed specifically for the post-war government to buy up land and relocate both the poor and those from bombed-out places into new areas, with similar waves occurring since then.

Governments could also support community land trusts (CLTs) in purchasing land, who then sell property on the land at an affordable rate, with decision-making democratic and the purpose of CLTs to be of benefit to the local community. While much of England is enclosed and we are trespassers merely for wanting to roam, Nick Hayes points to the alternatives all around us: in Finland, the right and freedom to roam is called *jokamiehenoikeus*; in Sweden it is *allemansrätten*, in Norway *allemannsrett*, and in Austria *Wegefreiheit*. Perhaps if people are able to see, touch, hear, and immerse oneself in the land – and nature itself – they might come to be more passionate about its impending doom.

DEFENDING BILLIONAIRES WON'T MAKE YOU ONE

'I sit on a man's back choking him and making him carry me, and yet assure myself and others that I am sorry for him and wish to lighten his load by all means possible... except by getting off his back' (Leo Tolstoy, *Writings on Civil Disobedience and Non-Violence*)

Trickle-down economics, premised on the fallacy that as the rich get richer everyone benefits, with economic growth leading to more jobs, high taxes being paid, and more disposable income, should be dispensed with if we are to follow any logic at all. Shareholders continue to take, hoard, and give little back – ably abetted by a state they collude with. Mentioned in the first chapter is this notion that we need the likes of Amazon more than they need us, as if they are performing some kind of public service by providing employment, albeit typically on precarious terms and alongside corporate handouts. This conception that the elites are somehow helping us is ruinous given that we are adjudging help to be confined within neoliberal, capitalistic ways that not only do not upset the present system (skewed enormously in their favour) but facilitates the exponential growth of inequality.

If this book has illustrated one thing, I hope it is that when we break everything down, the reality is that most of us spend our lives producing wealth for the capitalist classes – we do not receive a fair dividend for the share of the work we have put in (often living with debt) and certainly do not have as much free time as we want. And yet we seem resigned to this fate, as though this is all we deserve. The likes of Anand Giridharadas[490] well illustrate that our elites have done a fantastic job of creating a role for themselves in *seemingly* attempting to rid the world of ills that they themselves have created: from corporate social responsibility measures and establishing research centres geared towards tackling social problems to philanthropy. As a consequence, they have become leaders in problem-solving that has enshrined to them the power to offer solutions that ultimately will not harm them, i.e. to not actually change the system within which they benefit, be it the tax system, labour laws, and so forth.

A clear illustration of this is the tendency towards programmes designed to increase the upward social mobility of disadvantaged groups: a just, worthy cause and one difficult to argue against or denigrate. Yet such solutions are based on a business case, i.e. the benefits that accrue from a diverse labour pool (new perspectives, innovation, better reflection of customer base, to name but three) and from resultantly being an employer of choice. As they become the apparent problem-solvers, so the focus from them as chief causers of problems seemingly fades away. Corporations were central to slavery, colonialism, the under-representation of such groups particularly in managerial positions, and have prospered at the expense of communities since they began. David Harvey (*ibid*) questions whether any charitable donors would jump on board with movements away from anti-poverty causes to anti- (grossly unequal) wealth politics.

The seeds of change will undoubtedly have to come from below and again we can look to our compatriots abroad who have been fighting against the capitalist project that protects the interests of the wealthy[491]. We could take inspiration from the likes of the Ejército Zapatista de Liberación Nacional (the Zapatista Army of National Liberation), who gained the ears and eyes of the world at the inception of the North American Free Trade Agreement (NAFTA) on New Year's Day 1994 when declaring war on the Mexican government. This band of under 10,000 mainly indigenous Mayan peasants in the southern Mexican state of Chiapas have, and continue, to rebel against centuries of exploitation, genocide, racism, and neglect. As part of the preparations for

---

490 *Winners Take All: The Elite Charade of Changing the World* (2019), Penguin

491 It is no surprise that we hear little of mass protests elsewhere, but people in every corner of the world have fought the issues we similarly face, e.g. at the turn of the century there were general strikes in Bolivia, South Africa, India, and Puerto Rico in response to privatisation; in Ecuador (where a brief coup emerged victorious in 2001 and the neoliberal and anti-democratic leader Lucio Guiterrez ousted in 2005), Columbia, and Nigeria opposing neoliberalism

NAFTA with the US and Canada, Mexican president Carlos Salinas had revoked Article 27 of the Constitution – won by Emiliano Zapata and his comrades during the Mexican Revolution – which granted public ownership and communal right to land, water, forest, and mineral resources. Land was effectively being readied for parcelling up for sale, thus constraining the ability of the indigenous population to access what are vast natural resources in the state from which they already benefitted little.

While their immediate struggle had a face, that of their president, the Zapatistas knew that their fight was not against a national government per se but the interests of international big capital, the corporations that wanted to exploit their land, and those that wanted them to forgo their culture and traditions to simply become entities that sell their labour (much more cheaply than their counterparts north of the border), like many others. The Zapatistas clearly stand for many things, including a fundamental opposition to neoliberalism[492], a fight for the commons and sustaining the environment[493], and against a lack of power and representation in the national political system. In effect, they have created the first autonomous Maya territory for over a century despite the behest of the state. There are lessons to be learned in the issues they have faced, but certainly in their successes: notably solidarity has led to communal identity among disparate groups of indigenous peoples and thus dialogue around shared problems and interests (typically regarding healthcare, education, and land reform); values such as fairness and egalitarianism drive these communities; they have a common recourse to working co-operatives; and not least experiments in regional politics and governance. What they also demonstrate is opposition to those who show complete disregard for communities that have little use for neoliberal capital; many communities do not buy stocks and shares, do not own credit cards, and are a nuisance in their resistance when it comes to appropriating land as part of capital's accumulation.

Perhaps we should dispense with money altogether. Despite its centrality to our current lives money is a very recent invention on the human timeline, and not only detracts from the natural basis of our existence but reduces it to the economy's logic of 'value' and ultimately our exploitation. In Thomas

---

492 For example, their declaration 'For humanity and against neoliberalism' has been taken up internationally

493 As of February 2021 the Zapatistas are protesting en masse against a series of government projects, including mines, highways, train lines, and oil pipelines under the banner 'Defense of territory and Mother Earth'

More's 1516 *Utopia* people are able to produce plenty of what they need for comfortable lives, and with the absence of money no unnecessary trading takes place. He also makes the point that poverty, 'the one problem that has always seemed to need money for its solution, would promptly disappear if money ceased to exist'. In reality, so-called moneyless societies have tended to substitute money for other things that similarly denote value. Examples range from the Bristol Pound through to Local Exchange and Trading Systems (LETS), which involve bartering things based on values such as labour time. As a crude demonstration of how this works, a plumber can fix plumbing issues for an electrician, who in return can resolve an electrical problem for the plumber, taking note of the time taken and/or value of the parts involved. Within a LETS each has a pool of people to whom they can offer their services and who can reciprocate in kind. This does bypass money in a way and the incentive to accumulate, and provides the means for those with lower incomes to access otherwise extortionate services such as childcare.

Others argue that we already have the infrastructure for a moneyless society and via local councils the (local) supply of everything people need can be co-ordinated – be it transport, food, shelter, and so forth. These councils could communicate to a national body which goods are needed from further afield, to exchange with any surpluses they themselves have[494]. Naturally this cannot occur in a capitalist society and (eco)socialism would be required, whereby communities determine what is consumed and thus produced rather than the wasteful endeavours of the capitalist class[495]. Ecosocialism signals a commitment not only to common ownership of the things we need to live comfortably, but also to overcoming all social injustices such as patriarchy and decolonisation. Communities around the world offer us ideas and inspiration on how to achieve these things, with the aforementioned MST and Zapatistas, Kurdish resistance in Rojava and Northern Syria, the autonomous region of El Alto in Bolivia, and the *Piqueteros* in Argentina all demonstrating how resources can be fairly distributed in non-oppressive ways. Alongside the Zapatistas, the female-led El Cambalache moneyless project in Chiapas illustrates how value can be attributed to things differently than within the capitalist system, and exchanged in ways removed from capitalist notions of 'value'[496]. Any item,

---

494 See, as one example, *Life Without Money* edited by Anitra Nelson and Frans Timmerman (2011), Pluto Press
495 See Salvatore Engel-Di Mauro (2021) *Socialist States and the Environment*, Pluto Press
496 See Erin Araujo in *Why Don't The Poor Rise Up?* (2017) AK Press

knowledge, ability, or time that can be offered can in turn be exchanged for something else, which has included everything from cooking classes and massages, to puppet shows. Everyone is considered to have something to offer, and everyone has an equal say in matters relating to the project. Paul Foot (*ibid*) notes that parliamentary opposition to the propertied, elitist classes has always been measured – for the reasons set out in Chapter 3 – and it is only the people who can truly unsettle the status quo. A series of seemingly small acts may be all that is required to generate cultural and structural change, if control of 'the state' seems improbable.

NOTHING TO LOSE
BUT OUR CHAINS

'No people are really free until they become the instruments of their own liberation. Freedom is not legacy that is bequeathed from one generation to another. Each generation must take and maintain its freedom with its own hands' (John Henrik Clarke)

Any 'utopia' requires a leap of faith. Indeed, any worthy cause that people have fought for in the past has seemed a tall order to begin with and required lots of work and sacrifice. In the words of Nelson Mandela, it always seems impossible until it's done. Without understanding that change is needed and taking such a leap of faith, the Chartists would not have mounted the first genuinely democratic movement for social reform in modern history, civil rights activists would not have advanced efforts to end racial segregation, same-sex marriage would not have been legalised in 2014 (albeit with limitations), and feminists would not have ensured movements towards egalitarianism, reduced sexual violence against women, and so forth. We often look upon the historical figures who fought to end injustice, exploitation, and create a better world with great admiration, yet have been made to feel that such feats are beyond ourselves. Can I guarantee that this radical alternative world will be perfect? Not at all, but what I can guarantee is that whenever we do not know something, it is important to work at the answer – both practically and theoretically. To give change the greatest chance of success there needs to be two things:

a clear plan, and buy-in. The latter should be relatively straight-forward in principle: I am arguing that we need to replace a system of exploitation and alienation with one that gives everyone access to the things they need and freedom to do more of what they wish. We are not calling for the end of all work, as that would be impossible, just its centrality to our lives. We do not need to feel pressured into identifying ourselves with our jobs or feel that enquiring into one's line of work is the best opening conversation piece we can muster. This new reality requires us to establish exactly what it is that people wish and work backwards from there, which requires genuine widespread participation and democracy.

For a truly radical, alternative world the options here need to be better articulated than abstract notions of 'overthrowing capitalism' and replacing it with 'something nicer', accepting that this has been attempted. As Charles Umney posits in *Class Matters*, the problem with slogans like 'the 1% versus the 99%' is that conspiracies around a governing few masks the fact that, actually, society is chaotic and the elites are confused like everyone else. This is why we see Tory governments abandoning their so-called ideals because – quite simply – they do not have many beyond maintaining power at practically any cost. They are also more effective at appealing to the masses they continually subordinate than the 'left' are: beyond attaching blame to immigrants and so forth, but creating categories that people wish to belong to (e.g. 'hardworking people', 'proud Brits') than categories people do not want to be part of, i.e. the downcast 99%[497]. I see no good reason why individuals from the working classes and the well-meaning outside of it cannot co-exist in the same political movement.

There are so many things that could garner popular support: surely a significant proportion of people would like everyone to have access to adequate healthcare, education, and housing; to work less yet be able to afford more; have more time for themselves; and know that poverty has been tackled in a meaningful way? As one example, British attitude surveys show that hard work is a societal value that most people subscribe to, but

---

497 There is something to admire in the Tory PR machine: that the party established by hardworking people, i.e. the labour movement, in opposition to the elites who largely live off the hard work of said people, became the party associated with those considered workshy. During the recent cladding scandal there were frequent assertions to the Tories as the party of home ownership and treatment of leaseholders being uncharacteristic, despite their dismal record on housing (noted in Chapter 3)

polls also suggest that they question a society that demands more and more work at the expense of family life and friendships. We can provide a society that meets these values: cut down on work to just that which is useful for society and thus has meaning, noting that transitioning to an ecologically sound, localised, and truly democratic way of living will indeed require a fair amount of work itself. As one illustration, a move towards more localised and less intensive farming and fishing will undoubtedly require more labour.

The project could take various forms but must begin by creating greater awareness of the ills of our current system. This is well illustrated by Danny Katch[498], who asks us to imagine building a society on a deserted tropical island, and proposing that the people who do all of the work are to be paid as little as possible, and those who do next to nothing having more than they can spend in their lifetimes; to ruthlessly exploit all natural resources and animals; and construct nuclear weapons and prisons to maintain this social order. People simply would not agree to it, and yet we uphold this way of life ourselves. The second stage of this project would be to outline the benefits of socialism, which is essentially what is being propagated here. There appears to be a real lack of understanding regarding what this concept entails, but the fundamental principle of socialism is that all should be well-fed, well-housed, and well-educated. This is quite a difficult principle to argue against! Particularly as there is enough food, shelter, and education to go around if we choose to distribute it evenly and all decide to stop this rat race that we are the losers in, and unlikely to make it out of.

As with many other European countries, socialists have come to power in Britain, introducing things like the NHS and a welfare state, building council homes, expanding education, nationalising industries, etc., with millions of private businesses co-existing and democracy not threatened, as suggested by those who cry 'Stalin' at the first sight of any alternative to capitalism. Despite its own various problems, in Spain the new-ish, anti-austerity coalition left party Podemos (which translates as 'we can') is ensuring positive changes are introduced – sectoral collective bargaining has been restored, an increased minimum wage, more egalitarian parental leave policies, more funding for social housing, pension increases in line with inflation, climate action, and more – in coalition with the Spanish Socialist Workers' Party (PSOE).

---

498 See *Socialism... Seriously: A Brief Guide to Human Liberation* (2015), Haymarket

Whatever the future of Podemos, this is a clear indication that with enough grassroots support, left policies can galvanise support and improve the lot of the many.

We can begin by clearly expressing that we object to the way people are treated: the disabled, the poor, migrants, even those of us who may appear to be 'better off' than the aforementioned groups yet are still hugely exploited by the capitalist system and ruling elites. We should no longer accept poor working conditions; increased homelessness should not be normalised, nor should cuts to the health or education sectors. We need to draw these threads together, i.e. while they are analytically distinct issues they are all manifestations of the same system and those disparate fights need to be brought together. We have normalised celebrating the weekend and seemingly have been forced to accept that 70% of the week is not there to be enjoyed, which is quite remarkable. And yet our hours are getting longer and 'real' pay is down for the privilege of work intensification, as though this is the natural order.

The composition of modern trade union members demonstrates that working-class individuals have much more in common than they do differences along the lines of sex, ethnicity, and other demographic characteristics. Gone are the days of unions being 'pale, male, and stale', with membership density highest among black workers (27.2% compared to 23.9% for white workers and 19.1% for Asian workers); and members are more likely to be female (170k more in 2019, representing the biggest female increase since records began[499]). Likewise, those with a disability are more likely to be a trade union member than those without. The sharing of experiences and building rapport can spark the collectivism needed for the working classes to unite and target their frustration at the elites rather than each other. Sometimes it takes a 'victory' at workplace level for the fire to ignite that spurs us on to tackle larger political projects.

It seems sensible to establish a guiding set of principles – to be democratically chosen – for people to rally around. George Monbiot offers some examples of what these might look like in *Out of the Wreckage: A New Politics for an Age of Crisis*. They include:

---

499 Department for Business, Energy & Industrial Strategy, 'Trade Union Membership, UK 1995–2019: Statistical Bulletin', 27 May 2020

- We want to live in a place guided by empathy, respect, justice, generosity, courage, fun, and love
- We want to live in a place in which everyone's needs are met, without harming the living world or the prosperity of future generations
- We want to live in a place in which the fruits of the work we do and the resources we use are fairly and widely distributed, in which shared prosperity is a general project, and the purpose of economic life is to enable universal well-being
- We want to live in a place whose political system is fair and fully representative, in which everyone has a voice and every vote counts, and whose outcomes can neither be bought nor otherwise engineered
- We want to live in a place in which everyone has access to the information needed to make meaningful democratic choices, and in which political debate is honest, accessible, and inclusive

From these, people are able to develop an attachment when they see fit with their own personal values and view of what life could and should be like. From such principles policies and plans can be made. Equally, we do not have to go searching far for guiding principles in the political system itself – the Labour Party was literally founded upon socialist ideals. Clause IV in Labour's constitution, before it was rewritten by Tony Blair, rejected capitalism:

> 'To secure for the workers by hand or by brain the full fruits of their industry and the most equitable distribution thereof that may be possible upon the basis of the common ownership of the means of production, distribution and exchange, and the best obtainable system of popular administration and control of each industry or service'.

Probably the biggest question here concerns democracy itself – at present Parliament seems to be little '…but a vehicle of direct oppression to enhance the interests of an elite… minute and removed from everyday life' (Fleming, *ibid*; 147). The issues with our current system of democracy were outlined in Chapter 3, so too the inextricable links between those in government and their backgrounds/affiliations which are ultimately to serve elitist interests and not those of the majority. Even when an individual with anti-capitalist aims is elevated to a position of power there is an antagonism between their position and what they can achieve (as we see in the diaries of Tony Benn). It is the author's view that people need to be the vanguard for real change themselves[500], however, a more representative parliament better reflecting the make-up of the country it serves would of course be an asset. Being born into a family that can afford £42,500-per-year school fees or shoed in from the financial sector should not be the kinds of people we see as ideal for running the country; they fail us time and time again. Too many people from the same background stifles innovation, new ideas, and ultimately an understanding of the issues facing many members of the public – grossly divorced from their reality. In the interim MPs should also not be able to take second jobs. A typical counter to this is that we will not get the best people for the job if their salary will be no more than £82,000 or thereabouts (plus expenses) and thus we should allow for additional income streams to retain top talent. This would be a coherent argument if we actually had top talent in the first place[501]. Particularly if we are implementing a maximum salary cap then actually the best people for the job will want to be politicians as opportunities, for higher pay will be few and far between in this new system.

---

500 There are many examples of 'the people' as the vanguard themselves, or governments broadly orientated to socialism, embarking on radical reform. Even where short-lived or replete with issues there is much that we can learn from these challenges to the status quo. The most notorious examples are the Paris Commune of 1871 (see Prosper-Olivier Lissagaray), Catalonia during the Spanish Civil War (see Gaston Leval), and the Cuban revolution (see Helen Yaffe). Europe from 1918 is a hotbed of further examples: workers' self-management in Yugoslavia (see Gal Kirn), the Soviets in Russia (see Carmen Sirianni), Germany (see Ralf Hoffrogge), Hungary (see András Göllner), Georgia (see Eric Lee), and cities like 'Red' Vienna in Austria and Turin during the Biennio Rosso in Italy. Later instances include Portugal 1974–75 (see Raquel Varela) and Poland 1980–81 (see Colin Barker). Latin America has seen the 'pink tide' of left politics rise, fall, and rise again: prime examples being the Sandinistas in Nicaragua (currently back in power), Venezuela under Hugo Chávez, Bolivia (notably during the presidency of Evo Morales), Chile in the early 1970s (and has recently elected socialist Gabriel Boric), Guatemala before the CIA-backed military coup in 1954, and many more. Numerous African states pursued variances of socialism after gaining independence, Mozambique being one example, and there is much to learn from African socialists: first president of Tanzania Julius Nyerere, of Burkina Faso Thomas Sankara, and of Ghana Kwame Nkrumah to name but three. As the likes of China, Vietnam, and Laos adopt models that combine socialism with market principles, there are lessons from Asia to inform what our alternative future could look like

501 The ludicrous nature of expenses is highlighted by Tory MP for Southampton Itchen, Royston Smith, claiming from the taxpayer a £1 car park fee incurred while visiting a food bank – having voted against extending free school meals to poorer children and other measures that helped create the need for food banks in his constituency. At the other end of the spectrum, Liz Truss claimed £3k in expenses for a 'business lunch' at a restaurant owned by Zac Goldsmith's half-brother (and Tory donor) Robin Birley, including three bottles of £153 Pazo Barrantes Albariño wine

Undoubtedly a progressive state would be an effective vehicle to implement some of the initial stages of this utopian future, but if we are looking to move beyond capitalism then almost certainly not. The state is intertwined with capitalism in a number of ways, not least via taxing the capitalist market economy for income (thus incentivising the state to create the conditions for capitalism to be profitable, creating jobs, and so on). The state is effectively responsible for sustaining capitalism over the long term because, left to its own devices of environmental destruction, competition driving out other businesses, and replacing workers with technology, capitalism would probably not survive for as long. In conversations, most of the objections I hear to a socialist society with the state taking a fundamental role is that ultimately they become corrupt. This seemingly ignores how corrupt our current governments are! But it is possible to ensure that the state does not become too powerful with localised councils, a form of democracy that offers transparency, and the ability to relieve people of their duties – not having to wait four years to then elect somebody else who will then not be held accountable for another extended period.

With a genuine attempt to properly educate people on economic, political, and social matters the public would be better informed to make judgements and decisions. At present huge swathes of the population do not vote, do not know what the treasury or austerity is, and so forth. If we trust people for jury duty we can trust them for other important decisions, particularly once these matters are more publicly discussed. Examples we can look to include participatory budgeting, an idea that originated in the Brazilian city of Porto Alegre whereby parts of the budget are allocated based on direct democratic participation in decision-making, and whose model has influenced similar systems in over 1,500 cities (from New York to Hamburg)[502]. This is something that could be rolled out incrementally, i.e. those who live in a particular local authority area vote on a number of expenditure options (anything from improving the conditions of roads to additional teaching assistants in state schools, whatever is important to that particular community). To this end, there is a strong argument for moving part of Parliament and its associated agencies further north to make it less London-centric. This fits with more devolved, localised forms of governance, be they work councils or something similar.

---

502 Dmytro Khutkyy (2017) 'Participatory budgeting: An empowering democratic institution', OpenDemocracy

There are many possible names for a mixture of public enterprises, worker co-operatives, and democratically regulated private enterprises; for example, Erik Olin Wright described this as a democratic-egalitarian economy. Preston in Lancashire offers one example of a bold initiative – namely a focus on 'community wealth building' – to boost a local economy in the face of economic hardship and years of being starved of required investment in public infrastructure and services[503]. The local council helped to establish Clevr Money a non-profit savings and loans co-operative that offers both affordable loans and works with local employers to provide a range of services. The council has also led a drive for businesses in Preston to pay the 'real' living wage, itself becoming the second local authority to pay this back in 2008. After devising a vision and strategy with various think-tanks (e.g. the Centre for Local Economic Strategies), 'anchor institutions' in the area, notably Lancashire County Council, UCLan, teaching hospitals, and various colleges now work together to ensure that local suppliers are used, local jobs are created, and ultimately the local economy becomes more sustainable. Long-term goals include the expansion of worker co-operatives and the living wage to all workers in the area.

Not far from Preston, another left-leaning Labour council in Salford is working on its own 'model', what the Mayor Paul Dennett calls 'sensible socialism'. Writing in *Tribune*, Paul contrasts the fabled 'dirty old town' with its new titles of greenest and most sustainable council thanks to the huge investment in green spaces and infrastructure, including expanding public access to previously enclosed land. Work has started on hundreds of new, eco-friendly homes with nearly half designated for social rent and many others for affordable rent. Growth has been led by insourcing, including services lost during privatisation and PFIs, such as UrbanVision who are responsible for road maintenance, highways, and building control in the city. Partnership with trade unions has led to many benefits, including help to manage council job cuts during austerity and ensure pay rises for carers under the 'Salford Offer'[504]. Salford's vision is one different to 'the Thatcherite model of hollowed-out councils as procurement hubs for private contracts', based on a local economy characterised by well-paid

---

503 See the Democracy Collaborative, 'The Preston model: An overview' and Preston City Council's website, 'What is Preston Model?'

504 Relatedly, local and national government may only award public contracts to companies (where necessary) who demonstrate that they do recognise trade unions, are committed to ecological sustainability, and pay their full tax obligations. Any company who does not will thus become incentivised to do so

jobs, co-operatives, and community enterprises. Similar things are happening north of the border in Scotland, with North Ayrshire's socialist Labour council an accredited Living Wage employer (introducing the new rate six months early – just in time for Christmas), they have long provided free meals for poorer households during school holidays[505], and have reorientated business support services to focus on the solidarity economy (social enterprises, co-operatives, etc.) not just orthodox 'growth potential' metrics.

Other alternative concepts include Robin Hahnel's 'participatory economics' with a focus on (self-managing) worker councils who determine everything from designing jobs that balance desirable elements such as empowerment and lack of unpleasantness, to wider activity that compromises between productive efficiency and being environmentally sustainable. Others propose variances of a 'social and solidarity economy' that comprise co-operatives and a range of other enterprises (such as associations and mutual benefit societies) which prioritise the interests of members and community above profit, through to autonomous management and democratic decision-making[506]. Another approach is that of the 'democratic economy'[507], which is guided by a broad set of principles. Namely that people are not viewed as isolated, self-interested entities as is the case within capitalism, but rather as integral members of a community. As such, the guiding premise of transactions and activity taking place within this type of economy is to prioritise the common good, as this benefits each individual as a direct consequence. So too labour is prioritised before capital by way of a real living wage and dignity while working. This type of economy is inclusive to all members of the community, irrespective of their demographic characteristics or life histories, in the offer of opportunity, whether this be work- or non-work-related. Crucially it aims to build wealth that remains local such that this sense of community can be developed and sustained. Finally, that organisations within this economy are owned by those members of the community in a co-operative fashion. Kelly and Howard (*ibid*) offer many practical examples from

---

505 Taking responsibility of (locally sourced) food supplies for those in receipt of free school meals during lockdown as opposed to outsourcing to private providers as the Tories did in England – another privatisation debacle. Chartwell's, a subsidiary of Compass Group, was chaired by Tory donor and former advisor to David Cameron Paul Wash. Chartwell's were forced to apologise and review their practices after delivering grossly inadequate meals to children (all part of the profit motif)

506 For detail and examples see *Social and Solidarity Economy: Beyond the Fringe* (2015) edited by Peter Upping

507 See, for example, Kelly and Howard (2019) *The Making of a Democratic Economy: How to Build Prosperity for the Many, Not the Few*, Berrett-Koehler Publishers

the US and further afield to complement those touched upon here regarding how such a transition from an exploitative economy is achieved.

Kerala, a state encompassing around 40 million people, operates a modified form of communism which effectively translates as socialism, and regularly tops the United Nation's Sustainable Development Goals Index across India despite having a lower per-capita GNP. This index is a measure of progress across social (e.g. life expectancy, poverty, gender parity), economic, and environmental metrics. Via significant investments in healthcare and education, one of the world's first democratically elected communist-led governments has secured a range of citizen well-being titles, such as the highest levels of literacy country-wide. It began life opposing British colonial rule, desiring land reform (and re-distribution) and an end to India's caste system, all of the hallmarks of a progressive, equitable society, and continues to be elected into power by Keralites. Private property and enterprise co-exist with state-run worker co-operatives, different religions living harmoniously side by side; in fact, so successful is this approach to people's well-being that it may be Kerala's undoing. Churning out healthy, well-educated youth has seen a brain-drain to higher-paying jobs in India's big cities and the Gulf states, but the message is clear: typical economic metrics cannot be used to justify a lack of investment in health and education, and the returns on investment for a society are second to none.

Governments in Amsterdam, Copenhagen, Brussels, and cities in New Zealand, Canada, and the US, have decided to embrace Kate Raworth's theory of 'doughnut economics', recognising that we need to hit the reset button in the post-Covid world rather than return to an unsustainable social and economic system. Citizen-led groups across the globe, for example in Sao Paulo and Kuala Lumpur, are forming to push for a transition to 'doughnut cities'. Rather than paying homage to the god of GDP and infinite growth, the focus is on the 'social foundation', i.e. ensuring that everyone has what they need to live a 'good' life (water, food, health, education, housing, energy, etc.), and the 'environmental ceiling' (what the planet can handle in terms of climate change, ocean acidification, biodiversity loss, and so forth). While such places are still developing what this looks like in practice for their particular locale, the emphasis is on zero carbon emissions, social housing, and access to nature. In Amsterdam, for example, once residents entered into lockdown the city government collected unused and broken computers, recruited a company to refurbish them, and then distributed to those who needed them for work or to combat social isolation. The fact that such gestures are worthy of international recognition just demonstrates how far many of us are from having politicians 'doing the right thing' in representing the interests of those they are elected to serve. Equally significantly, Amsterdam's local government has a range of initiatives encouraging the public and industry to work together to recycle products rather than throwing them away/continuously producing more. Whereas the Tories continue to rig the system in their favour via the Elections Bill 2021 that will disenfranchise at least 1 million voters, other countries are attempting to widen democratic participation. For example, in Estonia digital voting was introduced in 2005 whereby voters receive personal cards, PIN numbers, and security questions which enable them to vote online with minimal risk of fraudulent or suspicious voting activity.

Capitalism cannot continue with 'more responsible' people heading major corporations or any other solution capitalist-sympathisers may put forward. Inherent in the capitalist system is the need to expand constantly – if a firm does not, others will continue to reinvest and outperform them, leading to their demise, unemployment, and ultimately reinforcing this need to grow at all costs (environmental or otherwise). Existing and new firms need to find new ways of driving up consumerism in order to compete and survive, and thus production too in cyclical fashion. Imagine a world where you buy a mobile phone and it can last for 10 years instead of two (as we know, they have the technology to provide this now if demanded; it is simply not financially prudent for them to do so). We participate in a financial system of credit and debt in order to sustain this until the next inevitable economic crash. To increase one's standard of living under capitalism, one inevitably has to trample on others. Is that really a better option than a society based around solidarity, where everyone can have the things they need and we do not need to trample/ be trampled as work becomes more precarious and wages stagnate? Where work is for the benefit of everyone, not overwork for the benefit of a few.

This is the kind of nationalism a progressive political party should be offering up as an alternative to the right-wing populism we see today. A sense of community and pride in that community; common ownership of land, public services and good provision of said services to all who need it; direct democracy and a say in what happens here – a true 'taking back control'; pride in our contribution to the planet's survival and recovery; finding happiness in things that are not conducive to over-consumption. It should not seem unrealistic to us when thinking about the present arrangement. In an alternative world, what would we say the chances are of masses of people repeatedly voting in parties that serve a small group of elites and simultaneously undermine their own interests? If anything, a party more in tune with what the vast majority of people need and one that would actually improve their 'lot' should find it a great deal easier to be elected. With people having more free time as they work less, there is much greater scope for democratic participation and improved education on political matters that should further cement this.

It is easy to fall into the trap of equating GDP with positive metrics such as life expectancy. Yet, there are countless examples of countries who achieve high levels of human development when their governments prioritise things like universal healthcare. Jason Hickel (*ibid*) notes as one example how Spain has a life expectancy of 83.5 years despite spending less than a quarter of what the US spends on healthcare per person[508], where the life expectancy is 78.7 years. Likewise, countries like Costa Rica have a higher life expectancy with 80% less income than the States. What this illustrates is that countries provide for their population's needs without the additional trillions of pounds' worth of extraction, production, consumption, waste, and environmental damage incurred by the US and others. It also demonstrates how much by way of resources such countries have at their disposal to change things for the better, rather than ploughing on as things are. Equally, one must question how we can use metrics like GDP to measure progress, when the very thing underpinning such 'progress' is likely to result in our extinction – a process already well underway. While it is positioned to us that the 'free' market decides our fate, the market only decides what the government allows it to, and occasionally under pressure from the working classes. British history is one long, unceasing class struggle to create a system that is fairer for more people. A battle that it can often feel like we are not winning, but one that we must continue to fight. As stated by Tony Benn, 'there is no final victory, just as there is no final defeat. Just the same battle to be fought over and over again. So toughen up, bloody toughen up'.

---

508 This should not be surprising; we saw in Chapter 2 that universal public services for such basic needs are much more cost-effective than when left to private corporations

Rise, like lions after slumber
In unvanquishable number!
Shake your chains to earth like dew
Which in sleep had fallen on you:
Ye are many—they are few!

(Percy Bysshe Shelley, *The Masque of Anarchy*, 1819)

AFTERWORD

It will be clear that the intention of this book was to provide an introduction to these major areas of our lives (work, money, politics, and the media) rather than offer a comprehensive review of each. The aim was to keep the text relatively short and accessible; therefore it was not possible to do full justice to each of these topics, merely offer a point of departure to then investigate for oneself. The recommended readings are certainly a fruitful starting point. The next step, I hope, is to engage others. If history has taught us anything, the chances of a fairer society with buy-in from the majority requires a building of consciousness that many people do not currently have, and this will take time. It is perfectly fine for me, sat typing in my ivory tower complete with Grenfell-style cladding to wait patiently for positive change; unfortunately others do not have that luxury and suffer on a daily basis. For them, begin the discussions – and ultimately the struggle – now.

Special mention is due to my comrade Chris Chimes for his honest assessment of earlier drafts of this text and wider offer of support. This book is for Cillian and Shea. So too for Alfie and Archie, whose future in 'the leisure society' envisaged here I will continue to agitate for. To Mick and Dave Ormsby, for their review and comments. And the countless many others, whose conversations, insights, and humour on the types of issues discussed here have impacted my journey in one way or another. Not least to the trade union activists and those who dedicate their time and energy to good causes in the face of open hostility; such efforts make a huge difference even when there are seemingly few immediate results. And of course to my family.

RECOMMENDED READING

Bregman, Rutger (2020) *HumanKind: A Hopeful History*. Bloomsbury

Bullough, Oliver (2018) *Money Land: Why Thieves & Crooks Now Rule the World & How to Take it Back*. Profile Books

Campagna, Federico and Campiglio, Emanuele (2012) *What We Are Fighting For: A Radical Collective Manifesto*. Pluto Press

Christophers, Brett (2020) *Rentier Capitalism: Who Owns the Economy, and Who Pays for It?*, Verso

Edwards, David and Cromwell, David (2006) *Guardians of Power: The Myth of the Liberal Media*. Pluto Press

Fisher, Mark (2009) *Capitalist Realism*. Zer0 Books

Fleming, Peter (2015) *The Mythology of Work*. Pluto Press

Graeber, David (2018) *Bullsh*t Jobs: The Rise of Pointless Work and What We Can Do About It*. Penguin Books

Harvey, David (2020) *The Anti-Capitalist Chronicles*. Pluto Press

Hayes, Nick (2020) *The Book of Trespass*. Bloomsbury

Hickel, Jason (2020) *Less Is More: How Degrowth Will Save the World*. Penguin Random House UK

Hodkinson, Stuart (2019) *Safe as Houses: Private Greed, Political Negligence and Housing Policy After Grenfell*. Manchester University Press

Lafargue, Paul (1883) *The Right to be Lazy*. Charles Kerr and Co.

Mellor, Mary (2016) *Debt or Democracy: Public Money for Sustainability and Social Justice*. Pluto Press

Rutherford, Adam (2020) *How to Argue With a Racist: History, Science, Race and Reality*. Weidenfeld & Nicolson

Ryan-Collins, Josh, Toby Lloyd and Laurie MacFarlane (2017) *Rethinking the Economics of Land and Housing*. ZED Books

Sangher, Sathnam (2021) *Empireland: How Imperialism Has Shaped Modern Britain*. Viking

Sayer, Andrew (2015) *Why We Can't Afford the Rich*. Policy Press

Seymour, Richard (2016) *Corbyn: The Strange Rebirth of Radical Politics*. Verso

Shrubsole, Guy (2019) *Who Owns England? How We Lost Our Land and How to Take It Back.* William Collins

Standing, Guy (2021) *The Corruption of Capitalism: Why Rentiers Thrive and Work Does Not Pay.* Biteback Publishing

Sunkara, Bhaskar (2018) *The Socialist Manifesto.* Verso

Umney, Charles (2018) *Class Matters.* Pluto Press

Weiss, Hadas (2019) *We Have Never Been Middle Class.* Verso

Whyte, David (2015) *How Corrupt Is Britain?* Pluto Press

INDEX